An Introduction to
PRIMARY SCHOOL
ORGANISATION

PRIMARY BOOKSHELF

An Introduction to
PRIMARY SCHOOL ORGANISATION

Ken Reid, Robert Bullock, Stephen Howarth

HODDER AND STOUGHTON
LONDON SYDNEY AUCKLAND TORONTO

ISBN 0 340 40249 0

First published 1988

Printed and bound in Great Britain for
Hodder and Stoughton Educational,
a division of Hodder and Stoughton Ltd,
Mill Road, Dunton, Green, Sevenoaks, Kent,
by The Eastern Press Ltd, London and Reading

Typeset by Wessex Typesetters
(Division of The Eastern Press Ltd)
Frome, Somerset

Contents

Foreword vii

List of abbreviations ix

1 Setting the scene 1

2 Contemporary issues 7

3 The shape of primary schools 18

4 General and specific responsibilities 31

5 Staff selection and organisation 40

6 Staff management procedures 52

7 Pupil organisation 65

8 The small school 78

9 Looking at the primary school curriculum 91

10 Resources 102

11 External agencies 111

12 Parents and primary schools 124

13 The law 134

14 INSET 142

15 Analysis of needs 152

16 The new teacher 161

17 Towards effective teaching in primary schools 172

18 Effective primary schools 184

Bibliography 196

Acknowledgments 207

Index 209

Foreword

An Introduction to Primary School Organisation has been written as a basic text for new and intending teachers, though experienced teachers may find many of the chapters helpful. We have tried to write the book in such a way as to make it informative as well as a good read. During the preparatory and writing stages, we have leaned heavily on the advice of practitioners and utilised our own professional experience to a considerable extent. Consequently, the text is sprinkled with actual case data drawn from primary schools in West Glamorgan, Nottingham, the West Midlands, London and Essex. Care has been taken to ensure the anonymity of those teachers and schools which allowed us to visit them and who have willingly assisted us in our endeavours. In Chapter 1, for example, Sally, Jane and Wendy are real people working in real schools with real children.

We have attempted to be comprehensive in our coverage of primary school organisation. The text, however, is practical rather than theoretical.

Inevitably in a book of this sort, there are some issues which receive less detailed coverage than others. Examples here include record keeping and primary–secondary school links. It is for this reason that we have endeavoured to provide an extensive bibliography and interested readers will be able to use our references to good effect.

This book was planned before the Baker Pay Deal in 1987. We deliberately held the book back, rewrote and amended it in the light of impending changes. Of necessity, therefore, certain sections lean heavily on the historical structure of primary schools. This is particularly true of chapters 3, 4, 5, 6, 14, 15 and 16.

Throughout the text, apart from some specific case studies and quotations from sources, primary school headteachers and teachers are referred to as 'she', to acknowledge the preponderance of female staff in the primary phase of the profession.

List of abbreviations

ACSET — Advisory Committee on the Supply and Education of Teachers

ACSTT — Advisory Committee on the Supply and Training of Teachers

A/T — Assistant Teacher

BEd — Bachelor of Education

BIOSS — Brunel Institute of Organisation and Social Services

CAPER — Children and Parents Enjoying Reading

CARN — Classroom Action Research Network

CATE — Committee for the Accreditation of Teacher Education

CDT — Craft, Design and Technology

CGS — Child Guidance Service

CNAA — Council for National Academic Awards

CRC — Central Regional Council, Scotland

CSE — Certificate of Secondary Education

DES — Department of Education and Science

EVS — Environmental Studies

EWO — Education Welfare Officer

GCSE — General Certificate of Secondary Education

GRIST — Grant Related In-Service Training

H — Headteacher

HMI — Her Majesty's Inspector (of Schools) or Her Majesty's Inspectorate (of Schools)

HMSO — Her Majesty's Stationery Office

ICI — Imperial Chemical Industries

ILEA — Inner London Education Authority

INSET — In-Service Education and Training

LEA — Local Education Authority

MSC — Manpower Services Commission

NAPE — National Association for Primary Education

NCPTA — National Confederation of Parent-Teacher Associations

NOR — Number On Roll

PGCE — Post Graduate Certificate in Education

PTA — Parent-Teacher Association

PTR — Pupil–Teacher Ratio

SPITE — Structure and Process of Initial Teacher Education Within Universities in England and Wales

TES — The Times Educational Supplement

TRIST — TVEI–Related In-Service Training

TVEI — Technical and Vocational Education Initiative

YTS — Youth Training Service

Primary school classes/ Age groups

N   Nursery Class
R   Infant Reception Class
I1   Infant One (First Year Infant Class)
I2   Infant Two (Second Year Infant Class)
J1   Junior One (First Year Junior Class)
J2   Junior Two (Second Year Junior Class)
J3   Junior Three (Third Year Junior Class)
J4   Junior Four (Fourth Year Junior Class)

1 Setting the scene

Background issues

The primary school is a complex social world. Its inhabitants – the headteacher, teaching staff, secretarial staff, cleaning staff, children, parents and other external agents – comprise a unique social organisation. Within this scenario, children are vitally important, perhaps as the clients of the organisation.

The needs of primary teachers these days are the focus of considerable attention. Yet, traditionally, students and new teachers alike have tended to learn about matters relating to schools as organisations 'on the job' rather than through prepared simulation or training exercises, or through other source materials. This process is, for example, heavily criticised by Her Majesty's Inspectorate in such documents as *Taking Stock* (Welsh Office, 1986), a report based on school inspections in Wales between 1983–1985. In this Report, the text is highly disparaging of both curriculum organisation and school organisation, as well as schools' links with such external agencies as pupils' homes.

Take the case of Sally. She is 21 years of age and recently undertook her first teaching practice in a Roman Catholic primary school in Wales. Previously, she had spent two years in rigorous academic study on Part One of her course. Suddenly, within some six weeks of commencing her professional training, she was thrust into a world she had last participated in at the age of 11. Moreover, her recollection of her own primary schooling in Devon was that it was very different from her own experience on teaching practice – so much had changed. Although her father is a successful secondary teacher and very keen on education, she is inclined to the view that he knows little about the philosophy, process and content of primary schooling. After completing a successful teaching practice, Sally wrote the following passage, in her file:

> . . . really I enjoyed being at the school very much. I am sure it will be very different from others I will soon visit and teach in. I suppose I will have to wait until I get my first job before I really understand why schools are so different and why schools are organized as they seem to be at present. In some ways I think teaching is unfair. For example, Miss Jenkins had a class of fifteen whereas Mrs Wallers' contained thirty-three . . .

On the same teaching practice and on the same course is Jane. She undertook her first teaching practice in a large primary school in a small town 12 miles away from Sally's. Whereas Sally spent most of her time with a J1 class, Jane was placed with a J3 group containing almost twice as many pupils. Unlike Sally, Jane was a mature student of 40, with two near grown-up children of her own. Consequently, she had only distant memories of her own primary school days and was immediately struck that her open-plan teaching practice school was unlike anything either she or her

1

The primary school is a complex social world, whether in a traditional . . .

own children had ever experienced before. Everything was different – the layout of the school, the styles of teaching, the integrated work carried out by pupils, the rapport with the parents and, most of all, the informality. For her the school was:

> . . . constantly buzzing. I was immediately struck by the pictures on display on every free piece of space in the school, by the atmosphere and by the friendliness of the children.

A few weeks later however, she wrote the following:

> I can see teaching is going to be very different from teaching practice. At present, everyone is very good to me especially the Head and Mrs Miles. Unfortunately, relationships in the staff room are a bit strained. No one likes the fact that Mr Jones has been given a scale 2 ahead of other claimants, especially as he has come from another school nearby which the staff claim is useless. Some of the teachers go into a huddle each break and just moan about everything to do with education. What I can't understand is why no one seems to consult them. The Head appears to make the decisions on a day-to-day basis. His deputy then carries out his orders. The rest of the staff simply seem to fall in line without question and then gripe to one another. The difference between the internal appearance of the school and the staff room atmosphere is most marked. Something is wrong somewhere but I can't put my finger on it . . .

Wendy is in her mid-twenties. She has been teaching for four years. Recently, she returned to the institution where she originally trained to follow a part-time in-service course. While on the course she expressed her exasperation with the way her school was organised. She claimed that at the beginning of term her head had called her into his office to offer her a scale 2 post for science. Although delighted at the recognition of her teaching qualities, she was upset and confused by the offer of a scale post for science. She professed a lack of interest in the subject, stating that she had taken no science since her O level days. Also, she now had charge of an infant class in which she felt the need for science was limited. The head had explained that all the other scale posts were already taken and there was no

. . . or a modern setting

possibility of redistribution. The problem was that there was no member of staff in the school with a background in primary science. Reluctantly, Wendy accepted the offer and promptly sought some in-service training to help her. A few weeks later her confidence had only slightly increased. She had not yet begun her first task – consulting the staff on the teaching of science in the school prior to beginning the process of writing some guidelines.

Before we consider the sort of information that new teachers and students like Sally, Jane and Wendy need to know, we will pause briefly to examine the meaning of the term 'organisation' when applied to primary schools.

What is an organisation?

What is an organisation? A rural primary school, the police force, ICI and a trade union are all organisations, but they are not identical. Is there some common thread, one unifying concept in all these 'organisations' which makes us use the same term to describe them?

It has been suggested that the use of the word 'organisation' is rather like the use of the word 'game' (Davies, 1976). We use 'game' to describe football, tennis or darts. They are not the same, but they are members of that family of things which we call games and which are distinct from other forms of activity. Gray (1985) suggests that:

All organisations have qualities that are common and qualities that are unique.

Hicks (1972) distinguishes five attributes which are common to all human organisations:

1 An organisation always includes persons.
2 These persons are involved with one another in some way – that is, they are interacting.
3 These interactions can always be ordered or organised by some sort of structure.
4 Each person in the organisation has personal objectives, some of which are the reasons for his actions. He expects that participation in the organisation will help to achieve his objectives.

3

5 These interactions can also help to achieve compatible joint objectives, perhaps different from, but related to, their personal objectives.

Hicks (1972) thus arrives at a definition of an organisation as, 'a structured process in which persons interact for objectives'. We are suspicious of lists of organisational attributes such as those provided by Hicks as they tend to over-simplify complicated issues. Nevertheless, as organisations are linked by family resemblances, they will have some attributes in common but no list will be complete.

Everard and Morris (1985) list some of the elements found in formal school organisations:

1 Technology. The 'technology' of an organisation is its processes – in the case of a school, the process of education and the plant (classrooms, workshops, gymnasia, blackboards, etc.) that goes with it.
2 Structure. An organisation's structure embraces the organisational chart, the committees, the departments, the roles, the hierarchical levels and authority, the procedures in the staff manual, the timetable, *et seq.*
3 People. The people in a school organisation are the teachers, their professionalism, knowledge, experience, skills and attitudes; also the pupils and the non-teaching staff.
4 Culture. The character (or culture) of the organisation covers such intangibles as its tone, its value system, the standards by which merit is judged, personal relationships, habits, unwritten rules of conduct and the practice of educational judgement.

So we can begin to see that an answer to the question of just what an organisation may be involves questions of structure, processes, people, and purposes. Musgrave (1976) defines an organisation as:

A system of co-ordinated activity carried out by two or more persons for a definite purpose.

A number of models of organisations in contemporary literature are drawn from outside the school. Teachers probably feel, understandably, that to draw comparisons with industrial models may not be very helpful in the primary school context. Schools do not seek, for example, to maximise profits or increase production in the manner of a business enterprise. Similarly, we may talk of organisations pursuing 'goals', but the 'goals' or aims of primary education are far from being universally accepted, even amongst teachers (Ashton, 1978).

Nevertheless, there are advantages in using theoretical models in educational circumstances. It is generally agreed that in order to understand the nature of organisation and the nature of change, it is necessary to adopt an analytical framework or 'model' to aid understanding, and from which to provide a rational basis for behaviour. It needs to be borne in mind that there is no one 'model' which is entirely complete. All models provide some insight. Most models so far devised are based on non-educational organisations and situations. These tend to be adapted to suit educational circumstances. Paradoxically, their lack of perfect 'fit' can help us to distinguish those elements which are applicable to the school situation as well as those which are not (Gray, 1985).

The reality of schools as organisations

There is comparatively little research material on the school as an organisation, especially on the effective organisation of primary schools. Those studies which do exist, and which we shall discuss later, tend to be on micro aspects of the organisation, such as issues relating to teaching styles and curriculum matters, rather than analyses of the advantages and disadvantages of different organisational structures. Hence Gray (1985) suggests that most of what has been written seems to be theoretical, conceptual and at best speculative.

Consequently, the study of schools as organisations is inclined to lean heavily on material emanating from industrial, commercial or public sector organisations, many of which focus on economic and management perspectives. While such information can be valuable, we need to remember that schools, especially primary schools, are very different places from industrial or commercial concerns. Therefore, although the evidence obtained from the organisational models or their frameworks can be useful, we must be cautious in extrapolating such findings too directly to primary schools. In industrial concerns, for example, the organisation has to acknowledge the requirements of profit making, competition and the like, and also of numerous different levels of employees – unskilled, semi-skilled, skilled and managerial staff. Generally speaking, managerial employees tend to have more organisational knowledge and clout than the lower echelons. Although to some extent the same is true of the relationship between headteachers and their teaching and non-teaching staff, schools have different aims and objectives from many other organisations, while their teaching staffs are comprised of professionally qualified people, often of similar knowledge and ability. Furthermore, in industrial concerns the end products are usually materials or artefacts. In schools the end product is improved pupils' knowledge or learning skills. Thus, the management and organisation of pupils' education is a very different kind of business from that involved in producing, for example, delicate drinking objects from sheet glass. Nonetheless, teachers should never fall into the trap of rejecting industrial analogies out of hand or of applying them uncritically.

Despite these fundamental differences, schools are equally complex, multifaceted, changing places which can only operate sensitively and responsively if the whole staff is actively engaged in the processes of the organisation at all levels, as participants rather than hierarchical 'agents'. It is becoming increasingly accepted that if a school is to develop, then it must do so from a basis of common collegiate responsibility in terms of its planning, development, organisation and evaluation (Campbell, 1985).

Yet schools remain unpredictable places. Ridley and Trembath (1983) suggest that it is, 'remarkable that so much in schools and classrooms goes so well, given the complexity and unpredictability of classroom activity'. Despite this, they also think, 'it is dangerously complacent to accept that schools are doing a reasonable job in the circumstances', partly because:

> . . . it is sadly rare to find a group of teachers able to be relaxed with one another on the basis of their own sense of personal worth, and further developing it through the professional sharing and cooperation generated by corporate group activity.

Therefore, they suggest that the organisation of primary schools should enable them to be:

> . . . the kind of institution peopled by individuals who are particularly skilled as a result of training and reflective experience, which enables children to act on their own experience of the world and literally create out of the symbolic constructs that school makes available to them, a pattern of order that both tells them something about themselves that they did not previously know, and something of the world they are growing up in. This meeting of child and institution is manifested through 'The Learning Experience'; the environment in which this takes place; and perhaps most importantly of all, the organisation that supports that environment.

In management theory, the basic assumption is made that all kinds of organisations have essential qualities in common. Models are derived from studying all organisations and applying the concepts to particular types and specific instances. It is assumed that all organisations consist of people interacting for some common purposes and that to do this the organisation requires a technical structure. The management process is concerned with helping the members of an organisation to attain individual as well as organisational objectives within the changing environment of the organisation. Because the environment changes, the objectives will change and be modified and the planning aspect of management is concerned with coping with this change (Gray, 1985).

So it is that most available research into the organisation of primary schools has focused on the micro level. In particular, the relationship between the organisation and classroom activities, especially those most obviously concerned with teaching and learning.

Barker-Lunn (1982) has reported on the organisational policies of junior schools. As part of a larger research project into teaching methods and practices in junior schools and departments, she obtained (by questionnaire) details of the organisational patterns existing in 732 schools. The findings confirmed that streamed junior schools or departments are very uncommon, but indicate that devices such as setting and the formation of enrichment or remedial groups are often used in attempts to provide more appropriately for the range of children's capabilities. She suggests that there has been a change towards more selective teaching groups over recent years as a result of the so-called 'Great Debate', calls for accountability, the findings of the National Primary Survey and the rest of the 1970s scrutiny of primary education. Barker-Lunn leaves the question of the effectiveness of the provision open, presumably deliberately. The survey indicated that a substantial minority of schools had shifted organisationally away from out-and-out mixed ability teaching. Teachers appeared to be using more ability groupings within mixed ability classes.

Another organisational issue on which there is quite a lot of research evidence is on the effects of open-plan schools. Open-plan primary schools have added much to the mythology and folklore of primary education. The findings and implications of the national inquiry into open-plan schools by Bennett *et al.* (1980) have been hotly debated (Brogden, 1983). Bennett's observational data reveals considerable differences between practice in open-plan units in schools, a finding which is supported to a greater or lesser extent by other studies (Bennett *et al.*, 1975; Arkwright *et al.*, 1975; Hurlin, 1975; Evans, 1979; Brogden, 1983).

What it is important to reinforce from an organisational perspective is that most primary schools tend to offer their staff considerable autonomy within their own classrooms on their teaching and learning styles. Moreover, teachers at all levels like to have a say in what goes on within their own classrooms but often feel less strongly about some of the major managerial or organisational issues at a macro level (Price, 1985). Even this, however, is changing as mounting evidence shows that primary teachers prefer to be consulted rather than 'managed' on most issues relating to primary school organisation (Price and Reid, 1987a, b, c).

It is within this context that we should see the experiences of Sally, Jane and Wendy, outlined at the beginning of the chapter. Their circumstances were by no means unusual as issues relating to school organisation, such as pupil and staff organisation, staff selection, the role of local education authorities, advisers and external agencies, resource management, staff development, in-service training, schools as effective institutions and primary school differences tend to be new or neglected topics, not least on initial teacher training courses (Reid, 1984a). An examination of data obtained from empirical studies tends to suggest that initial teacher education courses are deficient on organisational issues (Reid, *et al.*, 1981; 1982; Reid, 1984a; Bernbaum, Patrick and Reid, 1982; 1985a, b). Indeed, as early as their probationary year, many new teachers already feel in need of in-service training in aspects of organisation (Bernbaum, Patrick and Reid, 1983; Reid, 1985b). Thus, not only do new teachers learn from their different experiences but they do so in a haphazard fashion. Accordingly, although this book is intended to be a basic introductory text for new teachers and student teachers, it is highly probable that it will contain factual evidence which will be helpful to many experienced staff.

2 Contemporary issues

Changes since 1974

Since the mid-seventies there have been many important changes in education which have had a significant effect upon school and local education authority life. The scale of this change is probably best demonstrated by listing some of the specific milestones which have occurred over a 13-year period between 1974 and 1987:

1 1974 LEA reorganisation;
2 1975 Bullock Report: *A Language for Life*;
3 1976 William Tyndale Junior and Infant Schools Public Enquiry;
4 1976 James Callaghan and the Ruskin speech;
5 1977 Taylor Report: *A New Partnership for Our Schools*;
6 1978 Primary School Survey (England) by HMI;
7 1979 Education Act to repeal 1976 Act;
8 1980 Education Act encouraging more parental involvement and bringing in (more) parental governors;
9 1981 Education Act concentrating on Special Educational Needs;
10 1982 Cockcroft Report: *Mathematics Counts*;
11 MSC, YTS, TVEI, TRIST, GRIST and so forth with non-subject based curriculum change being brought about through central control of resources;
12 1985 Government White Paper; *Better Schools*;
13 1986 Education Act which requires annual reports from schools' governing bodies, increases parental power, the publication of LEA curriculum policies, amongst a number of other issues;
14 1987 Introduction of the new INSET;
15 1987 The Baker Pay Deal and the subsequent effects for teachers' conditions of service.

Let us briefly consider the Education Act, 1986, in more detail for a moment. Guidance on implementing the Act is given in Circular 8/86, issued by the Department of Education and Science. In a press release at the time from the Department, the Education Secretary, Kenneth Baker, stated that:

The Act provides for important changes in the way our schools are run. It pushes more power to the schools and strengthens their links with the parents and local communities they serve.

We are getting the Act's major reforms into place as quickly as possible. I am particularly glad that the new requirement for governors' annual reports and parents' meetings will enable all parents to make a fuller contribution to the life of their children's schools in this school year.

Among the provisions of the Act which came into force on Wednesday, 7 January, 1987, are those which:

—require each governing body to present a wide-ranging annual report to parents and to hold a meeting with parents to discuss this and other matters of interest (sections 30 and 31): the first meeting had to be held before the end of the summer term 1987.

—place a duty on LEAs to keep up to date and publish their curriculum policy (section 17).

—provide safeguards in the teaching of policies and sex education (sections 44 to 46).

—require local consultation in determining individual schools' admission arrangements (section 33).

—clarify the grounds LEAs have to take into account when deciding whether to provide free school transport (section 53).

—provide for more effective in–service teacher training through specific grants to LEAs (section 50).

—provide a revised framework for payments between LEAs for educating each other's pupils and students, in particular to extend to non-advanced further education the system of automatic reimbursement which currently applies to school pupils (sections 51 and 52).

Plans for implementing the remaining provisions of the Act included:

—the abolition of corporal punishment in the maintained sector from 15 August, 1987 (sections 47 and 48).

and, from 1 September, 1987:

financial delegation to schools (section 29).

—safeguards for freedom of speech in higher education (section 43).

—the reconstitution of school governing bodies to remove the LEA majority and strengthen the parental voice, and the clarification of governing bodies' powers (Parts I to III) to be completed by:
    1 September 1988 for county and maintained special schools; and
    1 September 1989 for voluntary schools.

Consequently, the subsequent organisation and implementation of this Act alone has meant massive extra work for teachers and administrators alike. Mr Baker's order of 1987 requires teachers to be available for work under the direction of the headteacher (directed time) for *up to* 1,265 hours per year. One hundred and ninety days will be with pupils and a further five days for other staff activities.

As well as the 1,265 hours of 'directed time' the teacher is required to work additional hours which may be needed to carry out her duties effectively. Cynically, it can also be noted that for the essential tasks of marking pupils' work and preparing lessons, material and teaching programmes, teachers will be expected to spend additional working time beyond that which is formally controlled. The fulfilment of the duties required must be judged by reference to the work done, hence, unlimited demands. Moreover, into the equation come voluntary activities – extra curricular, recreational, cultural and sporting. These activities are normally greatly valued by children and parents alike and, in a sense, should be regarded as part of the full professional role.

A second list offers the more diffuse, but nonetheless pervasive, changes in ideology and circumstances that have occurred over the same period:

1 the ever-increasing shortage of money since 1973;
2 falling and rising rolls;
3 the rise in perceived parent power;
4 the growth in the demands for accountability;
5 the movement of control of the curriculum away from the academic domain and into a public and very political arena;
6 the growth and effects of devolving financial autonomy to individual schools;
7 the changing public and political attitude towards education;
8 increasing cultural pluralism.

Added to these lists for primary schools have been:

(a) the effects of new technology such as microcomputers and word processors;

(b) the changes in positions of curriculum responsibility;

(c) the rise of primary science;

(d) the increase in nursery provision;

(e) the rising number of promoted female teachers in the profession and the continuing predominance of women in primary schools;

(f) the increasing numbers of pupils with special needs in schools and the integration of such pupils into the mainstream;

(g) the growth of teachers' in-service needs;

(h) the demands for management training for headteachers, deputies and scale post-holders;

(i) changes in resource needs, book provision and school–community attitudes.

When added to the educational changes, the contractual and legal demands upon teaching make it a constantly evolving profession which, in turn, means that no school as an organisation is static. There is always plenty going on. Teaching is becoming an increasingly demanding activity (NAS/UWT, 1987).

There can be little doubt that these changes have had a considerable impact upon LEAs, their advisory services, teachers and head-teachers, making the job of managing and organising education in schools even more complex. For example, falling rolls with their contingent school closures and teacher redeployment, the growth of more active governing bodies, the encouragement of parental choice and school–choice appeals, and the new requirements to have to 'bid' for central money, all mean extra LEA presence, representation and work. As a consequence, in some authorities the traditional primary adviser has acquired various parts of the conventional LEA officer role, while the education officer has begun to influence the curriculum and aspects of curriculum change (Stillman and Grant, 1986).

Constraints of space prevent us from discussing all these important and changing areas

further at this point. To highlight the effect of change on primary education we will now consider three aspects – autonomy, control of schools and appraisal – in more detail as being indicative of the implications of change upon primary education.

Autonomy

In this section we will concentrate on teachers' claims to exclusive rights in decision-making on curriculum and pedagogical matters. First, we will examine some of the traditional arguments for and against teacher autonomy on historical and professional grounds. Secondly, we will look at practical limitations on the freedom of action granted to headteachers. Lastly, we consider classroom teacher autonomy, suggesting that changes in school working relationships and school organisation may well force a reconceptualisation of the traditional view of the role of primary teachers especially if professionalism, in its fullest sense, is to develop.

Until comparatively recently, what went on in the primary school seemed to be left very much to the headteacher and the staff. It was apparently a private matter for them. Parents rarely entered the school and when they did so, it was usually by request. Primary education was non-controversial, and therefore not questioned. The seventies and eighties have seen great changes. What goes on in primary schools, what is taught and how it is taught are now the subjects of fierce debate (Richards, 1982a).

Arguments for autonomy

The claim that teachers have considerable freedom in practice is based on a number of different issues. Sometimes an appeal is made to history and tradition. 'We have always operated in this way' (by contrast with other countries, such as France). Then there is the 'teaching is a private activity' syndrome. In reality, however, this is historical fiction. White (1975) shows that until 1926 the state controlled the broad framework of the elementary school curriculum. The secondary school curriculum, incidentally, was prescribed until 1945. Even after 1926, elementary schools followed the guidance of the Board of Education's *Handbook of Suggestions* (revised in 1937) until after the Second World War (White, 1975; Lawton, 1981a). So justification for autonomy on historical grounds is hard to find.

A second often used argument is that teachers ought to be autonomous because of their particular group status. They are, after all, in a seemingly unique position to make decisions on educational matters by dint of training, expertise and experience. White (1979) makes a distinction between, on the one hand, matters related to pedagogy and teaching skills and on the other decisions on aims and curricula. The former, he says, are the province of the teacher – hence an area for granting limited autonomy. However, aims and curricula are inextricably bound up with wider questions about the kind of society in which we live and the kind of societal values we wish to promote. We are thus concerned with political matters in the broadest sense. White suggests that teachers have no more claims to expertise in these affairs than other societal groups like postmen or doctors. He argues, therefore, for democratic curriculum control, that is, no one group can be justified in claiming sole rights in these areas.

A third point revolves around the value of teacher autonomy. Both the HMI Primary Survey (DES, 1978b) and the Open Plan Schools' Survey (Bennett *et al.*, 1980) point to the wide and varying range of experiences which primary school children may or may not receive as part of their education. These findings have helped to raise questions of consistency and continuity in primary education, in turn prompting discussion of a national curriculum.

Some would regard this as the ultimate attack on teacher autonomy. Others would see it as releasing teachers from decisions on the curriculum which are not entirely or properly their area of decision-making, so they would be able to concentrate on their 'proper' task of using and improving their professional skills. The whole concept of teacher autonomy is open to fierce and continued debate.

Autonomy of the headteacher

The headteacher in the British primary school is traditionally seen as a rather solitary, omnipotent figure. Her unique position of responsibility is sometimes used to justify an autocratic leadership style.

Jones (1980) however, points out that the headteacher, in fact, has considerable restraints upon her freedom of action. There are, for example, obvious legislative restraints (she cannot eliminate religious education from her school curriculum, for instance).

Jones divides these constraints into three main areas: resources, societal and professional.

Resources come in three kinds – material, financial and human. Clearly, all three aspects control a headteacher's room for manoeuvre. For instance, her capitation allowance limits the number and kind of equipment purchases she may wish to make. Indeed, scarcity of resources in a time of contraction may force her to look outwards from school or local authority sources. She may seek to attract funds from outside agencies such as advisers or the parents' association, who in turn would wish to have a say in how monies are spent. Similarly, aspects relating to the school buildings themselves are likely to influence her actions. Societal changes during the last two decades have encouraged primary schools to regard themselves much more as part of a community. Parents have become involved in schools in a number of ways. They have the right, for example, to become members of school governing bodies and also to exert influence through parent teacher associations.

Nevertheless, even if all the other external agencies and pressures unite to support the headteacher the greatest influence on her professional actions remains that of her own teachers. If she cannot carry them with her then her plans will be frustrated – a fact made more complicated, of course, when she has not appointed the staff but simply inherited them and when their personalities do not 'gel', or their teaching and organising skills are not of the highest calibre.

Teacher autonomy

Clearly, if an organisation is to function smoothly and purposefully, the work of individuals within the organisation must be co-ordinated (Hoyle, 1974). From the post-war period to the mid-seventies, teachers in England and Wales enjoyed a remarkable degree of professional freedom (Evans, 1985). However, this kind of autonomy inside the classroom needs to be contrasted with 'the massive responsibility and power of the head at the school level' (Alexander, 1984), and other influences on the direction of the school as a whole in which the school has little choice – its catchment area, the law and the 'rules' of the local education authority.

While the primary school teacher has enjoyed considerable classroom freedom, her contribution to the overall policy of the school has been minimal, if changing. More recently, moves have been made towards increased teacher participation in school decision-making processes (Price, 1985). 'Whole school' reviews and policies have begun to dominate thinking. Indeed, publications from HMI such as *The Curriculum from 5–16* (DES, 1985b) imply a collegial approach to school policy formulation (Richards, 1986). Pedagogy has also been influenced, with teacher collaboration, shared expertise and team teaching approaches increasing. In many ways this kind of openness and the breaking down of boundaries within schools is a reflection of the rising democratisation of schools.

Hoyle (1974) points to the implications of these moves for teacher autonomy. Collegial ideas in decision-making and teaching involve a loss of some classroom autonomy. But, by the same token, influence on the school increases. If the teacher is to make an informed contribution to collaborative ventures, a degree of genuine professional understanding is required. Put simply, the teacher is required to be an 'extended professional', that is, conceiving of teaching as having a theoretical, rational basis rather than an instinctive practical basis. In this sense the teacher loses some autonomy but gains ultimate, professional control. In organisational terms, the problem becomes one of need for time, time to meet and plan with colleagues. Time is the commodity in shortest supply in teaching. The 1987 Teachers' 'Agreement' attempts to provide teachers with time which may be used for these activities.

It is interesting to note in passing that one of the intriguing suggestions made possible by the post-1987 in-service education regulations, is that arrangements can be made by local education authorities and schools for the purchase of time. That is, funds can be used to buy time (for supply cover or 'team-building' sessions) in much the same way as any other resources are purchased. Clearly, such decisions will reflect the priorities of the individual school.

The McGoldrick Case

Arguments were fuelled in staff rooms up and down the country by the media following the handling of the McGoldrick Case by Brent Local Education Authority. The facts first.

On 18 July, 1986, Miss Maureen McGoldrick, Headmistress of Sudbury Infants School was suspended from her position after allegedly making a racist remark during a telephone conversation with Mrs Sheilagh Szulc, a junior local authority officer. By all accounts Miss McGoldrick had been fully supportive of Brent's anti-racist policies. She had the full support of the parents of the school, a large proportion of whom were non-white, and had been praised for her multicultural work (Meikle , 1986a).

In accordance with disciplinary procedures, Brent Council asked the Governing Body of the school to investigate. On 26 August, 1986, the Governors found that there was no substance to the allegation. Spencer (1986) reported:

11

A Governors' meeting called under the authority's disciplinary proceedings, on August 26, unanimously found that there was no evidence she had made any racist remark. The Governors demanded her immediate reinstatement and remarked that the Authority had trivialised the whole concept of anti-racism.

On 29 August an LEA sub-committee met to discuss these findings and decided to hold a full disciplinary hearing. The disciplinary investigations were halted by the National Union of Teachers, representing Miss McGoldrick, until a High Court case was 'heard on the issue' (Hugill and Meikle, 1986).

After hearing the case:

Mr Justice Roche ruled that the Governors' findings that she should be reinstated were binding on the Council. He lifted her suspension and awarded her costs. (Spencer, 1986)

Mr Justice Roche pointed out that it was wrong for Miss McGoldrick to go through the ordeal of having been heard by the Governing body and then subsequently, to be subjected to a council disciplinary committee hearing. In effect she was being 'tried twice' (Spencer, 1986). In essence, the LEA had 'refused to accept' the decision of the Governors, after a hearing which had lasted for six hours, and was appealing to the court for support. In this case it was not forthcoming (Hugill, 1986a). Brent argued in court that the Governors had 'deprived the Authority of dismissing the head' (Spencer, 1986).

Miss McGoldrick then duly returned to Sudbury School but the Authority appealed against the High Court ruling 'forbidding it to hold a disciplinary hearing' (*Times Educational Supplement*, 7 November, 1986). This appeal was upheld and on 27 November, 1986, Brent announced its decision to hold a full disciplinary hearing.

On 15 December, 1986, Miss McGoldrick obtained a High Court injunction which prevented the Council from proceeding with a second disciplinary hearing until a judicial review had been held early in 1987.

On 16 December, 1986, the Secretary for Education and Science, Mr Kenneth Baker with a 'very unusual use of the severe power' given to him under Section 68 of the 1944 Education Act, ordered Brent Council to drop a further hearing. In Mr Baker's view, any new action was unreasonable; he considered the ordeal which she had suffered to be enough (Clare, 1986). This intervention may be interpreted by some as a reassertion of central power and control (Dowd, 1986). Certainly, Section 68 gives power to the Minister to decide that an LEA is acting unreasonably and to intervene as he thinks appropriate. Its exact implications are not clear and seem only to be limited by the Minister's view of what is or is not reasonable.

The Tameside Case of 1976, when central government unsuccessfully attempted to reverse a decision of a local authority over comprehensivisation plans, seems to weaken the authority of Section 68. But it still remains potentially an important source of power for central government (Evans, 1985).

The implications go far deeper than a vigorous promotion of a laudable anti-racist policy by an LEA. Walker (1986) concerns himself with the position of governing bodies. Just where does any power of final decision lie?

Should any decision reached by governors be open to checking by the local education authority?

He goes on to discuss the various contradictions and overlap in legislation concerning the government of schools. The 1986 Education Act goes some way towards clarifying the situation (Sallis, 1987). We are reminded, however, that the 'partnership' between schools and councils has been damaged. There are likely to be more disputes concerning teachers' conduct. Therefore, will the whole McGoldrick case, as far as the ordinary primary school teacher is concerned:

... enhance the value in teachers' eyes of union membership (Walker, 1986) and further decrease recruitment to the teaching profession?

Miss McGoldrick was 'given an assurance in the Court of Appeal' (*Times Educational Supplement*, 14 November, 1986) that her job would be safe. The Council seemed determined to hold a disciplinary hearing to underline its right to do so, even after the findings of the governors' enquiry.

Miss McGoldrick has returned to her school and the affair has faded from public gaze. However, certain questions remain. Just where does that leave the teacher and her autonomy? Is an alleged remark, a misunderstanding, words spoken under pressure (Hugill, 1986b) really sufficient to justify the subsequent turmoil? Is such a debate going to aid the partnership between schools and LEAs? Both headteachers and teachers need to feel a trust and confidence in their dealings with their LEA. The reverse is also true. Chance, unfortunate remarks, are sometimes made; this is a fact of life. The McGoldrick affair highlights the delicacy of relationships between schools and local authorities.

A third emerging issue which requires equally sensitive handling is that of teacher appraisal.

Teacher appraisal

Appraisal may be regarded as a process of forming qualitative judgements about activities, people or organisations. Assessment, on the other hand, implies measurement and grading against a set of criteria (Suffolk, 1985). The terms have sometimes been confused and discussion of appraisal has been clouded by the problems and fears related to grading of teacher performance.

Teacher assessment has been in existence in one form or another for a long time. The Victorians had a simple method of assessment: payment by results. The system was introduced in 1861, as a response to the Newcastle Report, which had criticised standards of education in elementary schools, on somewhat flimsy evidence. Charges were made

that the curriculum was sometimes too ambitious, neglecting a sound basis in the 3 Rs (May and Greer, 1970). Two-thirds of the Government grant to schools was made dependent on pupils' attendance and their end of term examination success. Of course, teachers 'taught to the test' and used all kinds of methods to make sure their children passed (Pickard, 1985). The system was abolished in 1895, but fears of a return to 'payment by results' perhaps underlay contemporary teacher hostility to the initial appearance of appraisal systems in education during the last decade. Some teachers feared that an attempt would be made to measure their classroom performance and that the complexities of teaching would be reduced to a checklist leading to a crude judgement being passed upon them.

Speeches such as that made by Sir Keith Joseph in Sheffield in January 1984 did little to allay such fears. He linked embryonic appraisal systems then developing in some local authorities with the need to weed out those teachers whose performance was unsatisfactory.

However, there has been a significant change in attitudes towards appraisal as assessment ideas have moved into the background, and appraisal has come to be seen as supportive and developmental in the career of the teacher, rather than a threat. It may be seen as a continuous formative process, sensitive to a changing context rather than a summative 'one-off' session. Parallel ideas of teacher self-evaluation and school development have also begun to grow.

Why appraise?

Any system of appraisal is set up to improve children's learning in school. A scheme which does not do this ought to be rejected (Nisbet, 1986). This seems obvious. Nevertheless, at a time when management courses proliferate and there is much talk of systems and structure, the question of what the primary school is about is in danger of being forgotten. It

13

follows, therefore, that the aims of a suggested appraisal system for the school are:

(a) to improve learning opportunities for all pupils;
(b) to improve the 'tone', or hidden curriculum, which influences all work in the school.

For the teacher, appraisal should:

(a) recognise and support effective practice;
(b) identify areas for development and improvement;
(c) identify and develop potential (Suffolk, 1985)

A supportive scheme of this nature, if it is to succeed, must clearly be kept separate from disciplinary procedures. The six local authority pilot schemes launched in 1986 seem to be emphasising different aspects of the process within their models, while in general reflecting these aims. For example, the influential Suffolk scheme seeks to provide a framework for overcoming teacher weaknesses. Mr Duncan Graham, Chief Education Officer, saw the scheme as a structure 'for professional development and to identify in-service training needs'. On the other hand, plans in Salford suggest teacher self-evaluation as a means of identifying the in-service training needs of schools and individual teachers. Similarly, Cumbria saw that individual teacher needs cannot be separated from those of the school. However, it is worth noting that the Croydon scheme views appraisal as a means of assessment for teacher promotion and improving cost effectiveness (Nash, 1986).

Answers to the question 'Why appraise?' from the wider perspectives of a local authority, are provided in part by mounting pressures in the last decade to examine the curricular provision in their schools. The development of curriculum guidelines and monitoring procedures are now a much more established feature of an education authority's work.

The Suffolk authority, therefore, sees appraisal as just one part of its four-fold curriculum provision. Each part – curriculum development, in-service management training, teacher appraisal and school appraisal – being linked (Graham, 1986).

How is it to be done?

Appraisal seems to involve three processes:

(i) Agreeing on what is expected of the teacher –
  (a) a job specification
  (b) criteria for appraising performance on the job
(ii) Collecting evidence on the teacher's performance
(iii) Making judgements, reaching decisions and acting upon them. (DES, 1986a)

These processes are included in all the appraisal schemes referred to so far. The work of the six pilot authorities will be to produce guidelines adaptable to the needs of all 104 local authorities and so assist them in setting up their own schemes. The pioneering work of Suffolk has been influential. An annual system is envisaged and several stages suggested. These are:

1 *Preparation*
Preparation for the school would include an introduction to the principles underlying the scheme and agreement about procedures. For the teacher areas for appraisal would be negotiated. It is important that these areas and these alone form the subject of a particular appraisal.

2 *Classroom Observation*
This would involve collecting data on mutually agreed criteria for structuring observations. This should be done at least twice a year (*Education*, 1985).

3 *The Interview*
This is designed to acknowledge professional strengths and weaknesses, assist the teacher's professional growth and set suitable targets for the coming year. It is 'job' and not 'person'-centred.

4 *Results*
Action of some sort is now required to assist

the teacher in working towards his targets. His effort should be maintained by provision for feedback.

5 *Monitoring*

Improvement must be acknowledged by recognition and praise. Advice and support will also be required.

6 *Moderation*

This is a form of quality control (Graham, 1986). It will be undertaken by the LEA to ensure consistency. There are resource implications in the provision of moderators who need to be experienced and trained in observation and supervision.

7 *Evaluation*

This is required to ensure that the scheme does not become a mere paper exercise failing to achieve its aims (Suffolk, 1985).

The emphasis in the model is on fostering a framework for a school-based appraisal system. However, the local education authority has a responsibility to establish schemes as part of its overall function in managing schools and a wider accountability to parents and public (Graham, 1986).

Problems and difficulties

Many ideas currently in circulation are based on industrial line management approaches. Each member of the organisation on this model has a specific role and responsibilities (defined in a job description) and is directly accountable to a superior. Some would argue that the qualities of flexibility and adaptability required in a primary school teacher do not fit easily into such a tightly defined role analysis. The job description in this context can only indicate duties in a broad sense. The achievement of sales figures, for example, is hardly appropriate in the primary school. There is, in fact, no one clear measurable educational 'output' which can be attributed to the teacher in the way that an industrial production outcome can be identified. It is perhaps heartening to note that industrial models of appraisal do not appear to be under considera-

tion by the Department of Education and Science at present.

Other professions, and industry itself, have become aware of some of the difficulties in the focus of their own existing appraisal procedures and have begun to change them. In the nursing profession, for example, appraisal which sought to analyse the behaviour of nurses has now begun to look at the patients' care and response to nursing. This is very much a client-centred approach (Dadds, 1986). It is perhaps also applicable to teachers who as, professionals, would see themselves accountable to their pupils or parents rather than to colleagues. Hence an industrial model based on subordinate accountability to a superior may not be appropriate (King, 1986). Current models of teacher appraisal seem to focus introspectively on what the teacher, rather than the pupil, does.

Who is to do the appraising?

If teachers are to have confidence in the system, it is essential that the appraisers have credibility. They must have experience in the work of the appraisee and be suitably trained in appraisal skills and methods. Worries expressed by teachers in the Suffolk study (1985) were 'about their confidence in and empathy with the designated appraiser'. It is suggested that the appraiser would normally be the headteacher in the case of the primary school. The headteacher herself in turn, would be appraised by other experienced headteachers of proven ability, perhaps seconded for this purpose. There is a clear need for training in observational skills. The question as to who will train the trainers remains, however.

The collection of information

One of the areas of greatest concern to teachers is classroom observation which may be used to gather information prior to interview. It is suggested that this is done at least twice a year and is central to the whole

15

scheme. The difficulties lie in three main areas:

(a) the procedure to be used,
(b) the skills needed for classroom observation,
(c) the need for a 'fair sample' of lessons to be observed. (Suffolk, 1985)

The procedure for observation should be negotiated with the teacher, and mutual agreement reached on criteria. The greater problem comes in actually observing teacher competencies. The observer may lack skill or exhibit bias. Nuttall (1986) warns:

> Methodology and instrumentation are not value-free, and even with the most structured of observation schedules, observers will not always agree.

Classroom observation techniques exist but are still developing (DES, 1986a).

Some of these issues will be examined in our discussion of the effective teacher (Chapter 17), but put simply, there is more than one way of teaching. An appraisal should take account of context. Even if it were possible to reproduce identical teacher behaviours, different variables such as resources, pupils and catchment area would produce differing results. Teaching is a complex art. All that can be said is that there is 'a spectrum of teacher competence' (Suffolk, 1985).

Many teachers are unhappy about what they perceive as intrusions which will change the normal classroom situation and give only a 'snapshot' view of their performance (*Junior Education*, 1985). We may even begin to question the apparently central role that classroom observation is accorded in appraisal schemes currently under consideration. There may be other ways of evaluating teacher performance which ought to be considered.

Confidentiality

Most schemes assume that a record will be kept of the appraisal interview. The question of who will have access to such records, and what form they will take, is problematic. One suggestion is that the final record takes the form of a version agreed by and acceptable to all parties. In the event of dispute, it is possible that this is a situation where the local authority's monitoring role may be brought into play.

Resources

Although many teachers would sympathise with the stated aims of appraisal, doubts have been voiced about the provision of resources needed to operationalise such a scheme.

The estimates of time required for the seven-fold model outlined above vary from some 10 to 12 hours per teacher per annum. This is a substantial investment of resources when considered alongside the training period required for appraisers. Financial implications, too, are considerable. For example, Brian Wilcox, chief adviser of Sheffield local education authority which has approximately 5,000 teachers, estimates that the initial cost of setting up a scheme on the Suffolk model would be at least £1 million (*Education*, 1986). This far exceeds his authority's budget for in-service programmes. The Suffolk Report (1985) cites an appraisal scheme in Georgia, Alabama, which suggests running costs of $1,000 (£660) per teacher per year. There are costs also implied in follow-up action after the interview. For example, a teacher may agree that she should update her pedagogical skills in the teaching of mathematics. If help in improving her performance, perhaps in the form of a course or leave of absence to observe good practice, is not forthcoming, then the system will be quickly discredited.

The resource implications have to be squarely faced. The commitment of a local authority to appraisal will be indicated by the amount of resources devoted to it (Graham, 1986).

Will it be worth it?

Great advantages are claimed for appraisal. They include ensuring teacher accountability, increased parental power, a weeding out of ineffective teachers and a positive increase in teaching performance levels. However, doubts still remain.

Appraisal has come to dominate our thinking, perhaps diverting attention from other equally important questions about raising the quality of our schools.

King (1986), for example, argues for individual and group evaluation, encouraging schools to develop a common sense of purpose. He suggests that:

> Appraising professional performance should also be part of this, but it should be in terms of sharing experience and seeking self-knowledge.

Industry has had many years of experience in appraisal. According to Ron Shepherd, a senior manager of the Ford Motor Company, an appraisal scheme cannot compensate for poor recruitment and lack of direction (*Education*, 1985). Systems, he warns, need frequent updating and cannot remain uncontaminated by incompetent managers. Education may be expecting too much.

Therefore, the seemingly simple task of teacher appraisal is in reality a very complex one. We have demonstrated that ideas have changed from measurement systems to supportive and developmental models. The needs of primary schools, in particular the small primary school, have not been addressed seriously so far. Is appraisal simply going to encourage teaching for appraisal? Indeed, are some things of value to the primary school non-appraisable?

The results of the Croydon approach, basing appraisal partly on pupil outcomes, will be particularly interesting in primaries. It would be all too easy for a strong emphasis on measurable outcomes to stifle primary teachers' initiative, and limit the curriculum they offer in ways that would also limit children's achievements. The challenge is to find appraisal methods that help primary teachers to offer the Government's ideal broad, balanced, relevant and differentiated curriculum. (*Times Educational Supplement*, 5 December, 1986)

If this did not happen and primary education lost its view of the child then the costs of appraisal would outweigh any of its advantages. If, on the other hand, systems can be developed which are supportive of primary teachers and their work and do improve the learning opportunities for children, then appraisal is welcomed.

3 The shape of primary schools

The structural organisation of primary schools is a topic about which comparatively little has been written in the existing literature. This is partly due to the uneven and patchy nature of research on the subject. For example, virtually no systematic research exists on the best or alternative ways of organising or managing primary schools. Until the ILEA Junior School Project almost nothing was known about why some primary schools are different from and more effective than others (Mortimore *et al.*, 1985).

As a new headteacher, teacher or student teacher you may ask yourself why the school is organised in this or that way and whether the present infrastucture could be improved. Without an understanding of organisational issues you will only be in a position to ask the question. You will be unable to do very much with the answers.

In the prevailing situation, one of the key managerial tasks of the head is to ensure that all staff are properly inducted into the structure and organisation of their school. Only then will teachers be able to play a full and active part in the running and organisation of their schools. Without such basic and essential information, teachers can unwittingly fail to comprehend the very real local and national constraints under which headteachers manage and organise their schools and local

education authority officials administer the educational service.

Hence this chapter is predicated on the assumption that knowledge breeds both insight and understanding. It attempts to provide a brief overview of some of the structural reasons which lie behind much present-day primary school organisation. Along with Chapters 4, 5 and 6 it focuses on staff organisation in particular. In any effective school, the proper use of teachers is crucial. The contents of this chapter include a discussion of important, but sometimes forgotten, background issues, such as: the number and sizes of primary schools, primary school structures in theory and in practice and the vexed question of staffing primary schools. The chapter actually reflects primary school organisational structure which pertained until 1987. The new contract, while altering the formal structure, is unlikely to affect the realities of responsibility and influence for several years to come. In fact, the differences between formal and actual structure can be more easily examined within the traditional scale post framework. The analysis in this chapter, therefore, deals with the traditional organisation which includes discussion of scale post responsibilities. Chapter 4 concentrates on the historical significance of posts of responsibility, scale posts and staff deployment, the role of postholders, the concept of multiple responsibilities, as well as the role of non-teaching staff. In Chapters 5 and 6 the themes of staff selection and organisation are developed.

Number and sizes of primary schools

By the mid-1980s there were in excess of 20,000 schools of all types which were deemed 'primary' by the Department of Education and Science. These included infant, first, infant/junior, first/middle, junior and 8–12 middle schools. Middle schools with age ranges other than 8–12 are deemed secondary by the DES.

Table 3.1 shows details of school sizes by the different types of primary school in 1981. From the table it is apparent that roughly half the schools were of the all-through primary type, i.e. infant/junior or first/middle. Over 60 per cent had between 100 and 300 children on their roll. Schools of this size will have a relatively small teaching staff of between four and 12 teachers.

There exist a diminishing number of one or two teacher schools. Smaller schools are most prevalent in parts of rural Wales and Scotland and in some regions in England, like East Anglia. Similarly, there are comparatively few large schools with a teaching staff numbering 30 or more.

Table 3.2 shows details of school sizes by the different types of primary school in 1984.

Over 60 per cent had between 100 and 300 children on their roll

	0 to 50	51 to 100	101 to 200	201 to 300	301 to 400	401 to 600	601 to 800	801 to 1000	Totals
Infant	104	546	2510	554	29	1	–	–	3744
First	398	424	1139	717	188	52	–	–	2918
Inf/Jun	1312	1779	2831	2475	902	347	23	–	9699
First/ Middle	4	12	65	163	83	57	4	–	388
Junior	6	42	661	1638	871	280	7	1	3506
Middle/ Primary	–	3	103	313	238	102	9	–	768
All Primary Schools	1824	2806	7309	5860	2311	839	43	1	20993
Percentage	8.7	13.4	34.8	27.9	11.0	4.0	0.2	–	100.0

Table 3.1 *Numbers and sizes of primary schools in England 1981*

(Adapted from DES, *Statistics of Education – Schools*, January, 1981a, Table A3/81.)

	0 to 50	51 to 100	101 to 200	201 to 300	301 to 400	401 to 600	601 to 800	801 to 1000	Totals
Infant	94	467	2153	458	22	5	–	–	3199
First	436	446	1202	591	123	24	–	–	2822
Inf/Jun	1325	1778	3243	2489	845	248	15	–	9943
First/ Middle	8	2	68	157	73	44	2	–	354
Junior	3	54	961	1423	476	79	–	1	2997
Middle/ Primary	–	5	146	312	167	54	2	–	686
All Primary Schools	1866	2747	7773	5430	1706	454	19	1	20001
Percentage	9.3	13.7	38.9	27.1	8.5	2.3	0.1	–	100.0

Table 3.2 *Numbers and sizes of primary schools in England 1984*

(Adapted from DES, *Statistics of Education – Schools*, January, 1984b, Table A3/84.)

A comparison between Tables 3.1 and 3.2 indicates the effects of changing rolls over a three-year period in England.

In addition to the main teaching complement, many schools have extra part-time or, occasionally, full-time staff concerned with such things as remedial help, community liaison or even French. A lot of schools also have visiting peripatetic staff whose deployment within the school is usually negotiated between the advisory service and the head-teacher. Nevertheless, in organisational terms, most primary schools can be categorised as 'small', especially when contrasted with comprehensive schools or industrial and commercial concerns. Primary schools also need a range of non-teaching staff to help run them. These will be dealt with later in the chapter.

The school hierarchy

The members of staff of any school constitute the key resource. Without the staff there would be no schools, a point which can sometimes be forgotten when teachers, like other professional groups, are subjected to unnecessarily harsh and 'abrasive' styles of leadership. As the long industrial action of 1984, 1985, 1986 and 1987 showed, even in times when shortages of materials, facilities and capitation militate against effective teaching and management, there remains a tendency for the everyday work of the majority of those involved in schooling to continue unabated. Sometimes, glaring deficiencies are glossed over by the endeavours of conscientious staff and caring parents. It is not unknown, for example, for teachers of first year infant classes to have to teach 40 pupils – hardly an ideal situation. Nor is it unknown for staff in primary schools to teach in dilapidated buildings with leaking roofs and damp walls, as confirmed by reports in the eighties (NCPTA, 1986). Thus many staffs are forced to do the best they can under difficult circumstances. Viewed from an educational or managerial perspective, this is hardly ideal, particularly as there are marked regional variations and even variations between schools in the same authority. When such matters come to the fore, it can easily be forgotten that the proper organisation of staff constitutes the single most important part of effective school management. And good management stems from the top. A school with a poor head is never going to function as well as one with a good head.

Since, with few exceptions, teachers in primary schools are heads, deputy heads or class teachers, it is not difficult to represent the formal hierarchy of the typical primary school (see Figure 3.1). In most primary

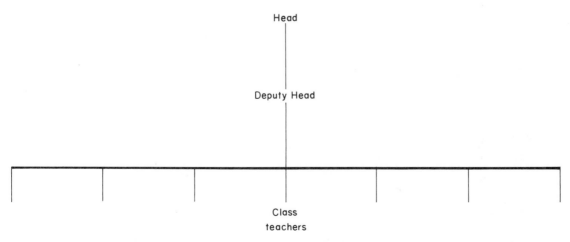

Figure 3.1 *Hierarchy of the typical primary school*

schools, deputy heads usually, and heads sometimes, are also class teachers.

Figures 3.1 to 3.3 are interesting in their own right. They show the differences between actual and apparent structures in the organisation of primary schools. Figure 3.1 indicates the conventional theoretical view. Figure 3.2 moves towards the reality, something that is reinforced and complicated by the situational interaction processes which are shown in Figure 3.3. Taken collectively, Figures 3.1 to 3.3 highlight the enormous gulf which can exist between theory and practice as most primary teachers will readily testify.

The pyramid presented in Figure 3.1 is, by comparison with secondary school structures or most industrial organisations, a 'flat' one. In the past, primary school teachers have tended to regard one another as equals, irrespective of status. Lortie (1969) makes the point that in many primary schools the responsibility and status of 'class teacher' tends to take precedence over other formal aspects of the role such as seniority and status. Until recently, for example, the deputy head's position tended to have little significance or impact beyond his or her role as class teacher or, as we shall discuss later in the book, curriculum leader (Alexander, 1984). Indeed, in many small primary schools, a senior assistant teacher fulfils the functions of deputy head.

In practice, therefore, the typical primary school structure is more like Figure 3.2. Of course, such a simplistic diagram does not do justice to the complexity of the structure in terms of what Paisey (1981b) calls jobs, positions and authority, and what Alexander (1984) refers to as tasks, status and authority.

Ordinary class teachers (other than the head or deputy) were generally paid on the basic salary scale (Scale 1), or as designated postholders on Scale 2 or 3 grades. The latter were usually termed 'scale posts' in staff-room jargon. Payments above the basic scale were almost always made, at least in theory, for the performance of additional tasks which were deemed to be necessary and required some expertise. These included teachers in charge of aesthetics, empirics, maths, science, art, music, needlework. Theoretically, they carried some additional status and, possibly, some kudos and authority. These experienced staff alter the rather simplistic organisational model presented earlier and give a more realistic structure which is represented in Figure 3.3.

The 'points system' linked salary scales to school size, age of pupils and, occasionally, special circumstances (see later). The fact that the deployment of scale posts (Scale 2 and above) was often, up to the rank of deputy, made entirely at the discretion of the head

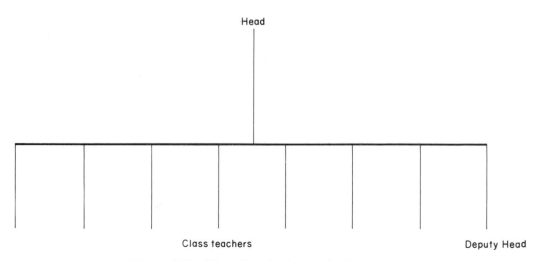

Figure 3.2 *The reality of primary school organisation*

22

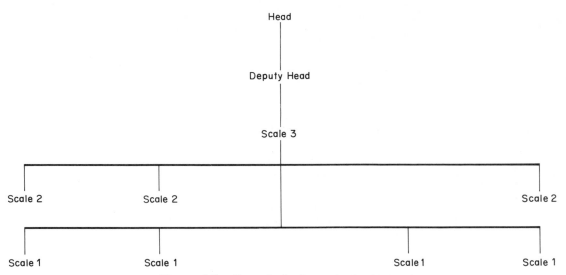

Figure 3.3   *Formal school organisation in practice*

acting alone or in conjunction with appropriate advisers, was not the most scientific process. Moreover, generally speaking, once a scale post was awarded, it remained with the recipient for the rest of his or her career, irrespective of changing individual and school circumstances. The best a head could hope for was a re-negotiation of the terms of the appointment. This meant that the actual structure of a school's hierarchy was often far more complex than the apparently straightforward formal structure depicted earlier. There were numerous reasons for this state of affairs, including complex interpersonal relationships and personality factors. We shall consider these matters further shortly by examining the case study of Homeland County Junior, a medium-to-large school.

But first, it is important to re-emphasise that primary education itself is in a state of flux due to implementing the 1986 Education Act, rising and falling rolls, new contracts, reorganisations, amalgamations, economic strictures and the increasing recognition which is being given to primary teaching by professionals and administrators alike (Reid, 1983; Hopkins and Reid, 1985).

As Bush *et al.*, (1981) point out, in the primary school, the deputy head is usually a class teacher and therefore holds two places in the management structure – teacher and deputy. A 'typical' structure for a two form entry junior school might have looked something like Figure 3.4. The ambiguity of the deputy's position in this structure arises partly from the duality of her role. She is both a class teacher on the same basis as her colleagues, and in the same relationship to the head as they are, and also in some respects superordinate to her colleagues in her position as deputy. It is scarcely surprising that, 'teachers may regard the deputy as one of themselves without the right to prescribe behaviour for them' (Coulson, 1974). Bush *et al.* consider that further ambiguity results from the uncertain position of the deputy in the primary school hierarchy. Much evidence suggests that the head maintains a direct relationship with primary teachers, as indicated in Figure 3.4. 'Research and informed comment indicate that charismatic elements form major components of the role conceptions of many primary school heads' (Coulson, 1974). The influence of charismatic authority is largely direct between the leader and his subordinate (Bush *et al.*, 1981). A head concerned to maintain this direct relationship with teaching staff gives her deputy little opportunity to find a meaningful place within the management structure. The deputy is in limbo, neither

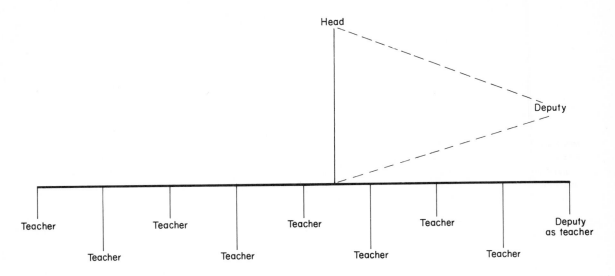

Figure 3.4 *'Typical' primary school management structure*

clearly on the same basis as her colleagues nor clearly in an authority relationship with them. The deputy's dependent role is emphasised by Coulson (1974):

> The implementation of a decision taken by a subordinate depends upon the extent to which the head supports it ... there is nothing in the primary school deputy head's role which assures compliance with decisions taken.

Homeland Junior

There is more to any organisation than a mere diagramatic representation of its structure. Therefore, we now consider the case of 'Homeland Junior' to bring some of our earlier points home in realistic terms.

The actual structure of Homeland Junior in 1986 (in terms of Pollard's (1985) concept of functional authority) might at first sight seem somewhat unexpected (see Figure 3.5). But Homeland Junior is, in fact, based on a school well known to the authors. We write from first hand experience and bluntly, in the knowledge that readers will understand the nuances. Like Homeland, most schools have their own idiosyncratic features.

Mrs Ward, the Head, was comparatively new to the school. She was keen, able and articulate. Unfortunately, she was deficient in her understanding of how to manage change in schools. As a result, some of her best endeavours were not bearing the fruit for which she hoped.

Mr Gregson, the Deputy Head of Homeland Junior, had, to all intents and purposes, already 'retired', except for the fact that he turned up every day and taught his J4 class. He has never got on very well with the 'new' Head after failing to land the post himself. All parties within and outside the school recognised that the only desirable solution was for him to take early retirement – something he showed little sign of doing. He was an old-fashioned teacher held in deep affection by his pupils and amused tolerance by other members of staff.

Similarly Mr Jones had a Scale 3 post which used to mean something but whose actual responsibilities have become negligible apart from his curriculum leadership function, which he does not really exercise apart from the ordering of stock. His former responsibilities were acquired over several years, under the stewardship of a previous headteacher with whom he served in the Royal Air Force. These gradually, and not unwillingly were taken over by upwardly mobile younger teachers such as Miss Court who looks after

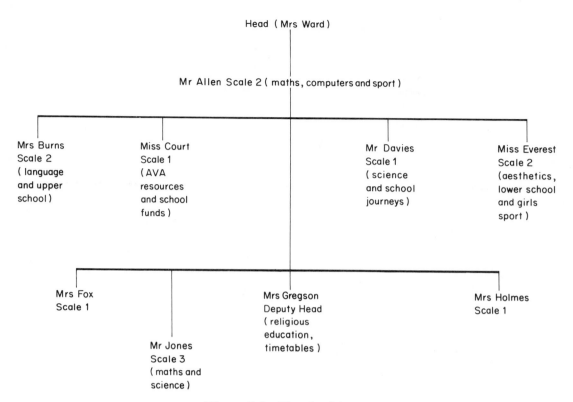

```
                              Head (Mrs Ward)
                                    │
                                    │
                    Mr Allen Scale 2 ( maths, computers and sport )
   ┌─────────────────┬─────────────────┬─────────────────┐
Mrs Burns         Miss Court        Mr Davies         Miss Everest
Scale 2           Scale 1           Scale 1           Scale 2
( language        ( AVA             ( science         (aesthetics,
and upper         resources         and school        lower school
school )          and school        journeys )        and girls
                  funds )                              sport )

   ┌─────────────────┬─────────────────────────────────┐
Mrs Fox                        Mrs Gregson              Mrs Holmes
Scale 1                        Deputy Head              Scale 1
                               ( religious
         Mr Jones              education,
         Scale 3               timetables )
         ( maths and
         science )
```

Figure 3.5 *Homeland Junior*

audio-visual aids and library resources, as well as being at the forefront of any fund-raising and social functions. Mr Jones' position in the hierarchy, as shown in Figure 3.5, was a reflection of the fact that, unlike the Deputy Head, he was not even considered to be a competent class teacher.

Mr Allen, who was a recent appointee, had a Scale 2 post which was supposed to encompass computers, mathematics and sport. He was well assisted in the latter by Miss Everest who looked after the girls' games as well as overseeing aesthetics on a 'voluntary' basis and having a nominal responsibility for the lower school. Mr Allen is undoubtedly the Deputy Head for which the Head, Mrs Ward, had always hoped. He was widely experienced, highly qualified and had a helpful, vibrant nature. Accordingly, he was looked up to by most of the staff. Mrs Ward was fearful of losing his talent. Nevertheless, she knew she had little choice but to hint and to await

developments from the incumbent – Mr Gregson.

Mrs Burns had nominal responsibility for the upper school. She was also in charge of language throughout the school. She was justifiably proud of the fact that she formulated and put into operation a coherent and relatively effective language policy for the school, shortly before Mrs Ward was appointed. She was a very competent class teacher whose Achilles' heel, like so many other primary teachers, was science.

Mr Davies had been at the school for three years, following his BSc in Biology and his PGCE. His keenness and expertise in science earned him his place in the hierarchy. His enthusiasm for shouldering the burdens of organising school trips gained him some respect, but mostly gratitude, from other members of staff. Formerly they had taken it in turns to prepare, execute and follow-up such activities – something which most of them secretly dreaded. Mr Davies appeared to be going places, provided he could recognise and rectify his limitations in certain areas of the curriculum, notably maths and aesthetics about which, in Mrs Ward's words, 'he is clueless'. Unfortunately, for a man so devoted to his own subject, his pedagogical knowledge was strictly limited. This was a constant source of irritation to Mrs Ward who laid the blame firmly on the way graduate teachers are trained without knowing the truth or otherwise of her supposition.

Mrs Fox and Mrs Holmes were unpretentious, steady class teachers with little long-term ambition beyond the well-being of their pupils. Mrs Fox had been at the school for many years with only a break for maternity leave. Mrs Holmes, while somewhat less experienced, looked and acted like a fixture and was the agent for much cohesion in the staff-room. Renowned for her expertise in needlework and herbal remedies, she was a down-to-earth teacher much liked by all.

Homeland Junior, then, was the kind of complex community which has to be organised and managed. Unlike many schools in the authority, it had a reasonable balance of male and female staff with, predictably, a preponderance of males in key scale posts. There is little evidence to suggest that the majority of infant, junior and primary schools are notably less complex in terms of structure or personalities than Homeland. Nevertheless, it should never be forgotten that every school is unique and has its own set of circumstances. This is one of the reasons why managing primary schools can be so difficult.

Therefore, in organisational terms, there is no such thing as a 'typical' primary school. As mentioned earlier (see Table 3.1), there are at least six different 'types' of school deemed primary by the DES. If we consider that a primary school with a nursery is a different kind of school from one without, the total of possible types is now immediately increased to 10. Add to this the further possibility of schools having classes for children with special educational needs, then it could be argued that there are around 20 different kinds of primary establishments in all, in England and Wales. When differences between primary schools in terms of their catchment area, socio-economic background and cognitive and non-cognitive outcomes are considered (Heal, 1978; Reynolds and Reid, 1985; Mortimore *et al.*, 1985), it is not difficult to appreciate that teaching in one school is inevitably very different from teaching in another. The same applies to organising and managing schools. Explicitly, being a success in one school is no guarantee of being a success in another. Every institution is a result of the mixture of the interaction between the personalities and temperaments of the staff, which, in turn, affects the organisational and management style of the school. Very often, these human dimensions are more important than anything else.

Staffing primary schools

One of the major differences between schools, irrespective of other factors such as geographical location, is their size. Much depends upon this variable (Patrick, 1985; Hopkins, 1985) particularly the 'points system', the consequent staffing levels for schools and the deployment of those staff.

The complexities and anomalies of the system of scale posts have already been touched upon. Clearly, a prime management function for headteachers and their deputies is to make the best use of the total number of staff under their charge. However, decisions related to the actual number of staff located in a school are usually made by officers of the local education authority based on the individual circumstances of each school. Factors influencing this decision generally include a school's size, catchment area, buildings provision and resources. Another contributory factor (pre-1987) was the number of 'above Scale 1' posts which were allocated to a school. Most local education authorities did retain the right to vary the points allocation to a school in the light of all the circumstances prevailing. This provided LEAs with the option of giving some schools extra staff for good social or educational reasons. For example, a split-site campus, remedial difficulties or multicultural needs, are still reasons for extra staffing. Sometimes, too, schools are protected for reasons of economic viability as when it is more cost-effective to lower pupil–teacher ratios than open new schools. Conversely, the reverse can sometimes be true. In times of economic restraint, it is not unusual for large schools to be made to wait before appointing replacements after losing staff for one reason or another.

The actual numbers of staff allocated to particular schools are usually easily calculated from the LEA guidelines and policies on central staff allocations. Often, however, these are not fully understood by many teachers.

Furthermore, obtaining the appropriate Pupil–Teacher Ratio (PTR) for a school within an authority can be complicated by:

(a) a tendency for different authorities to use different formulae for staffing their schools;
(b) the discretion allowed for identified special needs children (under Section 11 of the Local Government Act, 1966);
(c) the inclusion of headteachers and certain unattached staff in the overall PTR;
(d) unusual, peculiar or other local circumstances. Nationally, variations abound.

Table 3.3 presents the national statistics for overall pupil-teacher ratios in primary schools in England and Wales. Of course, such national figures say little about PTRs for individual schools. They say even less about actual class sizes, where the variation is enormous, even after accounting for such factors as special classes. Nevertheless, they are a guide and are frequently quoted in educational debates, especially, it seems, by politicians, thereby causing some teachers to disbelieve their ears!

It may be instructive to examine how *one* formula in an LEA works for staffing purposes. For reasons of discretion we shall refer to this authority as Loamshire. This authority adopts the principle that no single-age class shall exceed 32 and no mixed-age class 26 and calculations are based exactly on this.

The 'formula' is merely a mechanical method of deciding staffing levels in individual schools. It says nothing about how staff should actually be deployed within a school which is, as in most places, left to the discretion of the head. The formula is also an attempt to avoid disputes over staff numbers between schools. It is intended to be a method which is equitable and available for public scrutiny so that anyone can, in principle, calculate the minimum staffing entitlement for any given school.

As the calculation is a 'mechanical' process, it is carried out as though a school would be organised into single-age classes of 32 and mixed-age classes of 26 as far as is numerically practicable, starting from the J4 level and working downwards to infant, nursery and reception classes. The actual figures for one medium-sized primary school are given in Table 3.4. These calculations simply give the number of staff who are allocated to the school by the LEA, excluding the head.

The numbers in bold type in Table 3.4 are the actual numbers in each of the seven year

Mean primary PTRs	1981/82	1982/83	1983/84	1984/85
English counties	23.2	23.0	22.7	22.7
Welsh counties	21.1	21.3	20.7	21.0
All LEAs in England and Wales	22.5	22.3	21.8	21.9

Table 3.3 *Mean primary PTRs for England and Wales*
(Source: CIPFA Educational Statistics 1981–1985)

	N	IR	I1	I2	J1	J2	J3	J4	TOT	SPEC
Pupils	23	33	32	24	30	21	29	35	226	(22)
Split		(16)	(17 + 9)	(23 + 3)	(21 + 5)	(25 + 1)	(20 + 6)	(23 + 3)	(32)	
'Classes'		16	26	26	26	26	26	26	32	
Staff	0.5	1	1	1	1	1	1	1	1	8.5	(3)

Table 3.4 *Calculation of staffing for a primary school*

groups in the school. The figures in brackets show the notional 'split' of each year group into single-age and mixed-age classes. Thus there are 35 fourth year juniors, split into a notional 'class' of 32, leaving 3 pupils to be 'added on' to 23 J3 children to make a mixed 'class' of 26. As can be seen, this particular school, for calculation purposes, has almost all pupils in mixed-age groups – the one group of 32 J4 children and the small group of 16 reception infants being the exceptions. Ignoring the nursery and special needs children, the school ends up with 8 assistant teachers by the use of the formula, giving an overall PTR of 25.5 or, if the head is included, 22.7. In fact, Loamshire expects heads in schools with less than 130 pupils to teach a class four days out of five. Above this number heads are usually free of mandatory class responsibility. Added to this, the school is allocated three special class teachers for the 22 special needs children plus 0.5 for nursery, giving a grand total of 12.5 teachers for the school.

Staffing for the nursery children is calculated separately from the rest of the school on the basis of a straightforward allocation on numbers as follows:

Number of children	Staff Allocation
0–13	Nil
14–26	0.5
27–52	1.0
53–78	1.5

It should be noted that nursery children attend for half-days only and have the staffing allocation of 0.5 members of staff for each set of 26 nursery children. Every nursery group

also has a nursery nurse allocated on the same basis, i.e. 0.5 for each set of 26 children.

Special needs pupils are staffed separately and used to be in their own classes (termed 'observation units') for much of the time. At an accelerating pace, many special needs children are, since the 1981 Education Act, being integrated into normal classes. Staffing for these pupils depends on many factors, including the type and degree of handicap of the pupils. However, it should be noted that nursery nurses and staff allocated to special needs pupils are not included in LEA calculations of staffing ratios for particular schools.

We have seen (Table 3.4) how the LEA uses the 'formula' and the numbers in the different age groups to calculate 'notional' classes of 32 (single-age) and 26 (mixed-age) pupils. The real situation is quite different (see Table 3.5). In practice, on policy determined by the Head, the school puts children into single-age classes wherever possible. This is what is done for the junior classes. Thus, the J4 class actually has 35 children while the J1 class only 21. The staff generally agree with the overall policy and accept the inequities which arise from time to time. In fact, the Head gives the teachers of 'larger' classes (30 or over) the advantage of an extra hour of 'free' time, by taking the class on a *quid pro quo* basis. The infant department is organised so that the reception classes are kept as small as possible. In this case there are actually two reception classes of 16 and 17 respectively, split randomly.

The second and first year infants are then put together to produce two classes of 28 each with mixed-age pupils. These classes, too, are given the advantage of extra time from the

	N	IR1	IR2	I1	I2	J1	J2	J3	J4	SPEC	TOTALS
Pupils	23	16	17	28	28	30	21	29	35	(22)	226
Staff	0.5	1	1	1	1	1	1	1	1	(3)	11.5

Table 3.5 *Actual class sizes for same primary school*

Head which takes the form of the Head teaching alongside the class teacher for just under one day per week. The mechanism by which this system was agreed upon need not concern us, except to comment upon the fact that the staff do approve of it, particularly in respect of the Head's contribution. We should also note that the system has had to be modified more than once when numbers in particular years simply did not fit – a perennial problem for most heads.

Conversely, it is a point of complaint from teachers at the school that frequent demands made on the Head mean that the system is easily disrupted. For instance, classes often lose the Head's contribution when 'emergen-cies' arise or important visitors are in the school.

Although this is the way staff are allocated in Loamshire, there are numerous variations on the theme in other authorities. Primary teachers need to be aware of these local differences when they move between authorities. For example, in one Midlands LEA, primary staff are allocated on a scale based on the number on roll averaging about 1:30. A neighbouring authority uses different guidelines. It utilises a fixed scale as shown in Table 3.6, no account being taken of mixed-age classes. The weighting slightly favours and protects small schools. Headteachers are additional to the normal staffing establish-

Number on Roll Summer 1983	Primary
1– 20	H + 0.8
21– 30	H + 1
31– 42	H + 1.2
43– 50	H + 1.5
51– 58	H + 2
59– 72	H + 2.2
73– 83	H + 2.5
84– 99	H + 3
100–113	H + 3.5
114–128	H + 4
129–140	H + 4.5
141–160	H + 5
161–192	H + 6
193–224	H + 7
225–256	H + 8
257–288	H + 9
289–320	H + 10
321–352	H + 11
353–384	H + 12
385–416	H + 13

Table 3.6 *Staffing establishment in a Midlands LEA*

ment. In practice, in a few cases, 'estimates for schools, in areas of new housing or expanding population may err on the low side, but the staffing of these schools is reviewed term by term'.

These staffing ratios are not particularly generous and do not take into account the problems most schools encounter with wide variations in the numbers of pupils in different year groups. Staffing is, of course, only one element in the organisational equation, albeit a vital one.

4 General and specific responsibilities

In this chapter we concentrate upon four issues – 'points' scores, scale posts and staff deployment, multiple responsibilities, and non-teaching staff.

With the advent of the new main scale following the Baker Pay Deal of 1987, the traditional scale post has disappeared. However, the hierarchical organisation of primary schools is most likely to reflect the previous scale post system for the foreseeable future as individual staff continue to have specific in-school responsibilities for curricu-

lur and organisational functions. Furthermore, as we shall see, the reality of the situation has always been that many teachers undertake duties and have responsibility and influence irrespective of the formal structure. Before we can understand how the new contract has affected the organisational structure of primary schools, it is useful to examine the way 'points' scores used to operate and the ways which scale posts were allocated.

'Points' scores

If the way in which staffing ratios are determined is a mystery to some people, then the methods of allocating a school's scale posts were even less well known. Once the actual number of staff in a school was ascertained, the next burning issue was to determine how many points to award a headteacher for the distribution of scale posts to staff. The regulations governing the permitted range of allocations are set out in the Burnham Regulations Part 1 Section 2A (Primary and Secondary Schools Score Range). For calculation purposes, each pupil is given a notional weighting (or number of units) depending upon age. This simple formula is shown in Table 4.1.

Pupil age in years	Units
Nursery	1
Under 14	2
14–15	3
15–16	4
16–17	6
17+	8

Table 4.1 *Posts of responsibility – scale posts central allocation*

As this table shows, calculations for primary schools were relatively straightforward. Each pupil over five, irrespective of age or stage, was worth two units.

The fairness of the system to primary teachers was a matter of considerable debate since both overall resources and promoted and unpromoted primary teachers' salaries

were indirectly, and adversely, affected by the points system. For instance, a class of 10 upper sixth form pupils studying, say, English literature (usually not the most resource-intensive subject) was considered to be equivalent to a class of 40 juniors. It is not difficult to see, therefore, why some primary teachers regarded themselves as second-class citizens by comparison with their secondary colleagues.

The unit totals to which this system gives rise are shown in Table 4.2. This table also indicates the range of points towards scale posts which were permitted by the Burnham agreement, and the actual allocations which were decided upon by Loamshire local education authority. To calculate the number of scale posts available it is necessary to know that a Scale 1 counts 0 points, a Scale 2 post counts 1 point, a Scale 3 post counts 2 points and so on.

Using Table 4.2 it can be seen that a school with 226 primary-aged pupils would have a unit total of 452, making it a Group 4 school with a points score range (Burnham) between 2 and 6, and an actual LEA allocation of 4. The highest assistant teacher scale (excluding deputy head and head) allowed would be a Scale 2. This is shown in Table 4.3.

Therefore, out of a staff of 12 (not counting the nursery), there would be the head and deputy head, four Scale 2 teachers and six teachers on the basic scale. This is represented in Figure 4.1.

Because this is a Group 4 school, no Scale 3 posts are allowed. A Group 5 school, however, with, say, eight points allocated could have a variety of patterns of posts, including Scale 3 teachers. For example, the Group 5 school could decide to have either:

$$1 \times \text{Scale } 3 = 2 \text{ points}$$
$$6 \times \text{Scale } 2 = 6 \text{ points}$$
or
$$2 \times \text{Scale } 3 = 4 \text{ points}$$
$$4 \times \text{Scale } 2 = 4 \text{ points}$$

As will be seen, the implications of falling rolls upon schools with Scale 3 postholders could be very significant.

Under Part 1 Section 2(a) of the Burnham agreement it is proposed that the Unit Total for Primary and Secondary schools as from 1 March, 1975 be as follows:

Group	Unit total or Review average	Points score range (Burnham)	Proposed alloc. (LEA discretion) Primary	Comp.	Highest scale for A/T (Burnham)
1	0– 150	0– 1	0*	0	2
2	151– 200	0– 1	1	0	2
3	201– 300	0– 2	2	0	2
4	301– 400	1– 3	3	3	2
	401– 500	2– 6	4	6	2
5	501– 600	3– 8	5	8	2
	601– 700	5– 11	8	11	2
6	701– 800	7– 13	10	13	3
	801– 900	9– 15	12	15	3
	901–1,000	10– 17	14	17	3
7	1,001–1,100	11– 21	19	20	3
	1,101–1,200	13– 23	21	22	3
	1,201–1,300	14– 26	23	25	3
8	1,301–1,400	15– 28		27	4
	1,401–1,600	17– 33		32	4
	1,601–1,800	21– 37		36	4
9	1,801–2,000	25– 40		39	4
	2,001–2,200	30– 44		43	4
	2,201–2,400	35– 49		48	4
10	2,401–2,700	41– 55		53	4
	2,701–3,000	47– 60		58	4
	3,001–3,300	52– 65		63	4
11	3,301–3,700	57– 74		72	4
	3,701–4,100	62– 79		77	4
	4,101–4,600	68– 83		81	4
12	4,601–5,100	75– 90		87	4
	5,101–5,600	81– 96		93	4
	5,601–6,000	88–103		100	4
13	6,001–6,100	88–103		100	4
	6,101–6,600	94–109		106	4
	6,601–7,100	101–116		113	4
	7,101–7,600	108–123		120	4
14	7,601–8,100	115–130		127	4
	8,101–8,600	122–137		134	4

Table 4.2 *Primary and secondary schools score range*

*In schools with unit totals below 151 and with more than one assistant teacher on the establishment, i.e. no designated deputy, the *points score* will be *one*.

No. of Pupils	Unit total	Group	Points Score range (Burnham)	Allocation (by LEA)	Highest Scale
226	452	4	2–6	4	2

Table 4.3 *Score range for a school with 226 pupils*

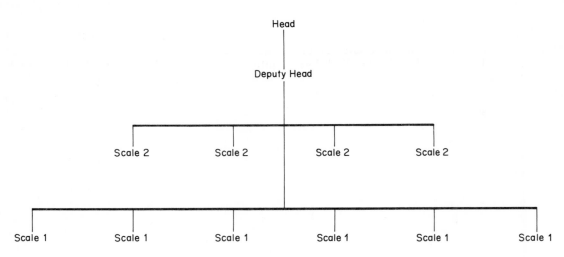

Figure 4.1 *The allocation of scale posts to a Group 4 school with 226 pupils*

Unfortunately, like most aspects of life, things were rarely as simple as Table 4.3 and Figure 4.1 suggest. The straightforward analysis is complicated by two major factors. First, the allocation of points to a school was done on a three-yearly basis, during what was called a triennial review. Thus the allocation of points could reflect a school's position anything up to three years beforehand. Second, in times of falling rolls, there was a considerable amount of protection practised for maintaining the status and salary levels of incumbents. For example, the salaries of heads and deputy heads were normally protected, even after a fall in roll had caused a school to be redesignated to a lower group (see column 1 in Table 4.1), while the existing incumbents remained in post. Furthermore, when numbers in a school fell, the school was only obliged to lose half of the points allocation which the fall in roll warranted. This was known as buffering.

Explicitly, a school whose numbers were

360 (10 points in Loamshire) which then fell to 330 (notionally 8 points) would, in fact, have retained 9 points. In addition, the Head and Deputy would have continued to be paid Group 6 salaries and any Scale 3 teachers on the staff would have remained so while they continued in post. Obviously, as teachers left in a falling roll situation, staffing could become quite complicated. One of the dangers of falling rolls was that although the buffer system protected existing scale postholders it also helped block promotion opportunities. This is one reason why so many local education authorities introduced early retirement schemes – to keep their school system fluid rather than stagnant.

Scale posts and staff deployment

From a managerial standpoint, the preceding information on the calculation of staffing levels and above Scale 1 payments is merely a prologue to two much more important issues – the actual deployment of staff within a school and the equally vital skill of delegation.

The primary head is in a very strong position of power within her school (Whitaker, 1980). Any tasks not performed by the head and any authority which other members of staff wield are all, in principle, delegated by the head. Even the term, 'assistant teacher' (which applied to the deputy head and senior teachers as well as Scale 1 staff), implied that the remaining teachers were all engaged in helping a head to carry out her wishes in the running of a school. In all but the smallest one-teacher schools, heads have the major managerial function of deploying staff and delegating responsibility – even if they do the latter with reluctance in some cases!

In the late seventies and early eighties there was an upsurge of interest in the role of scale postholders. The allocation of what used to be called 'scale posts' is part of the folklore of primary education. Most designated scale posts were given for performing additional tasks, such as taking charge of the 'library', 'boys' games', 'the infant department' or 'science'. However, many teachers have stories of other teachers who at one time or another have received above basic payments for curiously odd jobs, sometimes, but not always, hidden behind ambiguous titles. In our experience, these have been known to include responsibility for 'stock', 'display', 'wall charts', 'needlework cupboard', 'the bell' and even more surprisingly 'the bottom corridor' (Alexander, 1984).

Moreover scale posts could be self-defeating and restrictive. For example, a teacher in charge of the library often felt duty-bound to spend all her free time there, when she might have preferred to spend as much on music, drama or sport.

Retrospectively, perhaps one of the most surprising features of the way scale posts used to be allocated was the comparative variety of curriculum responsibility. In 1978, a survey in Salford showed that maths and language were ranked only eighth and ninth respectively (24 per cent and 23 per cent of surveyed schools) in a league table of posts of responsibility. By contrast, PE/games and library featured at the top (Rawlinson, 1982). Consequently, over three-quarters of primary schools surveyed did not then have designated scale postholders for such vital subjects as maths and language.

In the same year, the much publicised HMI primary survey (DES, 1978b) reported that when teachers with curriculum specialism skills were able to exert an influence over others, there were better standards of work inside schools. Since then, a great deal more attention has been given to curriculum leadership in general.

The HMI surveys of 1978 and 1982 (DES, 1978b; 1982a) divided responsibilities in primary schools into two distinct categories: organisational and curricular. The percentages of primary schools which had teachers with organisational and curricular responsibilities are shown in Tables 4.4. and 4.5 in rank order. These tables indicate the relative importance of tasks and subjects towards the end of the seventies. They also differentiate between perceived organisational and subject divisions.

Notice in Table 4.5 how low science

Library	54
Infant department	41
Remedial work	38
Resources	28
Year group leader	16
Junior department	14
Liaison with other schools	13
Team leader	13
Liaison between home and school	12
Nursery	12
Highly able children	2
Others	41

Table 4.4 *Percentage of primary schools having teachers with organisational responsibilities*

(Source: DES, 1978b; *Primary Education in England*. Reproduced by permission of the Controller of HM Stationery Office.)

appears to have been rated when compared with schools today. Different schools have, of course, different needs. Nevertheless, it is probably fair to say that much more thought should be given to curricular responsibilities in line with recommendations made by HMI (DES, 1978b; 1982b), committees of enquiry (DES, 1982c) and teachers' unions.

Music	70
Language	51
Games	48
Mathematics	45
Craft	35
Swimming	32
Art	31
Gymnastics	25
RE	19
Science	17
Environmental Studies	17
Drama	14
French	14
Dance	13

Table 4.5 *Percentage of primary schools having teachers with curricular responsibilities*

(Source: DES, 1978b; *Primary Education in England.* Reproduced by permission of the Controller of HM Stationery Office.)

Headteachers as managers always need to assess and determine their own priorities with respect to curricular, managerial and organisational tasks using, perhaps, the sort of checklist provided in Tables 4.4 and 4.5. Their next step should be to prepare job descriptions in conjunction with the people most directly involved. Writing succinct and apposite job descriptions is a difficult skill to master, as we shall see in Chapter 5.

Multiple responsibilities

There are rarely enough staff in a primary school to cover adequately all the subjects in the curriculum, let alone the organisational responsibilities. This remains true even when curriculum subjects are designated in terms of broad 'areas of experience' rather than individual disciplines. HMI (DES, 1985b), for example, list nine such combined fields. Any alternatives rarely list less than seven. These integrated subject areas include terms such as 'aesthetics', 'environmental studies' and 'human studies'. By fusing subject boundaries in this way, the challenge facing schools of covering every aspect adequately is often disguised rather than solved. In any event, the equation is complicated by whether there are staff available and suitable to take on responsibility. If we add on to this situation the not inconsiderable number of administrative and organisational tasks which curriculum leadership generates, the unfairness or bitterness which was caused by the scale post system can be understood. Consequently, within many primary schools it was and remains the norm for staff to take on more than one administrative or subject responsibility.

In a survey of postholders in 10 primary middle schools in Warwickshire, Campbell (1985) found that only two postholders out of 10 had a single responsibility. These two were used as specialist teachers. One other was a part-time member of staff. All the other seven had class-teaching as a major responsibility and up to three other designated functions, including aspects related to class teaching, year leadership, second subject work and managerial functions. There is no reason to suppose that the situation is much different in most schools today.

Campbell makes the point that such demands on teachers raise both questions of priority and of feasibility. It is a clear, but difficult, managerial function of a head to help prioritise the tasks demanded of teachers and to make sure that what is finally asked of staff is feasible. This is why accurate job descriptions are so important (see Chapter 5), provided they take account of changing professional, educational and school needs over time.

Teachers with multiple responsibilities need to plan their duties methodically and with diligence. They have to recognise that from time to time one need will outweigh another. An obvious strategy to employ is to tackle tasks in sequence and not either to overstretch one's ability to cope or to overload the system. The former may lead to inefficiency and stress, the latter to rebuke!

Task sequencing enables worthwhile routines to be established which are an efficient and effective use of time. Therefore, once a need is identified and a solution found, it should be encompassed in a total year or term plan. Heads as well as responsible teachers should devise such yearly plans. For example, contrast what could be considerable effort put into devising an acceptable means of assessment and record keeping with the relative ease of maintaining the records once established.

It is inconceivable to think that primary teachers will ever only have one prime responsibility within their schools (apart from their class teaching duties). A challenge facing headteachers is to ensure equity of workloads for their staff, dependent upon status and expertise. Failure to do so is sometimes a source of bitterness. It also can lead to gaps in the curriculum and holes in the organisation of schools.

Students and new teachers need to take note of the significance of the preceding discussion because the historical legacy of scale posts is likely to remain and impinge on the organisation of schools for many years to come. Teachers' existing salary levels, for example, will be partly determined by their previous position in the scale post structure.

Non-teaching staff

The general 'feel' of what a school is like has variously been termed the school climate (Halpin, 1966), the school ethos (Rutter *et al.*, 1979) or the school's 'institutional bias' (Pollard, 1985). In theory, the climate of a school is related to the interactions between all members of the school community – headteacher, deputies, teaching staff, non-teaching staff and pupils. In reality, it is more likely to reflect the perspectives of those with most power and influence in the school (Pollard, 1985).

Apart from certain occasions, it is often forgotten by educationalists that as well as the teachers and the pupils, non-teaching staff can and do have a substantial influence upon the day-to-day running and ethos of a school. The range of non-teaching staff in an average-sized primary school can be considerable. The actual number employed in any particular school will depend upon several factors, including LEA policy on the employment of, for example, ancillaries and infant helpers. The following list is the possible range of non-teaching staff available to any primary school. Many primary schools will not have people appointed to all these posts, partly because of their size:

School secretary
School keeper (Caretaker)
Cleaning staff
Kitchen staff (cook and kitchen assistants)
Ancillaries
Infant helpers

It is possible that infant helpers may be subsumed under ancillaries in some local education authorities. In some parts of Great Britain, there may well be other non-teaching staff engaged in regular employment who have been omitted from this list. In addition, some schools use parent-helpers as non-qualified, unpaid staff for general or specific duties such as helping children learn to read.

It may be thought that the organisation and management of non-teaching staff is not problematic; a view many educationalists have long since abandoned in the light of their own experiences. Theoretically, the responsibilities and duties of non-teaching staff are fairly well defined, subject to an unambiguous contract of employment. Most, for example, work a specific number of hours per week. However, the full picture is often greater than the sum of parts. A potential source of conflict may lie in perceived differing allegiances. For instance, caretakers may feel more directly accountable to their area supervisor than the headteacher of the school.

Consider the role of the school secretary. By the very nature of her work, the school secretary is privy to much of the confidential information which passes to and from the school and which arises within the school confines. She is likely to be the person with whom a non-teaching head has the longest contact, sometimes to the extent of sharing an office. She also represents the first contact outsiders and parents have with the school, in her role as receptionist. In a large primary school, many of the children may know her better than they know many of the teachers who have not yet taught them. Moreover, it is the secretary's work as the on-the-spot clerk/typist/office manager which releases the head to run the school. In fact, within many schools, some secretaries also take on additional, often unofficial, responsibilities such as running/organising/overseeing the library, accompanying groups of children on residential visits or being the first aid assistant. The legal implications of this work need not concern us here. There is little doubt, however, that the personality of the school secretary and the range of tasks she undertakes can and do have a profound effect upon the running of many primary schools.

Therefore, it is a prime management function to choose non-teaching staff, like the school secretary, with as much care as teaching staff and to ensure effective deployment by means of accurate job descriptions. Thereafter it is desirable for the head and staff to ensure that non-teaching staff are fully recognised for their work and included in as many of the appropriate functions as possible. Non-teaching staff, like their teaching counterparts, need to be made to feel part of a corporate team. This is one aspect of team building which can be overlooked or forgotten by some heads.

It is often said by some, in jest, that a school is only as effective as its caretaker. Frankly, this remark is too close to the truth to be funny. Some caretakers make an enormous, and undervalued, contribution to the life of a school, not just by being efficient at their job, but also through their extended role. Many caretakers take on numerous additional responsibilities within a school. Mr Jenkins, for example, a caretaker at a school well known to the authors, regularly accompanies parties of children on residential field trips. Because of his experience, his organisational ability and his empathy with staff and pupils alike, he makes an enormous contribution on these educational visits as a kind of extra teacher. The head recognises this service and attempts to ensure that difficulties which could accrue in Mr Jenkins' absence are minimised through sound planning.

Another school caretaker, Mr Howells, a former joiner, completely remodelled a redundant cloakroom in an old school, to make a first-class library and resource area. He now helps to keep it efficiently organised. Ironically, this project caused the head some difficulties when disgruntled cleaners complained that the scheme added unnecessarily to their workload. The head managed this problem in two ways. First, she instigated a very successful 'keep our school clean and tidy' campaign amongst the staff and children. Secondly, on a voluntary basis, she arranged for some parents to come to the school to help to organise and clean the craft and cooking sections which were the least favoured cleaning areas!

Many caretakers assume, or are given, responsibility for the daily organisation of non-teaching staff, under the overall control of the head. Where the caretaker and his cleaners and caterers have a good working relationship, the involvement of senior management in regular decision-making is minimal. Nevertheless, as we have seen, problems can and do arise in most schools from time to time on non-teaching matters. Sensitive attention to such problems is obviously essential.

Another example: dinner ladies (i.e. the staff who supervise the dining areas and playgrounds during the lunch-time period) are in an invidious position. They are almost invariably non-professional and non-unionised with few managerial skills and consequently of low status in the school. Yet they have to control large numbers of children for relatively long periods of time. They have to see that school policies on behaviour are maintained and initiate disciplinary proceedings when there are transgressions. All in all, dinner ladies have an unenviable task. Good management practice suggests that in order to maximise the effectiveness of the dinner ladies, they should be given a definite and clearly defined role which they themselves have helped to negotiate. They should be given some form of training, however limited. It is essential that they are 'backed up' by the senior management team and person on duty at all times. The effective use of dinner ladies undoubtedly contributes to smoother-running lunch-times in most schools.

Kitchen staff usually have a fairly clear and unambiguous role under the authority of the cook. Their physical confinement to the kitchen area helps to reduce their direct influence on the running of the school. However, they too help to put into practice rules on such things as 'how much has to be eaten' and the clearing away of plates. Being directly affected by the consequences of such rules, they may well wish to exert influence on behaviour which relates to the application of those rules. A sensible manager will be aware that such enthusiasm can be a helpful aid in maintaining order at a difficult time of the day. People who feel part of a team and who believe that they have some influence on the conditions of their job ought to be able to do their job better.

The term 'ancillary' can cover a multitude of different roles within a school. Ancillaries are usually unqualified part-time assistants whose actual tasks are, within certain guide-lines, at the discretion of the head. They may be limited to relatively menial tasks such as sharpening pencils and making topic books. Alternatively, they may, like 'infant helpers', be involved in the classroom with groups of children, helping them with their learning tasks. While they are excluded from the actual teaching role they may, under the control of the teacher, have considerable influence on children's learning. The dividing line – or even the difference – between 'teaching' and 'influencing learning' is at best debatable.

Working out the actual tasks which ancillaries will undertake is a proper management function. Job descriptions should be constructed in consultation with other members of staff who will be affected. As with any aspect of staffing, a well thought-out policy will increase the effectiveness of the staff concerned. This is particularly true in schools which cater for children with special education needs when the work of non-teaching staff is crucial to the well-being of pupils and teachers alike.

In conclusion, we can state that the rationale behind the structure and organisation of primary schools is learned by most people from experience. It is the sort of subject matter which is too often excluded from initial teacher training courses. However, without such basic information, even beginning teachers are unlikely to be fully effective. Nor are they likely to be sympathetic to the constraints under which headteachers and local education officials operate. Therefore, a basic understanding of the points system, scale post allocations and multiple responsibilities is crucial to teachers' comprehension of the organisation and management of primary schools.

5 Staff selection and organisation

Chapters 5 and 6 concentrate on staff selection, organisation and management in primary schools. They develop some of the themes begun in the preceding chapters. This chapter focuses upon staff selection, including job descriptions, the role of curriculum co-ordinators, interviewing and advertising procedures. Chapter 6 examines the use of staff in schools, staff management procedures, helping new staff, delegation, decision-making, communication and the teacher-as-researcher concept.

The proper use of staff in schools is vital to successful organisational and managerial practice. When staff are contented, they tend to perform better than when they are not. Maintaining staff-room morale however, is never an easy task, particularly because teaching is an all-professional activity (Roy, 1983). It is especially difficult at times when the profession is increasingly under attack from many sectors of society, not least politicians (Frude, 1984; Reid, 1986).

Staff selection

We begin this chapter with a discussion of staff selection. Perhaps the most fundamental aspect of staff organisation and management is choosing the right team in the first place. This is not as simple as it sounds because most headteachers tend to inherit a large proportion of their staff upon appointment. Moreover, there is a surplus of certain subject consultants and a shortage of others.

The selection of staff is a process which itself is capable of being subdivided into distinct phases. These include: defining needs, advertising, job descriptions and interviewing. The first of these – defining needs – is fairly straightforward. The rest require more thought.

Advertising and job details

National or county-wide advertisements tend to be very brief, giving few details, partly because of the costs involved. It is by no means unusual for a majority of applicants for particular posts to be unsuccessful simply because they do not match the requirements of the head, the appointing committee or those responsible for devising the short list. Appointment committees, for instance, often have preconceived ideas on the kind of candidate they are looking for, but these are seldom explicitly stated in the preliminary advertisement. Sometimes, for example, appointment committees are ideally looking for particular strengths which are unspecified in the original advertisement. These can include the sex, subject and preferred age of the ideal candidate, the degree of previous experience required and, such diverse factors as the additional expertise needed for extra-curricular activities or the ability to play a piano successfully in assembly. Generally speaking, once a candidate is short listed, much depends on his or her performance on the day, not least the view the appointment committee takes of his or her personality and the way he or she will fit into the school.

Framing an advertisment is a considerable skill in itself. Normally, there is a short national and local advertisement and a longer job specification. Reading between the lines of job descriptions is an acquired skill as they often say a great deal about the ethos of a school. Regrettably, such skills are super-fluous when posts have been 'filled' before they have even been advertised – a quite deplorable practice.

Information on specific posts varies by job, even within the same local education author-ity. Some contain more or less information about a school and/or vacancy as the follow-ing actual examples in Figures 5.1 to 5.6 indicate.

It is interesting to note that all these jobs were advertised in the same month in 1985 under the old salary structure. Incidentally, part of the interest of these details lies in the fact that the schools were all located in the same authority within approximately 10 miles of one another.

Figure 5.1 Details for Post A

1 Infant Teacher – Scale 1
This post requires a teacher with experi-ence of mixed age/mixed ability group-ing at infant level.

Sound practice in reading techniques is required, including a knowledge of diagnostic testing procedures and assessment leading to individually planned reading programmes, where necessary, to ensure the sequential de-velopment of each child.

Applicants should possess the neces-sary ability to work as a member of a dedicated team where project and sub-ject area development is not necessarily limited by the confines of the school day.

Figure 5.2 Details for Post B

The school is situated in a pleasant residential area in the west of the city. Built in 1894, the building is a two-storied brick structure with modern ex-tensions and some remodelling in the infants' department. The upper floor has a large assembly hall/gymnasium, with six classrooms and a library-resource room. The lower floor accommodates the younger junior children in four classrooms, the infants' department in six rooms and there is also a dining area, a hall for infant use and a television/projection room.

The previously separate infants and junior schools were amalgamated in September 1982, creating a two form entry primary school catering for chil-dren aged 5 to 11.

The organisation is on a mixed ability basis: there are six class groups in the infants' department and eight in the juniors. There is also provision for re-medial teaching on a part-time basis and an additional full-time teacher who works with those children for whom English is their second language.

The provision of this support is neces-sary because of the comparatively large number of children from overseas whose parents study at the university, in addition to a small number of immi-grant children.

The curriculum and ethos of the school is, in many respects, traditional, there is a comprehensive scale post structure that serves the main curricu-lum areas and a great deal of goodwill and co-operation from the staff who give freely of their time and efforts.

The school is near a foreshore, and two parks, all of which are used by the school; regular use is also made of the City's 'Recreation Ground' for organised games, as the immediate environs and hard play areas are severely limiting. Swimming instruction is provided at the local baths. There are numerous extra curricular activities, team sports include: rounders, netball, rugby, cricket and athletics, also lunch-time activities including chess, table-tennis and guitar clubs. There is a successful school choir which plays a leading role in school functions.

The older pupils make annual visits to the Authority's Field Studies Centres.

The flourishing PTA works in close harmony with the school and has been instrumental in acquiring books and equipment that have enriched the school's resources. There is also an open door policy towards parents who are encouraged to visit the school and a tradition of sound relationships has been built up over the years.

Vacancy: Assistant Teacher Scale 1
Primary trained teacher required for September 1985, to be employed in the first instance in the Infants' Department. It is anticipated that the successful applicant will take a full part in the activities of both the Infant and Junior Departments. For example, an interest in Junior Girls' games including netball and rounders will be an added recommendation. A willingness to help with some extra curricular activities will also be an advantage.

Figure 5.3 *Details for Post C*

Appointment of Assistant Teacher. (Scale 1)
The Post Assistant Teacher re-

quired in the Infants' Department.

An interest in Environmental Studies would be an advantage.

The School Number on roll:
210 full-time children.
30 part-time Nursery Class children.

Age range: 3–11

St H's Primary School was formed in 1978 following the amalgamation of the Infants' and Junior Schools. The present teaching establishment is composed of Headteacher, plus eight full-time teachers and one part-time Nursery Class teacher.

The school is situated in the Bulfields area of S—— and is in close proximity to the Marina and the Maritime Museum. It serves the central area of the City of S——.

The school enjoys the support of a flourishing PTA which has been responsible for purchasing a number of major items of equipment including a photo-copying machine, colour television, music centre and a video recorder.

Figure 5.4 *Details for Post D*

The school
St T's Primary School was built in 1897 on elevated ground to the East of S——, overlooking the docks and S—— Bay. It is designated a social priority school, but there exists a good social mix.

The area served is one of predominently private houses, with some council houses, and the school has the advantage of close liaison with the parents through a thriving PTA.

The building which is of traditional design has its accommodation on four floors. The first and second floors are occupied by the Junior Department whilst the Infant Department is housed on the lower ground floor and the ground floor. There is a TV-AV room and the school is currently setting up a library-resource room.

There are three halls which are utilised for activities such as PE, dancing and games, etc.

There are 265+ children on roll between the ages of 4 and 11. The staff consists of the Headteacher plus 11 teachers and one nursery assistant.

The curriculum is implemented through a flexible organisation, allowing for the children's freedom of choice within a structured framework. The ethos of the school fosters a happy, caring social environment encouraging individual academic progress.

Vacancy: Scale 1 Assistant Teacher

The successful candidate will be initially responsible for a reception class. He/she should have a full knowledge of the aims and practice of Primary Education in Mathematics, Science, Language Development and Arts and Crafts, and be aware of new teaching approaches across the age range.

The ability to be able to teach drama would be an advantage.

The school is currently taking part in the CAPER Scheme — the success of which depends very largely on the good relationship between the class teacher and the parents, and applicants should be aware of this co-operative venture.

Figure 5.5 *Details for Post E*

The School (NOR 217)

G—— School, built in 1934 is situated on the north side of T——, S——, in a well established residential area. Part of this area, of local authority housing, is the northern end of a large estate desig-

nated as social priority, while the western half of the school catchment area is, in the main, private housing.

The school is a single storey structure built around an open garden quadrangle. In addition, there are two temporary classrooms adjacent to the playground. The main building houses a library and resources centre as well as a TV/AVA room.

There is a two-form entry and the classes of mixed ability are served by a teaching staff of eight. Provision is made for remedial reading on a part-time basis.

The curriculum is broad-based giving the children a width of educational experiences that will help to develop within each child a real desire to learn and to extend individual talents. While there is a great emphasis on the basic skills of literacy and numeracy, the school is working towards a more integrated approach to the whole curriculum. At present the school has two computers.

Various physical education activities include netball, rounders, soccer, rugby, gymnastics and athletics (swimming instruction is provided for the upper school).

Full use is made of the Authority's residential and day field study centres, the school mini-bus has proved invaluable on these occasions.

Parents are encouraged to visit the school to discuss their children's progress. A Parent's Association helps to foster home-school links.

Job Description

The post requires a person who is first and foremost an enthusiastic, imaginative classroom teacher who is prepared to be part of a teaching team and who is fully cognizant of modern educational theory, practice and technology.

He/she should have the ability to organise his/her class effectively to ensure that each child is given every opportunity to develop his/her individual talents in stimulating and caring environment.

An appreciation of the importance of aesthetics in the curriculum is expected and an interest in science and discovery work will be an advantage.

Figure 5.6 *Details for Post F*

LOAMSHIRE EDUCATION
COMMITTEE
FELTON PRIMARY SCHOOL
Headship Appointment

1 Applications are invited for the post of Head of the Felton Primary School, Clarke Street, from January, 1986. The vacancy is due to the appointment of the present Head to the Loamshire Advisory Service.

2 The school is situated on the inner northern side of the City of Loamester and serves a large muli-cultural community. Much attention has been given to the vigorous development of the curriculum since the former infant and junior schools were amalgamated. Both sets of buildings are modern, replacing Victorian schools a short distance away, and the school occupies an established place in the local community.

3 Amalgamation of the former nursery/infant and junior schools took effect from August, 1984. The primary school has two buildings which are closely adjacent and the accommodation comprises:

Lower School	*Upper School*
Nursery Unit	12 class bases
6 class bases	2 mobile class-rooms
2 resource areas	2 resource areas
Hall	Hall (used for dining purposes)
Small library	
Secretary's room	

Medical room
Staff room
Staff Kitchen
Playground
Play area
School kitchen (not in use at present)
Caretaker's store

Library
Children's quiet reading area
Head's room
Deputy Head's room
Reprographic room and store
Studio
Kitchen
Caretaker's room
Teacher's work-room containing audio visual aids
3 playgrounds
Playing field

At the present time there are 31 full-time children and 49 part-time children in the nursery.

4 There is no school house.

5 In January there will be approximately 436 on roll aged from 5 to 11 years. The teaching staff at present consists of Head plus 22.6 teachers. The school also receives 2029 hours per annum clerical assistance and 1976 hours per annum ancillary assistance.

6 An advisory and consultative staff based at County Hall is available to give assistance to Heads and teachers on request.

7 The school is currently Group 6 and the Head's salary will be in accordance with the Burnham Report.

8 In Loamshire, secondary education in the whole County is fully comprehensive.

9 In 1976, Burton Hall was opened as an in-service education centre for Loamshire teachers. This fine Victorian mansion, situated at Woodham, near Notton, offers excellent facilities for courses and conferences. At present, Burton can cater for over 100 teachers on a daily

basis, but there are plans to provide residential accommodation.

10 Candidates should include a statement on their application that they have not canvassed a member of the Council or any Committee of the Council, either directly or indirectly in connection with their application and will not do so. It is also necessary to disclose any relationship with a member or employee of the Council. Failure to disclose any such relationship may disqualify and if discovered after appointment could result in dismissal without notice.

11 Candidates should note that it is planned to hold interviews for the post on 26th October, 198—.

There are no forms and applications containing full particulars and the names and addresses of two referees, other than your employing Authority, should reach me *not later than* 14th September.

J. N. Hitchcock

Director of Education,
County Hall,
Loam,
Loamshire.

Descriptions of posts are sent out by the 'office' or by the school upon request in the form of job details. Usually, though not always, as the details of Post E above show, these give a more detailed picture of a school's and county's set up than the original advertisement. As the earlier posts in Figures 5.1 to 5.5 were for new or Scale 1 appointments, it is worth noting that much the same procedure applies for senior posts, including headteachers (see Figure 5.6).

Once applications have been received by either county hall or the head, a sifting process begins which culminates in a shortened selection of candidates for interviewing, dependent upon county or school policies, or both. Generally speaking, references are obtained prior to the interviews being held. These normally take place in county hall or the school.

As all the details show, there is comparatively little information about the kind of candidate sought, even in Figure 5.6. Therefore, applicants are left to make up their own minds about whether to apply or not. The information provided in Figures 5.1 to 5.6 is typical of many educational appointments. In some LEAs it is common for more information to be given for senior posts. However, Figure 5.6 provides little indication of what the local education authority is looking for in the new head. Presumably, someone in county hall had a clear idea beforehand!

Responding to advertisements also needs considerable skill. In fact, applying for posts requires much thought and is a time-consuming activity when done properly. Ideally, candidates should prepare a typed curriculum vitae beforehand. In addition, candidates normally (though not always) have to fill in the appropriate form/s from the school or office and compose a letter of application. Canvassing in advance usually disqualifies applicants.

The format of curricula vitae may vary but, generally speaking, relevant items from the following list should be included: name; address; marital status; school and higher education establishments and courses attended; qualifications; honours, distinctions and awards; previous employment and educational history; subject specialisms; other relevant work or vocational experience; special skills and professional interest; membership of professional bodies; relevant and/or recent courses attended; extra-curricular interests; general interests; publications.

The design of application forms varies too, but completing them is usually relatively straightforward. You should not be concerned if there are sections of the form which do not apply to you. Honesty and integrity are better than waffle and half-truths. Most forms include space for a letter of application. We suggest that great care be taken when composing the letter. It is important to ensure that the crucial features of your application are not lost in a welter of less significant detail. Explicitly, your Brownie handicraft badge is probably less relevant than your last post, teaching practice, your ability to play the piano or use a computer.

Some local education authorities ask for only a letter of application and curriculum vitae when advertising posts. These are in a minority. Obviously, even greater care needs to be taken over the letter of application in such circumstances.

Leaders, co-ordinators and job descriptions

Some vacancy sheets provide detailed job descriptions, often devised by the head. Other job descriptions are given to staff in schools after taking up their posts. Others are negotiated and jointly constructed by the head and individual teacher after a period of deliberation. There is a growing consensus that all teachers should be given job descriptions which are written down and periodically reviewed and revised in accordance with a school's needs and a teacher's professional development.

Job descriptions or specifications are simply statements of the major duties associated with a particular post. A weakness of many job descriptions is that they fail to recognise that schools' needs are constantly changing and evolving. Moreover, not only is there a trend towards more precise specification of responsibilities, but the number of duties seen as important is also increasing perenially. For example, liaison with parents is now frequently referred to in job descriptions. Recently, in some parts of Britain the plentiful availability of primary teachers has meant that staff find themselves in a 'buyer's market'. Hence most headteachers and local education authorities now have expectations of specialist inputs even from new appointees. The amount of

scrutiny which is currently given to job descriptions (following the publication of the 1978 HMI survey and teachers' revised contracts) has considerably clarified the kind of roles which are envisaged of primary staff. Therefore, the basic grade teacher is no longer thought of as somebody whose sole responsibilities begin and end at the classroom door. Rather, in pursuit of what Campbell (1985) calls the 'collegial primary school', every teacher is now seen as having a vital role in the overall smooth running, efficiency and effectiveness of a school.

There has been a great deal written about developing curriculum responsibilities in primary schools, some of it more relevant than others (Plowden Report (DES, 1967); Bullock Report (DES, 1974); DES, 1970; 1978b; 1980; 1983a; ILEA, 1985; Campbell, 1985). For example, in the 1978 HMI Survey, it was argued that there are positive associations between the achievement of higher standards in primary school classes and the effective performance of a particular role by the responsible teacher. HMI considered that the effectiveness of the curriculum postholder's role was related to:

1 Planning programmes of work in consultation with the head, advising other teachers about the programme and encouraging a consistent approach in the school. In addition to planning a programme, the postholder should be involved in the 'supervision' of it.
2 Achieving a better 'match' of work to children's abilities in schools, particularly when they exerted a strong influence throughout schools and not just in their own classrooms. Although this was true for all age and ability groups, it was especially noticeable with the work set for more able children.
3 The postholder's level of knowledge and expertise, especially when she was able to give a strong lead in planning, carrying out a programme of work, and influencing others.
4 The status of postholders. HMI con-

sidered that in general their standing in schools needed to be improved both in terms of position on the salary scale and in their perceived social position, both inside and outside the school.

5 Curriculum postholders developing acceptable means of assessing a scheme's effectiveness within schools. This might, for example, involve visiting other classes in the school to see work in progress and evaluating outcomes.

6 Allocating curriculum postholders with sufficient time for performing their range of duties. HMI acknowledged that some duties probably had to be conducted outside school hours, while others needed to be carried out when the school was in session.

The debate about teachers' responsibilities is related to arguments about subject specialisms in primary schools. The Cockcroft Report (DES, 1982c) recorded its unease about the mathematical background of general class teachers in primary schools. It suggested that one way of remedying this situation was to improve the efficiency and competence of the 'mathematics co-ordination' in the school. The Committee saw part of the duties of the 'mathematics co-ordinator' as:

(a) preparing a scheme of work for the school in consultation with the headteacher and staff and, where possible, with schools from which the children come and to which they go;

(b) providing guidance and support to other members of staff in implementing the scheme of work, both by means of meetings and by working alongside individual teachers;

(c) organising and being responsible for procuring, within the funds made available, the necessary teaching resources for mathematics, maintaining an up-to-date inventory and ensuring that members of staff are aware of how to use the resources which are available;

(d) monitoring work in mathematics throughout the school, including

methods of assessment and record keeping;

(e) assisting with the diagnosis of children's learning difficulties and with their remediation;

(f) arranging school-based in-service training for members of staff as appropriate;

(g) maintaining liaison with schools from which children come and to which they go, and also with LEA advisory staff.

Cockcroft added that it would have been easy to extend the list by considering, for example, the need to keep up-to-date with current developments in mathematics education, assisting with probationary teachers as well as contributing towards colleagues' mathematical confidence.

It is common practice for appropriate literature to be sent out with application forms before appointing new staff. We therefore now present and examine some actual job descriptions from posts known to us. As there are so many forms of job description in use, we cannot hope to cover every kind in this chapter and therefore we simply provide a few examples.

Below is a job description obtained from details for a curriculum leader in science in an infant school in Wales.

Teachers in this post should be infant trained and should be prepared to lead other members of staff and organise the development of *Science* within the Nursery/ Infant Departments, including the organisation of resources. In addition the teacher is expected to be responsible for the use and maintenance of Audio/Visual equipment at the school.

A more detailed description than this was not available. Thus, it is likely that the exact nature of the post was subject to negotiation between the postholder and the head upon appointment.

Here is another, more detailed description from an English junior school for a post in environmental studies:

Environmental Studies – Job Description for Curriculum Leader.

1 To devise, in consultation with colleagues, a scheme of work for the school, taking due account of current developments.
2 To aid colleagues in the implementation of the scheme of work.
3 To ensure that the curriculum is adequately resourced in terms of material.
4 To ensure that sufficient equipment is organised, available and kept in good condition.
5 To liaise with secondary schools and other feeder schools in order to maximise as far as is possible co-ordination and continuity of provision.
6 To co-ordinate the setting up of a wildlife reserve on land adjacent to the school and subsequent work in the area.
7 To devise a system of assessment for environmental studies in the school.

This is a formidable, and in some ways, unusual list which is much more precise than the first one. Yet, it too begs many questions – probably because these had not been worked out at the time the advertisement was placed. Specifically, what was the form of 'aid' to be given to colleagues over 'the implementation of the scheme of work' and what was to be the nature of the 'consultation with colleagues'? However, without being too pernickety, all these matters could be resolved with reasonably open discussion.

The third example is of a slightly different kind since it is a specific part of a total description related to the work of a junior school deputy head in Nottinghamshire. Not surprisingly, this deputy had multiple responsibilities. The precise details were worked out between the head and the deputy in order to clarify a situation which had developed by chance over a period of time in response to a perceived need. It is a useful check-list for a fairly varied role. It is also probably as precise as could be devised in the circumstances.

Secondary School Liaison

In order to improve liaison and communication between ourselves and the secondary school, the deputy head will:

1 Discuss the purpose and nature of liaison with staff from both schools and draw up a policy.
2 Attend with other teachers the information exchange meetings at the beginning and end of the year.
3 Arrange exchanges of staff between the two schools on a basis to be negotiated.
4 Arrange for liaison meetings on specific subjects or issues.
5 Arrange such other liaison activities as may be deemed fruitful.

These then, are three different sorts of job description. Clearly, it is important in a job description to strike a balance between an unhelpfully vague indication of responsibility and a dauntingly detailed specification of every movement and activity. It is certainly necessary for aspects of any particular job to be subject to negotiation and development, to take account of changing needs and strengths of the people involved. Job descriptions should be negotiable and can and do change over time for any number of reasons – not least changing school and educational circumstances.

As we have seen, therefore, the main purposes of job descriptions are:

1 To identify an area or job which requires particular attention and the means by which developments and/or changes can take place.
2 To make explicit to the rest of the staff, and others with a legitimate interest (such as governors and advisers) the exact expectations of the teacher in her specific role.
3 To give the teacher a ready-made basis to assess his or her overall performance.
4 To have a means of assessing to what extent a teacher fulfils a school's or a local authority's objectives.

Item 4 is, of course, a long term aim (see Chapter 2 – Appraisal section).

The best kinds of job description are those which have been negotiated. Although management teams can make a start in this direction, teachers should be encouraged to make their own contributions. When this is done, they should feel more disposed and committeed to performing the tasks well. Such negotiated procedures also provide headteachers and staff with a useful framework against which performance can be considered.

Finally, job descriptions can help in getting the right person for the post in the first place. Even when there is not the element of choice a job description can guide a potential postholder, both in terms of what to do and, possibly, in terms of what new knowledge or skills are required for the work. This, in turn, may stimulate staff development and school-focused in-service work. After all these points have been considered, it may appear surprising that explicit job descriptions have been so comparatively rare in the past.

Part of the skill in framing job descriptions is to get the tone and detail right. If a job description is too precise it can restrict both sides. If it is too loose, it can be virtually meaningless.

The role of curriculum leaders

A major national debate currently revolves around the role of curriculum leaders. Campbell (1985) provides a list of the curriculum and interpersonal skills required of curriculum coordinators if they are to be effective. These are shown in Table 5.1 but others are available (DES, 1982a; DES, 1982c; Alexander, 1984).

Campbell's classification of postholders' skills into curriculum and interpersonal skills is a very useful analysis which can be used as an 'aide memoire' in the construction of any job description. The content of a thorough specification should reflect all the aspects referred to in Campbell's list, at least implicitly. However, it is unrealistic to expect every actual or potential co-ordinator to be equally skilful in all the areas. Nor is it reasonable to expect that all sought after skills will carry equal weight or priority at any given point in time.

Such lists illustrate the formidable tasks which face modern curriculum leaders if they are to keep up to date and prove competent. The head's managerial function is to ensure that the curriculum and other co-ordinators are supported in terms of resources, time and

---

Curriculum area or phase responsibilities
(a) Knowledge: The coordinator must consistently update her knowledge of the relevant curriculum area (or phase) including appropriate teaching styles.
(b) Management and organisational: The coordinator, in consultation with colleagues, should draw up a school policy document, oversee its implementation and institute an effective evaluation mechanism.
(c) Resources: The coordinator should be aware of various materials (including human resources) appropriate to her responsibilities and oversee their effective deployment.

Managerial skills
(a) Social: The coordinator should work with colleagues (including teaching alongside them) to encourage their professional growth and competence, lead discussion groups, etc.
(b) External agencies: The coordinator should liaise with all external agencies including advisers, governors, parents, etc.

Table 5.1 *The skills needed by curriculum phase leaders or coordinators*

'facilitating systems' (initiating structure) through the use of meetings, workshops and information – dissemination sessions (Nias, 1980). It is important to ensure that the person with responsibility has a share in appropriate decision-making (Price, 1985). Otherwise, a head will fail:

(a) to give the person a chance to exert an influence in his or her specialist area;
(b) to give the leader a chance to accept responsibility and exercise his or her professional judgement;
(c) to take a creative lead in staff development.

One of the main functions of leaders or co-ordinators is to manage and 'resource' their sections. Too often, however, heads fail to involve or give sufficient information to all their staff on the financial and administrative aspects of running schools. This can lead not only to ignorance, but also to professional jealousies developing – frequently because of misconceptions. Scale postholders should never be afraid to ask a head to explain the reasons for a decision – especially when it affects their area of responsibility.

Finding sufficient time in schools for forward planning and necessary administrative exercises is another problem for postholders. Innovative postholders can sometimes manage to create time when none seems to exist. Formally, postholders can only be released for their organisational tasks in school time by another teacher, often the head, taking class responsibility or by enlarging or combining groups/classes. Too few schools are fortunate enough to have the resource of a 'floating' teacher other than the head. To staff it can often seem that everything must be achieved from within existing resources. Within secondary schools, all teachers are given a minimum number of free periods which increase with responsibility and need.

Interviews

Interviews are used in many ways in educa-tion. Most teachers, for example, are interviewed before being appointed to their posts. This was not always the case in the halcyon days of the sixties and seventies when teachers were in short supply and when primary schools were organised and operated rather differently from those of the present and when some teachers were recruited by LEAs before being placed in particular schools. Interviewing techniques are also widely used in, for example, staff development exercises within schools, for the selection of teachers to in-service courses, for seeing parents about their offspring and for many other purposes.

Formal interviewing before appointing junior or senior staff is a widely accepted procedure, partly because it satisfies the needs of all those actually involved in the enterprise. In theory, it should also show that justice is done. Regrettably, this is not always the case. Consequently, some people believe that the outcomes of interviews are no more positive than when this procedure is ignored.

Throughout Britain, some schools, local education authorities and educational organisations implement variations of the standard interview. These can include the use of psychological tests and other instruments, the timed formal statement with or without questioning and the observation of potential new staff in teaching situations. All of these schemes have their merits and shortcomings. In industry, it is common practice for managers to be regularly assessed and re-assessed before being promoted. One such scheme involves formal interviews and the use of a battery of instruments which, amongst other things, measure intellectual effectiveness (numerical and verbal ability, logical and critical thinking), work approach (general picture, mastery of detail, productivity, quality of work, decision-making, tolerance of pressure, flexibility, ambition), personal relationships (general impact, relations with superiors, colleagues and others), pattern of work interests, personal and vocational strengths and weaknesses (strong points and primary limitations) and career development potential. Within the armed forces and civil service, annual career reports and follow-up interviews are a normal part of staff development programmes and accepted as such, irrespective of the merits or otherwise of the system. There is now increasing momentum for similar procedures to be introduced into the education service from administrators and policy makers.

The selection of assistant teachers differs regionally. In some cases, headteachers are heavily involved in the enterprise and have the major say. In other areas, the main input is made by advisers and/or elected members of the local authority.

Before reaching headteacher status, few staff have experience of short-listing (sifting) procedures or of writing job descriptions or handling advertisements or external enquiries for posts. In some regions all of these four aspects are handled by education office staff only.

Appointment panels, too, vary in size and composition. A typical appointment panel could include the head, *or* the head and an adviser, *or* the head, adviser/s, district/assistant education officer, elected members, chairman of governors, *or* any number of variations along this theme.

Appointment panels for heads and deputies tend to be more powerful. These are usually comprised of a larger number of people including advisers, district/assistant education officers, elected members, governors, parent-teacher representatives and even directors or deputies of education or their nominees, especially for large schools or 'sensitive appointments'.

Questions asked at interview vary by committee and post. So do interview styles. In one authority, for example, no formal questions are asked of candidates. Interviewees are given five minutes to make a prepared statement on why they should be given the job. In others, there is more than one interview in, for instance, the school and in county hall. Usually, however, there is only one day, morning or afternoon, interview.

Nevertheless, most interviews go through two distinct stages – the formal and the informal. Irrespective of stage, never be in any doubt that people are making judgements about you all the time. As a general rule, it pays not to be too quiet or too garrulous at any stage. Most questions usually centre on applicants as individuals, their qualifications and subject interests, general knowledge, experience as well as the qualities they think they can bring to a post or school.

Finally, although you may be unsuccessful, the impression you have created will undoubtedly influence your chances of success in subsequent applications within the same authority. Also, the experience will not be wasted.

6 Staff management procedures

Apart from job descriptions, curriculum responsibilities, staff deployment and the use of scale posts, there are a number of other ways of utilising the staff in a constructive manner. These include the regular use of full or departmental staff meetings, the setting up of working parties or committees, and the proper oversight of new or probationary teachers within a school (see Chapter 16) as well as student teachers.

Staff meetings

Schools vary in their use and frequency of staff meetings. Many primary schools endeavour to hold a short staff meeting at least once a week. Often, these gatherings are mainly of the information-giving type. Formalised staff meetings which concentrate on major matters such as curriculum development, parent-teacher relationships and, in a different order of magnitude, amalgamations, tend to take place less frequently as and when required. It is important that the purposes of meetings are made clear. Traditionally, primary school staff meetings are chaired by headteachers. Headteachers, too, tend to keep the minutes and formalise the agenda. In many schools, however, formalised agendas and minutes are unusual. At the very least, records of decisions should be kept. These may be important as a means of keeping new or absent staff informed.

Staff meetings are one of the major ways in which information is disseminated to teachers and decisions taken. Some headteachers tend to be autocratic in this role, others democratic, while others move between the two extremes depending on the nature of the issue under discussion. Inevitably, some headteachers feel more comfortable chairing meetings than others, depending on their personalities, interests and abilities.

Chairing a staff meeting is a considerable skill in itself. Many headteachers never chair any kind of meeting until they start their leadership role in a school. This, too, is unfortunate. Until staff have experience of chairmanship they cannot always foresee the difficulties which are likely to occur at such times, nor develop the best and most appropriate style for their particular personality and school.

As the following extracts show, it is important for every head or chairperson to think precisely about the aims and objectives of meetings – beforehand. Failure to do this can be costly. It is a totally unnecessary error which some people regret at their leisure! Careful preparation of meetings, including relevant papers and agenda, normally pays dividends.

People perceive meetings and their usefulness in many different ways. Some typical perceptions of meetings are:

1 'A camel is a horse designed by a committee'

This perception of committees is well known. It is an attitude summed up rather well by Ted Wragg in an article in the *Times Educational Supplement*:

> Why is it that when sizeable groups of human beings meet together to make decisions, the level of united wisdom drops like a stone? Eisenhower once observed that governments were less intelligent than their people. Had he been a teacher he would probably have said that the staff meetings were much dafter than any individual member.
>
> After years of suffering at meetings, I have formulated my one and only law. It states that the collective intelligence of a meeting falls by one IQ point for every person present in excess of four. Thus a university senate of 80 professors, with an average IQ of about 150, operates at ESN level.

In spite of this cynicism there is evidence to suggest that 'better' decisions are arrived at by groups – although they take longer. Even if one takes the view that groups are not particularly effective, there are other arguments as to why people should be involved in discussion, for example politically it can be more expedient; meetings help to 'develop' staff; wide perspectives can be gained on problems, etc.

2 'What's the point?'

Very often the purposes of meetings or of parts of meetings are not clear to the participants (let alone those not attending). Agendas are often vague and very general. The aims of the meeting can be equally vague resulting in varying expectations about whether members are participants in decision making or merely being consulted; whether the purpose of meeting is to provide information or to seek it.

3 'We spent hours not getting anywhere'

Meetings often seem longer than people expect. Everyone else seems to talk for too long on irrelevant topics. Often, in reality, the subtle process of bargaining and negotiating takes time. People need a forum to clarify issues in their own minds and to express their opinions.

4 'The meeting was poorly chaired'

Poor chairmanship can prolong meetings and be very frustrating. There is little doubt that some people find chairmanship skills difficult to master. Poor chairmanship can result in a host of problems including very lengthy, rambling meetings, unclear decisions, repetition, irrelevant discussion, etc.

5 'The Chairman manipulated things to his advantage'

Possibly he did! Chairmanship can provide considerable opportunities to influence the direction of a debate. The chairman is theoretically in a position to determine who should speak and for how long; what topics will be debated; whether points are taken up or shelved. There is not necessarily anything wrong in this but discontent can be reduced if the participants understand their roles.

6 'We seem to spend most of our time clarifying procedure'

Many meetings in organisations do not operate under clear standing orders and there is often room for debate about procedures to be followed. Indeed, people often try to manipulate procedures in order to increase their chances of gaining from subsequent decisions. There are, of course, advantages in operating without rigid rules and procedures, but in such cases skilled chairmanship is all the more important. In particular, procedural issues should not mask important factual information.

7 'Nothing ever seems to happen after our meetings'

Even when participants are clear about what decisions have been taken (and this is often not the case), all too often subsequent decisions about who is going to disseminate information and implement decisions are glossed over.

Working parties

Working parties are generally instigated at the behest of local education authority personnel, headteachers or school staff to look into particular aspects of education or schooling within a county, school, or group of schools. Occasionally, these working parties are inter-county, interschool, multidisciplinary or localised with a brief to look at specific problems. Sometimes headteachers in large schools will set up a working party to investigate matters and report back to staff. Usually, these working parties are a prelude to change of one kind or another.

Local education authority working parties tend to look at major issues of concern to large groups of schools and/or their staff. These might include, for example, the problem of small schools, the teaching of science in the authority, the use of assemblies and how to handle amalgamations. Intercounty or regional working parties are less common and might be instigated to look at such matters of mutual interest as transportation, bilingualism and the use of outdoor centres. Very occasionally, teachers are co-opted onto national working parties, such as curriculum development projects. Some authorities use working party procedures more frequently than others.

The composition of working parties can be a delicate matter. Elections are rarely held for appointments. Normally, selected staff are invited to apply or simply appointed because of their particular expertise in a field. These appointments are generally filled through advisory service and headteacher contact. Experience of serving on working parties can be exceedingly valuable for a number of reasons. It gives teachers an opportunity to work together on matters of mutual interest, to develop their knowledge in a specialist field, to make useful contacts and, in some cases, to contribute to the writing of reports. From time to time, staff contributing to working parties will also be involved in subsequent action, dissemination and feedback exercises. Such participatory activities look good on a curriculum vitae.

Committees

Like working parties, some primary staff in most authorities are engaged in out-of-school committee work of one kind or another. This can range from being a teacher governor to being involved in local or national enquiries. Most authorities have a number of education or education-related committees or sub-committees. Positions on these committees are often filled by representatives from teacher unions, other official educational bodies and local representatives. Local or national agreements often determine or affect their composition. For instance, the West Glamorgan Institute of Higher Education Local Committee for the Accreditation of Teacher Education (CATE) consists of several nominated union representatives, selected staff from primary and secondary schools, advisers, HMI, a parent governor and officials representing the health profession, commerce and industry as well as staff from the Institute. It is independently chaired by an eminent person who is not associated with the Institute or local education authority. The sub-committee on school–Institute links is comprised of nominated representatives from each spectrum of the larger body. Teachers selected to sit on working parties are normally highly experienced.

Perhaps at this point it is worth pausing for a moment to reflect upon the plight of some of those teachers who come into the inexperienced category – probationary teachers. Although probationary teachers have been the subject of a great deal of research since the seventies, the consensus from studies on good practice is not always implemented by local education authorities. This is partly for reasons of cost, partly because of time and partly because induction programmes are either badly handled or non-existent in some schools and in some LEAs (Reid, 1985b).

Helping new staff

As we consider many of the organisational issues associated with probationary teachers in Chapter 16, we will only briefly touch upon a few aspects here which are pertinent to good practice with new teachers, appointees and student teachers. In *The New Teacher in School* (DES, 1982b), we are presented with the extraordinary fact that when most new teachers take up their appointments in schools, they are reasonably competent, having acquired essential survival kits, but they are lacking in experience. How very surprising! The study goes on to show that new teachers tend to know less than experienced staff. This is often manifest in the way they structure and plan their lessons, react to social discourse with staff and pupils, handle administrative matters and cope in classroom situations. The Report suggests that such knowledge and skill is not easily acquired. New teachers often suggest that it is mostly learned by a process of trial and error, sometimes accompanied by considerable anxiety (Evans, 1976).

Research suggests that well-qualified postgraduate probationers need some form of in-service training (Reid, 1985b) and general advice (Reid, 1984b) shortly after taking up their appointments. This is not always forthcoming (DES, 1982b; Patrick, Bernbaum and Reid, 1983). Student and probationary teachers often report being overwhelmed by their initial experiences within the classroom and they typically express concern about their own performance and competence as teachers (Taylor, 1975; Bernbaum, Patrick and Reid, 1982; Reid, 1985b). In order to cope with new or demanding situations in the classroom, they often devise their own means of coping with incidents which frequently differ from those of experienced staff (Calderhead, 1979; Gould, 1985).

Headteachers, deputies, curriculum leaders, advisers and others differ markedly in the amount of formal or informal advice they give to new teachers in schools. Policies for assisting probationers to settle and adjust vary nationally, although there is some consensus that most beginning teachers receive less help than they should or would like to receive. Moreover, this help is often obtained from unpromoted colleagues just as much as from those holding positions of responsibility (Patrick, Bernbaum and Reid, 1983).

Likewise, assisting new appointees from other schools (promoted or redeployed staff) to integrate harmoniously is another grey area. Frequently, such personnel are not utilised as effectively as they might be partly because of imprecise job descriptions, skill duplication and poor management. Short in-house induction schemes are one way of overcoming this problem. Another is through integrated school based in-service work. Developing and encouraging beginning and new teachers is one of the most important facets of staff development and management programmes within schools; something which some heads are better at than others.

Finally, it is very important for experienced staff to play a major contribution in the training of student teachers, particularly on teaching practice. School–training institution links are often not as well developed as they should or need be; a constant source of criticism in teacher education programmes (DES, 1984; Reid, 1985c). Enlightened headteachers and other staff should always endeavour to participate to the full in the training and well-being of student teachers, both in their schools and inside the training institution on appropriate courses. After all, they have a vested interest. They are training the teachers of future generations, some of whom will not only teach their own children but also find themselves back in their own schools on a permanent basis.

Delegation

Current notions of good management favour a shift towards collaborative decision-making and the devolution of authority and power by the head (Coulson, 1978; Campbell, 1985; Price, 1985). Such principles are, indeed, embodied in recent school-based curriculum development systems such as GRIDS (McMahon, 1984) and school-focused in-service approaches (Bolam, 1982; Rudduck, 1984).

The headteacher is in a very powerful position within the school. Good corporate managerial practice requires heads to diffuse power downwards by involving others in decision-making and sharing responsibility. This is one way of enabling good team work to develop. Generally speaking, heads are amongst the most widely experienced members of staff. There is no such thing as the omnipotent and omnicompetent head – apart from in the minds of those select few who have read and follow Plato!

Good delegation is not simply about tasks and responsibility but also about authority and power. It is these latter aspects which many heads are loathe to forego. In the survey undertaken by Becher, Eraut and Knight (1981), for example, a lot of postholders complained at the lack of delegated authority which was given to them to carry out their tasks, including their major curriculum development function.

There is also more to delegation than merely devolving power. Part of the skill lies in determining *what* needs to be delegated. Primary teachers tend to accept two forms of responsibility – organisational and curricular

as outlined in the HMI surveys of 1978 and 1982 (see Chapter 3). Both of these functions bring with them an administrative burden which is properly taken on by the person responsible, usually working in conjunction with the head or deputy.

Within primary schools, many teachers perform necessary administrative functions on top of their other duties. These include the collection of dinner monies and the collation of daily dinner numbers. It is important for the educational well-being of a school that these are not the only, or major, responsibilities delegated by the head. The main delegated responsibilities – and power – should lie in the two professional areas outlined by HMI, suitably modified or arranged to fit in with local and school needs. This, of course, is much less easy in small than in large schools. Generally, the smaller the school, the fewer the range of extra-curricular activities, ancillary and secretarial help and subject expertise. There is also a greater probability of the head having to teach. This tends to militate against delegation and can mean the head becoming a jack of all trades, often undertaking many additional routine chores in or out of school time. It is factors like these which have led to suggestions about minimum viable sizes for primary schools.

Most primary teachers as extended professionals (Hoyle, 1974) are willing to accept extra responsibilities and appreciate having some authority delegated to them. Many heads make a point of giving every member of staff specific responsibility for some aspect of school life (Campbell, 1985). Having been given this responsibility, it is necessary for postholders and the rest of the school to know what is expected of them – which brings us back to the issue of job descriptions! By devolving duties and power, headteachers contribute to the daily in-house training and development of their staff. For many teachers, it is the only informal training they will ever receive before taking on posts of responsibility at every level.

Decision-making

There are various kinds of decision-making. Reflective decisions involve much thinking and evaluation. For example, when a person decides upon a career, he normally considers various possible alternative occupations, acquires information about them, imagines himself in these different occupational roles and compares and contrasts their possibilities before making a final choice. Immediate decisions depend upon quick judgements which are usually based on intuition and experience. The evaluation of alternatives is unlikely to take place before the action, although it may occur afterwards, particularly if the action leads to an unsatisfactory outcome. For instance, if while driving along a road a boy runs out in front of the car, the immediate response is to slam on the brakes – not ponder the alternatives. Finally, routine decisions are those which are made so often that they have become automatic and routine – when to change gear, to accelerate or slow down or how to cross a road.

Teachers' decisions also vary in their nature. Some are reflective, such as the selection of appropriate teaching methods, curriculum content and curriculum development programmes, which can be made over a fairly long period of time. These often require consultation with other staff, and involve considerable thought and evaluation. Other decisions are immediate. Various kinds of interruptions in lessons normally require immediate and appropriate responses in order to minimise classroom disruption or unforeseen problems. Finally, teachers tend to take routine decisions many times daily as part of their normal practice. This kind of decision-making includes coping with excessive noise, coping with pupils who raise their hands in the air because they wish to ask a question or leave the room, or defusing pupils' ebullience when the bell for morning break rings!

There are, however, a number of constraints upon teachers' decision-making processes. These include physical constraints, such as the size and composition of the class and the materials available, and ideological constraints consisting of commonly held beliefs, values and expectations about the content and methods of teaching and the policies being followed by headteachers, curriculum leaders, advisers and the local education authority as well as the needs of the syllabus. Teachers who ignore these latter aspects do so at their own risk (Auld, 1976).

Generally, these constraints are taken for granted by teachers who have grown accustomed to working within them. Indeed, some constraints are often welcomed for the security they offer. A prescribed syllabus, for example, relieves teachers of the need to make certain decisions. Therefore, in order to develop an understanding of teachers' classroom practice, of how it can be changed and improved, and of the capacity for teachers themselves to bring about such improvement, the study of teachers' thinking and decision-making must include an investigation of the teaching context, the extent to which teachers are involved in establishing that context and the way in which it limits or constrains teachers' thoughts, decisions and actions (Calderhead, 1984). Observational studies of primary classrooms (Galton *et al.*, 1980) have found that teachers spend much of their time in interacting with pupils, asking questions, obtaining responses from their pupils and, in turn, reacting to their pupils' responses. Research has shown that inexperienced and experienced teachers tend to act differently in similar situations (Calderhead, 1979). This suggests that some aspects of decision-making are an acquired skill which can be improved through training or experience.

After reviewing a vast research literature on organisational decision-making, Owens (1970) proposes two generalisations that are applicable to educational institutions. These acknowledge the fact that:

(a) teachers do not want to be involved in every decision, nor do they expect to be;
(b) headteachers need to be able to distinguish between the decisions in which

teachers should be involved and those which should be handled in other ways.

Owens elaborates on the second generalisation by reference to what Barnard (1938) has called the 'zones of indifference'. Barnard's thesis is that there are some areas in which the decisions of the administrator (headteacher) will be accepted without question by organisation members. Cohen (1976) suggests that the headteacher who engages his staff in areas of decision-making which they feel lie within their zone of indifference is likely to court not just irritation but a good deal of resentment too: 'It's his job to make those decisions – that's what he's paid for.'

Price (1985) investigated the perspectives of 495 headteachers, promoted teachers and unpromoted teachers with regard to teacher participation in decision-making in primary schools within one county. For the purposes of the study, his analysis encompassed nine decision-making areas – finance, curriculum content, teaching method, parents, teachers, discipline, communication, evaluation and resources. His findings show that participatory decision-making is becoming a reality in many primary schools but is by no means universally accepted, with widespread variations occurring between and within schools. He suggests, therefore, that establishing criteria for joint decision-making is extremely difficult. The best approach may be to state that any decision which does not meet the criteria for the teacher taking the decision alone or the headteacher taking the decision alone should be taken by the headteacher and teachers acting together.

Price found that:

(a) teachers expected to participate in decisions about what is taught in school, the syllabus of a subject and decisions about their timetables;
(b) teachers wanted even more involvement than they had at present in decisions about finance, teaching method, resources, discipline and school policy;
(c) teachers in general wished to be involved in joint decision-making rather than autonomous decision-making practices;
(d) there were few differences between the views of promoted and unpromoted teachers, the major differences occurring between headteachers and all other staff;
(e) the length of time for which respondents had held their professional titles was relatively unimportant;
(f) headteachers were found to be more satisfied with existing decision-making practices than teachers;
(g) there was evidence to suggest that the level of importance attached to each decision-making area by both headteachers and teachers depended upon their satisfaction with existing decision-making practices in that area.

Price's work shows that the size of schools is an important variable which affects decision-making practices. In small schools (schools with less than 130 pupils), there was movement away from joint decision-making processes. It seems that decisions in schools with teaching heads are taken by the headteacher or teachers acting alone. Joint decision-making practices are probably considered undesirable because of the time such decision-making takes. It is a case of needs must. In schools of 131–275 pupils, the movement is towards joint decision-making practices and away from teacher independence. In schools with more than 275 pupils, the overall movement is away from joint decision-making practices and towards teacher independence. In particular, in these schools headteachers are less interested in joint decision-making. This may be due to the problems of organisation within a large school or, possibly, because headteachers in large schools tend to be the most experienced (Price and Reid, 1987a, b, c, d).

Unlike Grover (1972), but like Richardson (1981), Price, and Price and Reid, report that gender is a relatively unimportant factor in relation to perspectives on participation in decision-making. If anything, it is female headteachers who wish to move away from joint decision-making. Where the sex variable is important in the case of teachers, it is female teachers who seek autonomy in their decision-making rather than male teachers. In particular, female teachers appear to want a major say in deciding the appropriate classroom practice they have to carry out, possibly because this is the one decision-making area which most affects them. This finding is in accord with previous studies (Hilsum and Start, 1974) which have shown that female teachers' major concern in schools is with classroom practice, with less concern being shown for other facets of school life.

Decision-making and authority

Thus the decision-making process when related to primary education is a complex matter. There are four arenas for decision-making to take place – national, regional, institutional and individual. Parties involved in national decision-making include personnel in the DES/Welsh Office (in England and Wales), Her Majesty's Inspectorate, pressure groups (such as the NFER, APU, SEC, parent associations, national examination bodies), relevant trade unions, the church, politicians and others. These tend to deal with decisions on laws, policy matters, directives, guidelines, research, monitoring of standards, finance, manpower planning, etc.

Regional decision-making typically involves LEAs and their officials, advisers, local trade unions, local examination bodies, elected members, local pressure groups and other interested educational and local parties. Their decision-making is related to such matters as co-ordination, advising, finance, resources, buildings, staffing, assessment, and the monitoring of standards as well as formulating policies for schools and schooling.

Institutional decision-making tends to in-

Initiator	Unit	Example	Power/Influence
Government	National system	Introduction of GCSE	POWER
LEA Committee	LEA	Tertiary reorganisation	
Principal	College	Allocation of resources	
Headteacher	School	New resource policies	
Curriculum leader	Department/or school	New scheme of work	
Teacher	Class	Learning	INFLUENCE

Figure 6.1 *Levels in the decision-making process*

volve governors, headteachers, HMI, advisers, parent–teacher associations, teachers and other interested neighbourhood groups. Their decision-making tends to be about school staffing, curriculum, syllabi, methods of teaching, materials, fund raising, extra-curricular activities, in-school assessment and innovation and a host of similar issues.

Individual decision-making by teachers normally involves pupils, colleagues and others and is related to teaching method, lessons, curriculum issues, individual needs, innovation, resources, extra curricular activities, etc.

All these aspects are reflected in Figure 6.1 which indicates the initiators in the decision-making process at the national, local, school, department and classroom level with examples.

Decision-making therefore, is closely related to sources of power.

French and Raven (1959) postulate five potential sources of power that people can use to influence others in social settings:

1 Reward power – the control and distribution of rewards valued by others.
2 Coercive power – the control and withholding of rewards valued by others.
3 Legitimate power – authority legally vested in or assigned to a position.
4 Expert power – the expertise of special knowledge, skill or experience.
5 Referent power – personal attractiveness or membership of someone's primary reference group.

In general, the more of these sources someone holds, the more powerful they will be, although 4 and 5 tend to be especially important. According to Hornstein *et al.* (1968), teachers find more satisfaction working under heads who employ 4 and 5, than those who impose 3 and 2. These findings support Weick's (1976) position that 1, 2 and 3 are only loosely coupled to action.

These, in turn, are linked to leadership stereotypes which relate to headteachers. Likert (1967) suggests there are five kinds of heads.

Exploitative authoritative	:	Dictatorial (Undemocratic).
Benevolent Authorative	:	Paternalistic (Explains the reasons for decisions).
Consultative	:	Progressive Approach (Confidence in staff).
Participative	:	Shared responsibility (Expects total involvement).
Laissez-faire	:	Abdicates responsibility (Teachers do their own thing).

Nias (1980) undertook a study on leadership styles and job satisfaction in primary schools. She distinguished between three types of leaders: passive, positive and Bourbon. 'Maximum job satisfaction for primary teachers went hand-in-hand with humane but positive leadership: leadership to which teachers felt they were encouraged to contribute but which gave them in return the chance to perform effectively the main role for which they believed they were employed.'

In practice, however, it is probably fair to say that most heads are not always consistent in style and their stance will vary according to the people they are dealing with and the particular situation.

Furthermore, there are probably seven stages in problem solving and decision-making. These are:

1 Identifying the problem (where you are and where you want to be).
2 Analysing the problem (facilitating forces, restraining forces).
3 Generating multiple solutions (brainstorming).
4 Planning for action.
5 Forecasting consequences of intended actions.
6 Taking action.
7 Evaluating the action.

Finally, decision-making and the power game are related to the communication network. This, therefore, is what we will discuss next.

Communication

The communication network – who, what and how

Even small primary schools are complex organisations, especially when the web of external communication networks are considered alongside the internal. Few other organisations have quite so many diverse interested parties which, in practice, range from children and parents to the Secretary of State for Education. Good communication is an absolute pre-requisite for the efficient running of any primary school. The importance of constructing effective communication systems cannot be overstressed.

As managers, headteachers and their staffs should at the very least:

1 Be aware of the crucial importance of communication.
2 Be aware of the totality of the communication network for their school – something which is not always the case, especially amongst new or fairly junior staff.
3 Be prepared to review and revise communication systems within and beyond the school in order to improve their effectiveness.

The complete communication network will vary by school and local education authority. Figure 6.2 shows a typical list of those involved in the total picture, including internal and external participants. To some extent, it can be argued that the list also reflects, very approximately, the relative importance of the various communication networks, although the reality is, of course, much more complex, dependent upon a host of factors.

Headteachers need to decide what information is imparted to staff either informally or formally. If too much information is given informally it may not be acted upon.

There are two ways of communicating

Figure 6.2 *The communication network*

within school	Headteacher
	Staff (teaching)
	Staff (non-teaching)
	Children
within and external	PTA
	Parents
external	Secondary schools
	Local primary and special schools
	Administrators ('the office')
	Advisory service
	HMI
	Welfare agencies (EWO, social services, child guidance, probationary service, etc.)
	Support agencies (school psychological service, medical services, etc.)
	The community at large (local business, industry, Round Table, police, fire service, etc.)
	Colleges, polytechnics and universities.
	Educational supplies (LEA)
	Local press (publicity, etc.)

information – formal and informal. Formal methods tend to take place via staff meetings (usually with an agenda), on staff notice boards, through head's notes or letters and a range of other kinds of meetings. Informal communications tend to include impromptu staff meetings, corridor talk, common room dialogue and a variety of *ad hoc* notes.

The head of a school is, or should be, at the

centre of the communication network both within and across the school boundary. In practice, the vast majority of communication from outside will be addressed to the head who will then decide what information needs disseminating and why and how this information should be imparted. In primary schools this is usually done orally, although some schools use bulletin sheets or tannoy systems. Such discretion is a considerable source of maintaining a head's authority, particularly as she is generally 'free' to put her own interpretation upon events (Alexander, 1984; Pollard, 1985).

There are, of course, some communications which come directly to teachers. These include, for example, union matters and sports fixture arrangements. Generally, however, these tend to be of a routine nature and are not problematic. Communications between schools and external organisations are normally sent out in the head's name or vetted by her beforehand – part of the bureaucratic

tradition in primary education. The general approach tends to be to discuss a matter, form a policy on it, review the decision and then, finally, communicate it to the appropriate people concerned. In the daily routine of school life, it is very easy to overlook communication difficulties, ignore them, or to dismiss them in the belief that 'we use the personal touch here'. Resource and time constraints, too, often adversely affect communication. One local primary school, for example, recently sent out an oral message via five-year-olds to inform parents of their lower school sports day arrangements. Only one mother duly arrived on the day. Subsequently, the head had to deal with a host of complaints, not least from a proud father whose daughter had won the sprint and egg and spoon races!

Leaving human nature and the complexity of interpersonal relations to one side, the matter of what information needs imparting to whom is fairly obvious on most occasions – children's reports, records, stock require-

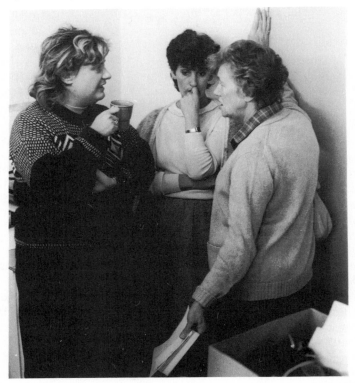

Informal communications are important but cannot replace organised meetings

ments, appeals, publicity leaflets and so on. There remain some grey areas, particularly in relation to confidential or policy matters. As a general rule, all staff should keep heads informed of anything which might have a bearing upon the well-being, efficiency or decision-making processes within the school. This includes applying for jobs, information on pupils and potential problem areas, in fact, anything which does or can affect the reputation of the school, progress of pupils, parent–school or LEA–school relationships and, most importantly, matters with potential legal implications such as the non-attendance of pupils or suspicions of ill-treatment or educational retardation. Teachers are not always aware that one piece of information can add to another, giving a clearer total picture, or that a head may be about to embark on a new strategy because of certain events. Hence it is never easy for individual teachers to judge when incidents or information should be passed on, or where the precise boundary of their autonomy lies. These aspects form part of teachers' professional judgements. Headteachers and teachers can overcome such inherent difficulties by keeping log books of information received, information processed and information passed on (to whom and why). New staff in particular need to be given immense detail on the daily routine of school life. If they are not given this information, it is hardly their fault when they make a mistake.

It is probably impossible to produce a list of information which should be communicated in primary schools, since it would be endless. But the following aspects should always be available to all staff:

Social records, including social service reports
Educational psychologist's reports
EWO reports
Other reports (health, etc.)
Information on school policy and organisation
Fire and safety regulations
Curriculum responsibilities
In-service courses

A school's in-service and staff development programmes
Names of external contacts, governors, parent–teacher association members, advisers, etc.
The school diary, giving list of arranged events
Timetables

Some schools keep confidential information separate from other records and out of the reach of many staff. This is bad practice. If staff do not have access to critical information, how can they be at fault for not complying with crucial recommendations? However, it is at least equally wrong when staff fail to keep such information to themselves.

Ideally, schools should produce their own booklets giving their curriculum guidelines and curriculum development policies. This information is invaluable for parents and a useful way of keeping a school's work schemes co-ordinated.

This is similarly the case with school-focused INSET. As so much INSET is located in teachers' centres, colleges, universities or elsewhere, dissemination has long been problematic. The dissemination of the benefits gained from attending in-service courses should be an essential built-in feature of school life (Clark and Reid, 1986).

Traditionally, courses on effective communication or communication management tend to be outside the scope of initial training or in-service courses. Nevertheless, many teachers-as-managers would benefit from an understanding of non-verbal and verbal communication systems.

Teacher-as-researcher concept

Undertaking research in their own classrooms is a significant way in which teachers can take increased responsibility for their actions, critically reflect upon their craft, and improve their teaching. Hopkins (1985) explores the reasons for doing classroom research and examines the types of research possible and those suitable for teachers to undertake. He draws on many examples of research done by teachers in describing how research problems are formulated, how the information is gathered and how it is analysed. He also discusses the reporting and publishing of teacher research and how it can be linked to the curriculum and used in school improvement strategies. In general, he provides a rationale, and a practical guide for teachers engaged in researching their own teaching and for those thinking of doing so.

Notwithstanding potential methodological problems, it is surely appropriate for teachers to act as researchers within their own schools in order to uncover original data on the real processes of schooling. Their findings can then be used to improve the quality of the teaching as well as the organisation and management of their own primary school.

The teacher-as-researcher concept (Stenhouse, 1975; Pring, 1978; Hopkins, 1982) potentially offers a most valuable medium for promoting relatively cheap and effective projects which can help to stimulate and promote better and more effective in-service work, schooling and personal development as well as contributing to the knowledge-base of education. Given the shortages of resources which are apparent in primary education and the limited public funds that are available for research, the notion of teachers undertaking research in their own classrooms is one way for primary education to move forward and for teachers to acquire new skills (Gould, 1985).

This latter aspect has been endorsed by the decision of the Department of Education and Science and Welsh Office to award small-scale grants to assist staff interested in undertaking research in their own schools and classrooms.

Undertaking 'action research' within schools on top of everything else is no easy matter. However, it is one way for primary teachers to develop their expertise to the mutual benefit of themselves, their schools and their pupils. In the past, too many primary teachers have taken higher degrees or been on in-service courses which have been too secondary or subject-orientated. Becoming a teacher–researcher provides an opportunity to 'problem-solve' within one's own arena. Teacher–researchers will probably play an increasing part in future school improvement/change exercises as well as in the debate about teacher effectiveness.

A consideration of the issues discussed in Chapters 5 and 6 suggests that effective staff management in primary schools is a considerable skill. Too often, these skills are learned 'on the job' rather than through specific forms of training. It is now necessary for headteachers and teachers as managers to receive appropriate training to develop their staff management and interpersonal skills. These courses should include sessions on staff selection, the role of curriculum leaders, job descriptions, techniques for managing staff in schools, delegation, decision-making and communication.

7 Pupil organisation

This chapter considers various aspects of pupil organisation in the primary school. First, the constraints and opportunities of school buildings are discussed, which leads on to a consideration of how schools organise pupils at the institutional level. Quite often head-teachers have little room for manoeuvre or choice about how best to organise pupils into class groups, due to the small number of pupils in the school and LEA regulations on staffing levels (see Chapter 3). Nevertheless, in most schools some choices about pupil organisation do exist. Second, various aspects of the physical organisation of classrooms are discussed, which, in turn, are followed by an exploration of some of the different ways of grouping children for learning in classrooms. This discussion is related to the purposes of the activity or experience concerned.

Institutional influences

There are numerous ways in which the pupils in a primary school can be organised. School systems are influenced by a host of situational factors. These include the type of school (infant, junior or primary), the size of the school, the school's yearly intake of pupils, staffing levels, the design of the buildings and, not least, the educational beliefs of the head and staff. Each of these aspects will be

discussed in more detail as the chapter progresses. First, however, we begin with a brief consideration of what for most schools is a relatively fixed resource – the school buildings. The quality of the plant and design of buildings certainly influences the way some schools are organised and managed.

School Buildings

Schools are housed in a wide variety of buildings of different ages and characteristics. In essence, there are two broad types of buildings which can be distinguished, usually designated as 'traditional' and 'open-plan'. Of course, we are not suggesting that the buildings alone dictate styles of school organisation. Nevertheless, the possibilities are often limited by the nature, as well as the extent, of the accommodation.

Traditional schools, of whatever age, are based on the idea of an individual classroom for every class group of children. That is, each teacher in the school has her own room in which to work with her own class of children, relatively independently and in comparative privacy. This is the embodiment of the 'teaching is a private activity' syndrome. Or, as Bennett (1976) graphically labels it, the 'box' system. There are, in almost all schools, other spaces and rooms available for different purposes (for example, a hall, cloakrooms, TV

65

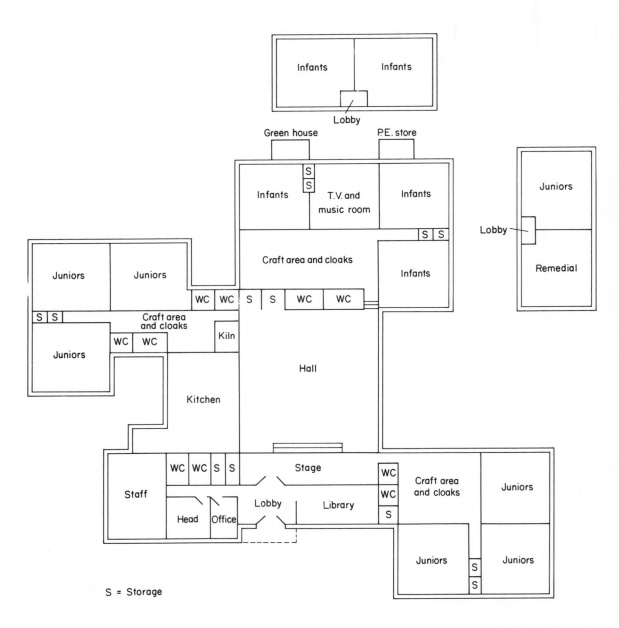

Figure 7.1 *Plan of a recently amalgamated primary school built in the late 1960s*

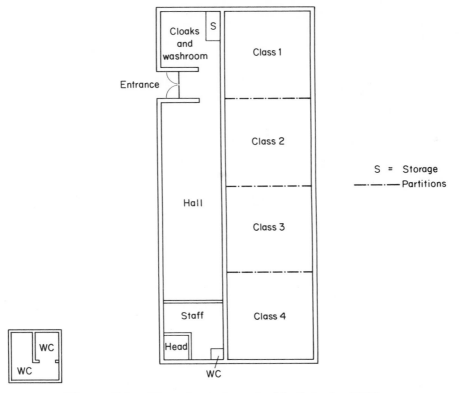

Figure 7.2 *Plan of an infant school built in the 1920s*

room, library) but the basis of the traditional system is a classroom, or 'box', for each teacher. Figures 7.1 and 7.2 show, in plan, two traditional layouts. One is a farly modern, large primary school; the other is a small infant school constructed in the 1920s.

Note that the infant school has the opportunity to fold back partitions to make bigger teaching spaces if desired. This arrangement has the advantage of flexibility, but even the best partitions allow a significant amount of noise to percolate through.

Clearly, where box-type classrooms exist inflexibly in a school, organisational options are reduced. Thus, schools are almost bound to adopt some form of 'single-class' organisation, with one teacher to one class group in their own accommodation.

By contrast, open-plan schools (generally of recent construction) are based on much larger teaching areas. These are shared, in one way or another, by two or more teachers and the

pupils for whom they are responsible. Even in these, however, many different designs are possible. Figures 7.3 and 7.4 show two different open-plan designs; one being a purpose-built primary school and the other being a redevelopment of the small infant school shown in Figure 7.2. (This school in the West Midlands is now part of an amalgamated primary school but retains its separate accommodation.)

Many schools built on open-plan lines have extra, separate classrooms added at a later date to form what might be called mixed systems. Mixed systems are quite common. In these circumstances, part of a school is open-plan while another part consists of discrete classrooms. The reasons for mixed systems are numerous. They may be due to a deliberate policy decision – for example, open-plan for the nursery and infant ages, 'classes' for the juniors. However, mixed systems often arise because of the necessity to accommodate

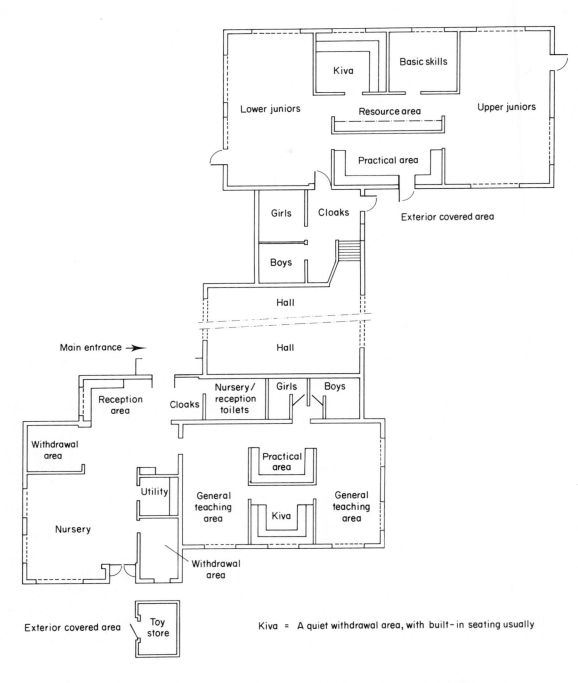

Figure 7.3 *An open-plan primary school built in the late 1970s*

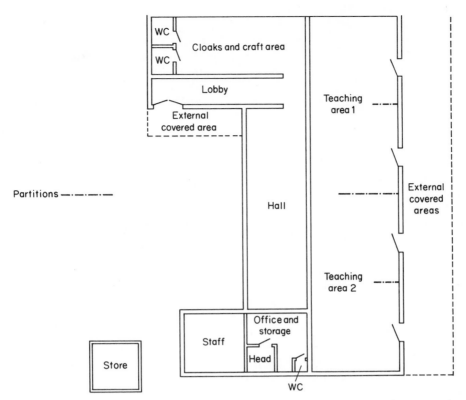

Figure 7.4 *An infant school built in the 1920s reorganised with extensions into a semi open-plan layout in the 1980s*

more children than the number for which the open-plan building was originally designed. Local education authorities have occasionally been known to slot larger numbers of children into schools than the buildings were originally designed for, either by changing their own accommodation guidelines or by redesignating non-teaching space (for example, cloakroom or storage facilities) as teaching areas. Despite this, there comes a point beyond which additional accommodation simply has to be provided. Normally, in an era of rising rolls and economic restraint, the extra space tends to come in the form of some sort of 'temporary' classrooms separated from the main buildings. Occasionally, when numbers in a school are confidently expected to remain at a higher level, the additional buildings may be substantial, or even new purpose-built schools erected. More usually the buildings are less permanent. They are then variously known as 'huts', 'terrapins' or 'mobile class-rooms', although their mobility is, to say the least, not very great!

Obviously, in times of falling school rolls, the numbers of pupils accommodated in this way are substantially reduced. Where such additional accommodation exists, schools do not normally have the option of organising the school so that all pupils are taught in open-plan situations, although semi-open-plan teaching remains a possibility when the 'mobiles' provided are very large. Irrespective of the provision of buildings, staff need to decide on some form of organisation for the children in their school. It is to this issue that we now turn our attention.

Organisation of classes

The most important factor to be taken into account when organising classes is usually the age of the children concerned. The common practice is to arrange for each class to contain pupils born, or admitted to the school, during one school year. This is usually referred to as horizontal grouping. If a school is large enough, there may be two or more classes in each year group.

Increasingly, the form of class organisation adopted is forced on a school by the numbers entering the school and by the staffing policies of the local education authority (see Chapters 3–6). In 1986, the Secretary of State for Education, Kenneth Baker, stated that all primary schools should have at least a two-form entry (i.e. two full classes of children starting school each year). The main reason he gave for making the assertion was that this safeguard would enable schools to offer as broad a curriculum as possible by having on their staff sufficient teachers with different kinds of subject expertise. In addition, it would also enable schools to have more flexibility to organise classes as they saw fit, rather than having organisational systems forced upon them.

Inevitably, when relatively small numbers of pupils enter a school year after year, some classes of mixed age-range tend to become the norm. Even in these latter circumstances, however, there are several alternative possibilities. To begin with, different local education authorities have different school admission policies and many LEAs also give some discretion to the schools about the age they first start accepting pupils. By law, in England and Wales, children must be in full-time schooling by or at the age of five. Nevertheless, LEAs do have a great deal of freedom about how they arrange their own school-start policies (Reid, 1985a). In particular, authorities may allow children to start school earlier than is strictly required. Therefore, in some parts of Britain, pupils tend to start school at the age of three or four; in others at five. In practice, staffing is so crucial that most LEAs tend to have specific age-related admission policies and staff schools accordingly.

Some of the regional variations in practice are now listed below:

1 Children are admitted to full-time schooling on their fifth birthday or as soon as practicable thereafter. (This means that admissions take place piecemeal throughout the school year with a small 'bulge' after the longer summer break.)
2 Children are admitted at the beginning of the term in which they have their fifth birthday. (This implies three admissions per year.)
3 Children are admitted at the beginning of the academic year in which they have their fifth birthday.
4 Children are admitted to school in one or other of the ways above (but most commonly 1 or 2) following their fourth birthday. (This is becoming more common for a variety of reasons.)

It should be pointed out that any attendance at school before the age of five years is at the discretion of the local authority (i.e. they do not have to provide places for under-fives) and the headteacher. It is also voluntary from the parents' point of view. They do not have to send their children, even if the places are available, although in practice most do.

Clearly, with any arrangement except 3, the numbers in the reception class will build up over the year. Schools taking in more than one full class per year then need to decide how to arrange the reception classes to give children continuity and security. This may be achieved by allowing two or more classes to fill up gradually or by deliberately arranging to have mixed age groups in each class, a system known as vertical grouping or family grouping.

In principle, in schools organising children in single-age classes, the cohort of children admitted to a reception class in any given school year moves up into the next class (first year infants or I1 for short) together. In practice, the numbers entering any school in any year often mean that such neat groupings and movements are not possible (see, for example, the numbers shown in Table 3.5). At best, the class sizes moving through the school will tend to vary quite a lot; at worst, single-age grouping may be impossible (for example, in small schools). In between it is often possible to ensure reasonably equitable single-age groupings in the junior phase by judicious juggling of children's movements from class to class in the infant section. This is especially true where numbers entering the school are relatively large. All this means that infant pupils often do not progress through the school neatly in cohorts. Rather, they move up in groups of varying sizes as the need arises. Whatever is done, unless children are in classes with a wide mix of ages, it is rarely possible to have classes of nearly equal size throughout a school, even in adjacent year groups. In any event, most teachers believe in the desirability of having rather lower numbers in those classes in the nursery and infant departments which induct pupils into the social and educational realities of schooling.

A typical arrangement of 'single-age' classes in a primary school might be:

	Class	Age Range (approx.)
Infant School or Department	Reception class (R)	4–5+
	First year infants (I1)	5–6+
	Second year infants (I2)	6–7+
Junior School or Department	First year juniors (J1)	7–8+
	Second year juniors (J2)	8–9+
	Third year juniors (J3)	9–10+
	Fourth year juniors (J4)	10–11+

There are several reasons why the majority of schools strive to organise classes on a single-age basis. For example, the range of ability and of social and emotional development in a single-age class is likely to be less than in a mixed-age class which makes it easier for teachers to organise the class and to provide appropriate work and learning experiences. Certainly, HMI (DES, 1978b; 1982a), have found that work in single-age classes is better matched to the aptitude of pupils than it is in mixed-age classes.

In principle, with individualised learning, the range of ability in a class should not matter. In practice, however, relatively little primary school teaching is truly individualised (DES, 1978b; Galton *et al.*, 1980). While children frequently work alone, they most often do so on similar work given to the whole class or a group.

The idea that single-age classes are easier to teach and organise because of the greater homogeneity of child development led, in the past, to the form of pupil organisation known as 'streaming'. Under this system, classes are not only organised on a single-age basis but an attempt is made to put children in classes of similar intellectual ability. The assumption in streaming is that the smaller the ability range, the easier it is for teachers to organise work appropriately for the class. While there are elements of truth in such an assumption, the advantages of streaming are far outweighed by the disadvantages (Barker-Lunn, 1970; Boydell, 1979; Bailey and Bridges, 1983). Despite this, the streaming of pupils was the commonest form of organisation in junior schools, especially where numbers were sufficient, up until the early 1960s (DES, 1967). Since then there has been a dramatic decline in streamed classes (Bealing, 1970; Boydell, 1980) so that streaming is now very rare indeed, except in a few of the most traditional areas. Clearly, as Boydell (1979) points out, de-streaming is one aspect of the 'Plowden philosophy' which schools have accepted and incorporated. To the best of our knowledge, there is no known case of a school in the primary sector de-streaming and then going back to a streaming form of organisation.

Some primary schools, though large enough to arrange classes in year groups, deliberately choose to have classes with mixed ages. Others have little choice because of their small numbers. According to HMI (DES, 1978), there are three categories of mixed-age classes. There is the situation in which the majority of children in classes are the same age, with just a few from another age group. Generally, these are in schools where year group sizes are particularly uneven and mixing age groups makes it possible to even up the sizes of classes. The second category is where classes contain substantial numbers of pupils from two age groups. The third category is where classes contain substantial numbers of children from three or more age groups. It is these last two categories to which HMI apply the term vertical grouping.

Small rural schools with a low yearly intake of children usually have little choice in the matter of pupil organisation. There are still some one- and two-teacher schools in places such as rural Wales and Suffolk, although these numbers are dwindling as LEAs implement closure policies. However, in such schools it is not uncommon for one teacher to cope with the whole age-range from 5 to 11, or for one teacher to have charge of the infants and another the juniors.

Vertically grouped classes are sometimes adopted in infant schools and departments to avoid the necessity of moving children to new classes during the year or, with bigger numbers coming in, to avoid ending up with an 'older' and 'younger' reception class. We might note in passing that it is inevitable that some children spend longer than others in the infant department. Research suggests that these children tend to benefit from the extra time in school (Davie *et al.*, 1972).

Junior departments, too, sometimes need to mix age groups due to uneven numbers in different year groups. For this reason, or as deliberate policy, junior schools may opt for restricted vertical grouping (two age ranges together) or extended vertical grouping (three or more age ranges). It is comparatively rare for schools deliberately to opt for the mixing of the whole primary age range in each class.

There are several reasons why some schools choose to adopt vertical grouping, aside from the 'numbers game' already discussed. First, it is considered by advocates of the system that a genuine 'family' atmosphere can be generated by having younger pupils with older ones. Older pupils are said to benefit from the opportunity to help look after and guide the younger ones and vice versa. Second, as pupils move into established classes in small year groups, older hands can help to settle them in and provide a welcoming atmosphere. In theory, transition problems

and time 'getting to know the ropes' should be reduced. Third, there is an opportunity for pupils to be with one teacher for more than a year, giving coherence and continuity and reducing the time taken by teachers in getting to know pupils (see Chapter 8 for fuller discussion).

There are, of course, possible disadvantages to vertical grouping which make many teachers dubious about the system. First, there is the possible problem of matching work and experiences to the wide range of pupils. Second, it is sometimes considered that younger pupils and their needs might distract older pupils. Alternatively, teachers might be tempted to let older pupils deal too much with younger ones – thereby distracting the older ones and depriving the younger ones of attention from the teacher. Third, an extended time with one teacher might actually deprive children of exposure to the different methods, personality, expertise and knowledge-base of other teachers. Bluntly, not all teachers are equally effective. Thus some children are going to spend longer with less effective teachers. In fact, even the best teachers have their own particular strengths, perhaps, for example, in a curriculum area. Thus it seems sensible to allow as wide a range of pupils as possible to have direct experience of each primary school teacher.

Summarising, it appears from the evidence that systems work best when the people operating them believe in them and, consequently, try to make them work. Unfortunately, with respect to the notion of individualised learning, the circumstances pertaining in our primary schools make some things impossible to achieve due to staffing, resourcing and economic constraints (Galton and Simon, 1980).

Organisation within classrooms

We now turn to a consideration of pupil organisation within classes and the general environment of the classroom. Obviously, there are many natural constraints on how a classroom can be organised. Equally, there are opportunities for teachers to use their skills and imagination. The ensuing discussion relates particularly to single classrooms (Bennett, 1976) although much of what we write also refers to organising open-plan situations.

In principle, an open-plan classroom is more flexible and gives greater organisational opportunities than single classrooms. For example, team teaching is more possible under the former circumstances. Also, there exist more opportunities for producing larger open areas, sections or corners for specific learning purposes such as reading. On the debit side, quiet and privacy are more difficult to establish. It is also harder to monitor individual children's whereabouts. Similarly, wall and storage space can be reduced. In addition, in open-plan settings, the timetable and resources have to be more rigidly controlled because of the number of shared resources and facilities such as wet areas. This necessity for extensive planning is exacerbated when certain kinds of team teaching are practised since the teachers involved often have to specify and organise the curriculum areas or parts of the timetable in which they are going to take a major role. In spite of these challenges, dedicated and imaginative teachers who capitalise on the advantages of open-plan situations provide exciting, effective meaningful and fulfilling learning experiences for the children (Bennett and Hyland, 1979).

In the single classroom or box system, a teacher usually has much more freedom to organise things the way she wishes. But there are constraints here too. For instance, the size of the room and its overall shape will need to be taken into account when organising the learning environment. Many teachers in primary schools would dearly love to be able to have their own wet area, maths, reading or library corner but are constrained by the lack of space, resources and, often, facilities such as running water. Having said that, even in the smallest classroom there is ample room to display books and to produce other features

for exhibition such as objects to examine. Again, a teacher's will and imagination are the two main requirements here. Enthusiastically organised, the classroom or learning area is a potent teaching aid. Rightly, the literature on primary education puts great store on the learning environment which a teacher and the school manage to create. Children learn from, and with, their immediate classroom environment. The standards which a teacher sets in the organisation and atmosphere of the class provide models and yardsticks for the children's own work. We believe strongly that every primary classroom should reflect the range of subjects and topics being taught through well-constructed display features including examples of children's work.

Amongst other constraints, we must include furniture in the list. Unfortunately, too many of our primary schools have to make do with old, poorly maintained and often inadequate and unsuitable furniture. Even in these circumstances, however, imaginative and enthusiastic teachers can provide the type of environment which facilitates the kind of learning they wish to promote. Happily, many primary schools do have modern, lighter, more adaptable furniture which enables teachers not only to set up a particular organisational structure within the classroom, but also enables teachers to change and adapt the system to suit different purposes.

Hence a good classroom should display several features:

1 It should be a pleasant working environment which children enjoy and where they feel happy and relaxed. Attitudes towards school and learning are formed early in pupils' education. Undoubtedly, the attractiveness or otherwise of the physical environment contributes towards these attitudes. By judicious use of displays of childrens own work, commercial material and natural objects as well as teachers' contributions, along with items from, for example, museums or resource centres, a delightful environment can be created. Teachers do not need to be artistic to make

use of proper backing paper, drapes and 'stands' (for example, boxes) to produce good displays and a pleasing environment.

2 The classroom should contain examples of good work in a variety of media, modes and curriculum areas. As well as providing a pleasant environment, this will motivate children to do well and provide exemplars for them to emulate.

3 The good classroom will provide interesting and stimulating experiences. The right sort of displays will include artefacts and objects to handle and explore as well as things to look at and read. Properly planned, tactile and exploratory displays will not only give children interesting and valuable experiences, but will also raise questions and encourage the beginnings of investigation. Children need to be given time and, often, overt encouragement, to explore the materials or situations provided. It cannot be assumed that the mere presence of displays will automatically lead to productive and worthwhile experiences and investigations.

4 In the classroom should be both the incentive and the means for finding things out. A range of reference books and resources for investigation (for example, measuring and observation instruments) should be readily available.

5 Any classroom should be functional and well-organised. All commonly used materials and apparatus should be accessible and organised. Rules about how and when things can be used should be common knowledge. Children can easily be trained to look after most aspects of the provision and organisation of materials and apparatus. Such delegation of responsibility has many advantages. Children enjoy accepting responsibility. Usually they make an excellent job of it when appropriately encouraged. Feelings of worthwhileness and usefulness are engendered. Also, teachers are released for more important teaching tasks. Furthermore, the items themselves are usually more effectively maintained and conserved.

A primary classroom should be well-organised and kept clean, active and exploratory. Experiential methods mean, however, that it is neither possible nor desirable that classrooms should be pristine at all times. Explicitly, it does not take too much effort, especially with children's help, to make sure that the classroom is at least tidy and organised ready for a new start at the beginning of the next day. The cleaning staff will bless you too!

Organising for learning

Even in open-plan schools, children are almost invariably organised so that each teacher has a 'class' of children who relate first and foremost to her and for whom she has responsibility and oversight. Thus it is the class teacher's responsibility to register her children first thing in the morning, take the main responsibility for record keeping and be available for consultation with parents, even if at some times responsibility for organising learning is shared with other teachers. So-called 'team teaching' (Warwick, 1974; Boydell, 1979; Cohen and Manion, 1981) is often like this, when two (occasionally more) teachers share responsibility for two or more classes of children in an open or semi-open-plan environment. Even in a traditional 'one teacher, one class, one classroom' arrangement it is not unusual for children to be taught by teachers other than their own in certain subjects. Music and games are probably the commonest examples. It is also quite normal for teachers to exchange classes for subjects as diverse as science, religious education and creative writing. This sort of exchange arrangement should be differentiated from team teaching.

Whatever the situation – open-plan, semi-open-plan or box – attention needs to be given to different ways of grouping children for learning. Nowadays, the overwhelming majority of children sit (when they are seated) in groups. The sizes of groups usually vary between four and eight. However, these groupings refer mainly to seating arangements rather than to pupils working together. Indeed, one striking finding of the ORACLE (Observational Research and Classroom Learning Evaluation) study of English classrooms was that the majority of children sat in groups but that actual co-operative group work was very rare in practice (Galton *et al.*, 1980). Children worked in groups, not as groups. If we accept the recommendations of the ORACLE report and HMI (1978) we are left in no doubt that the promotion of genuine co-operative work in primary schools is one of the biggest challenges facing us in the near future. Not only is co-operative work claimed to be effective in promoting learning (Tann, 1981; Yeomans, 1983) but it also represents a way of working which most people experience in adult life. Not all learning, however, is necessarily facilitated in group situations. Thus children can, and should, be organised in different ways depending on the objectives of what they will be doing, the nature of the task, the particular needs of the children involved and, of course, practical considerations such as the numbers of children and the space and facilities available.

We are now in a position to look at the range of different pupil organisations available and at some of the purposes, advantages and disadvantages of each.

Individual work

Galton, Simon and Croll (1980) and HMI (1978; 1984; 1986) seem agreed that pupils in primary schools spend too much of their time working individually and in relative isolation from their fellows (and their teacher, come to that). However, they do not suggest that individual work has no place in the primary school. It is certainly necessary for all children to develop the ability to work on their own since this is a valuable ability in secondary education and later in life. To an extent, children (and their teachers) need to be aware of what they can achieve on their own initiative. Furthermore, much individualised work is designed to be completed in a relatively

sequential way at the child's own pace. This would apply, for example, to SRA (Science Research Associates) language development materials and to some maths schemes such as SMP (Schools Mathematics Project). In these cases, co-operation might be counterproductive. There are those, however, who claim that even with such materials the benefits of co-operating outweigh any disadvantages, especially if the participants are well-matched for ability and speed of working. And, of course, many activities, even within schemes like SMP, require help from others. Perhaps silent reading is the only activity where working together is always inappropriate!

Paired working

There is some evidence that children prefer the ease and intimacy of working in twos to any other grouping (Boydell, 1976). Certainly it is a form of grouping which has a lot to offer. Pairs of children working together gain considerably from being able to talk through an activity, from the necessity to see someone else's point of view and, occasionally, to have to explain or justify their own. Indeed, many of the newer curriculum schemes explicitly attempt to promote work in pairs or bigger groups. For example, full benefit from newer teaching techniques such as cloze procedure is only gained when children co-operate and discuss their tasks (West Glamorgan County Council, 1987).

One great advantage of groups of two is that each child has plenty of opportunity to contribute and is less likely to opt out. It is a commonplace finding that the larger a group is, the more reluctant some children (and adults) are to interact in that situation. Thus not only is the notional 'share' of time increased in a pair, but the propensity to take part is also greater. It is possible for children to benefit from working in pairs in most curriculum areas and in cross-curricular activities such as topic work and sensory/ environmental work. Arguably, it is a way of working which is under-used and should be adopted more often.

Working in threes

A group of three is a very small group and shares many of the benefits of working in pairs. There is always the possibility in a group of three of one member being singled out. But this is unlikely if the groups have been sensibly 'constructed' by the teacher (for example, allowing pupil choice on a friendship basis).

It is an advantage of groups of three that a slightly wider range of opinion, knowledge and strengths may be available. In many activities, like maths, science and drama an extra person or pair of hands is often essential.

Small groups

A small group can be anything from four up to eight or nine children. Groups of this size are often used by teachers who have been described in the ORACLE survey (Galton *et al.*, 1980) as 'group instructors' and 'rotating changers'. Children in a group will, typically, be engaged on the same task or working in the same curriculum area (but not necessarily working co-operatively). This sort of organisation enables the teacher to interact with one group while other groups work independently. There is no doubt that a small group can benefit from working closely with the teacher, although HMI have reservations about the value of the work other children are often doing while the teacher is occupied (HMI, 1978). Some of the difficulties and dangers of working in this way can be overcome by team teaching, but team teaching remains a minority method.

If it is desired to promote co-operative work with groups of this size – particularly the larger ones – activities need to be carefully chosen (Yeomans, 1983). Often what is involved is a joint effort rather than total co-operation – for example, as when seven or eight children contribute items towards the construction of a large model, a big display or a group newspaper. Of course, there could be elements of co-operation (for example, in planning the overall model or the newspaper), but much of the work might consist of individual efforts which are eventually brought together.

Group work of any sort can be enhanced by the involvement of other adults in the classroom. Many schools use parents in a variety of roles, as described in Chapter 12. Some schools receive secondary school pupils, trainee nursery nurses and trainee teachers and their tutors into their classrooms. Such people can provide help, ideas and materials.

Irrespective of these situational variables, the small-to-medium sized group is particularly valuable for activities such as discussion, drama, certain types of musical activities and in circumstances where particular skills and concepts are taught to a group of pupils of fairly similar ability. This latter set-up is probably most often used in maths where, quite properly, teachers feel the need to introduce, develop or explain new topics with children in a face to face manner.

Large groups

Having defined a small group as containing up to nine pupils, we suggest that a large group is comprised of ten or more children, up to a full class, or even larger numbers in a team teaching situation. Interestingly, the ORACLE study (Galton *et al.*, 1980) found that teachers whom they labelled 'class enquirers' were the most likely to ask open and enquiry-promoting questions; the sort of question often thought to encourage cognitive development. Clearly, class teaching does have things to recommend it, used in the right circumstances. However, in a large group it is much more difficult to ensure that all children are attending and not opting out. Furthermore, when teaching *per se* is taking place in a whole class situation (for example, telling, instructing, explaining), it is very difficult to do other than 'teach to the middle' range of ability with all the difficulties this can cause for less and more able children. The fact remains that the 'class enquirers' (i.e.

those teachers who used class teaching as a strategy more than others) did produce very worthwhile cognitive gains in their pupils according to the ORACLE findings.

Aside from 'teaching' large groups, there are many situations in which children work in such groups. Many classes do drama together and produce plays, or take part in collective assemblies. Some forms of music-making are carried out in large groups and team games frequently involve larger numbers. Potentially, all these things provide children with valuable learning and social experiences.

As we have seen, different types of grouping have their own uses, strengths and weaknesses. The most important thing for the class teacher is to consider what form of grouping is appropriate for each particular purpose. If teachers think carefully about using co-operative learning whenever children can benefit from it, they may well find that situations in which children need to work alone occur less often than common practice would indicate. Helpful information can often be obtained from the teachers' guides of published schemes such as Language Patterns (Moyle, 1981, 1982), Mathematics for Schools (Howell et al., 1982) and Learning through Science (Richards et al., 1980) and the many books and articles now being produced on the newer teaching techniques such as fiction-centred and resource-based learning.

8 The small school

In this chapter we piece together some of the organisational problems usually associated with small primary schools. We have not attempted to argue a case for or against their retention.

Much of the discussion which has taken place in the early eighties about small schools, has expressed concern regarding the breadth of education which they are able to provide. In the main, the debate has focussed on rural communities but the declining birth rate of the past few years has meant that many of the erstwhile larger urban schools are now entering the small schools category. The recent avalanche of official documents has added a new dimension to the debate, and interest and concern regarding the viability of the small school have been rekindled.

Just what is a small school? Small schools can be defined in a number of ways. The term is a relative one (Mountford, 1984). A report by the West Glamorgan LEA (1985), for example, takes a roll of 130 pupils or less 'where the Headteacher has full time responsibility for a class', as its definition of a small school. 'Full-time responsibility for a class', incidentally, in this context, was four full days per week, as the local authority allowed at that time 0.2 teacher cover (one full day equivalent) to give the headteacher time for administrative duties. A sliding scale dependent upon numbers on roll has since been introduced.

Some writers (Paisey, 1981a) take a slightly higher figure on roll (below 200) as being a useful definition of a small school. Below this number:

(a) it is highly likely that the headteacher will perform significant class teaching duties;
(b) mixed age classes are very likely to occur.

These factors may, of course, be found in a larger primary school, though perhaps within these schools there is an element of choice. For example, headteachers often allocate themselves a particular teaching 'load' voluntarily.

The number of small schools is surprisingly high. In 1984 there were 20,001 primary schools and middle schools deemed primary in England, of which 12,391 fell into a 'below 200' category (DES, 1984b). In fact, 1,866 primary schools had less than 50 pupils on roll. These are by no means insignificant figures.

Small schools can probably be sub-divided into four categories. These are: village small schools; rural small schools; semi-rural small schools; and urban small schools. Generalisations must be made cautiously since schools which are apparently similar in size or environment can reveal important differences in several aspects of practice such as their internal organisation, decision-making procedures, educational objectives, curricula, and pupil achievement (Hopkins, Delyth, 1985).

The majority of the issues discussed in the

Many of our small schools are rural schools

remainder of this chapter may be applicable to all four kinds of school. However, some small rural and village schools are affected by problems of professional isolation – distance from colleagues, teachers' centres, resources (for example, museums) and institutions for in-service training.

The teaching head

It is worth considering for a moment the traditional position of the headteacher in British primary schools. The head is a head-teacher rather than head administrator. There is something of this sentiment contained in the contemporary view of the head as a 'leading professional'. Some heads, in fact, will go to great lengths to expound on their aversion to 'administration'. Coulson (1976) explains:

> It is part of the traditional concept of headship in Britain that the head is consi-dered a teacher rather than an administra-

tor (an emphasis symbolized by the word head*teacher*). Because of this, most heads subordinate administrative means of shap-ing their schools to interpersonal strategies. In particular, the head expects to influence teachers by his own example and to per-suade them to identify with his aims and methods.

The role of the head as teacher, therefore, is not unexpected and sits easily within the British 'headteacher' tradition which sees teaching as an opportunity to set standards and show headteachers' leadership skills (Welsh Office, 1985). However, it is necessary to distinguish between a 'voluntary' load and a situation where the necessary teaching load is so great that other important aspects of the headteachers' role have to be neglected.

The National Association of Head Teachers (1975) has argued that no head-teacher should be responsible for the full-time teaching of a class because of the disruption caused by interruptions of one sort or another which is often intolerable. The same interruptions can, of course, affect headteachers' classroom teaching in large schools. In far too many small schools the teaching head does not have enough time for the duties of headship. Frequently, teaching heads undertake much of their administrative responsibilities in their own time after school.

It is interesting to note that a Commons Select Committee (1986) controversially recommended that:

> Every primary head should be legally compelled to do some teaching (Hagedorn, 1986).

We would suggest that primary heads should teach to some extent. They should not teach so fully, however, that the effectiveness of the whole organisation is impaired.

HMI (Welsh Office, 1985) in a survey of leadership in 79 Welsh primary schools, reported that:

> Most heads are active in the work of the school and in a position to monitor and assess pupils' work. Approximately three-quarters of heads are either teaching heads (30%) or have a regular teaching commitment (40%).

A major impact of contraction in primary education has been a demand for an increase in the teaching commitments of headteachers (Walsh *et al.*, 1984).

There is a view which is held in some quarters that the headship of a small school should be regarded as 'training' for a later, large school headship. Davies (1975) argues that:

> A headship in a small school enables a teacher to be at the same time and in the fullest sense, teacher and administrator.

Others take a different view, arguing that 'in the fullest sense' a head cannot be both a class teacher and a head.

Walsh *et al.* (1984) outline a range of activities which heads regard as likely to suffer with an increased teaching commitment:

- meeting other teachers and working with them in the classroom;
- dealing with emergencies such as ill children;
- clerical and administrative work;
- curriculum development work;
- liaison with secondary schools;
- planning;
- meeting parents;
- relations with psychological and welfare services.

The West Glamorgan Working Party (1985) on *Resourcing the Small School* came to much the same conclusions. They stated:

> The central problem in the role of the teaching head appeared to be the conflict of interest created by the dual role, i.e. that of manager on the one hand and teacher, responsible for a class, on the other. At certain times the conflict imposed unreasonable demands on the headteacher and unfair educational opportunities on the children.

So much for the problems. We now consider some possible answers. Some will be internal, others demanding a response from local education authorities.

An obvious solution, of course, is to allow more and more flexible, supply cover to release the headteacher. Provision of this sort seems to vary from authority to authority, some allowing an increase in accordance with a sliding scale as numbers rise, others preferring an 'across the board' fixed supply cover allowance. As long ago as 1967, the Plowden Committee reported:

> There are striking differences between authorities on the size of school in which headteachers are expected to take charge of a class. In some areas, the head must teach full time when there are as many as 200 children in the school; in others, he is free of a class in a school of 100 or fewer. We are clear that, except in one class schools, all heads need part time assistance so that they can get to know both children and parents

and advise the staff, including probationers. (para. 938)

It seems clear then, that a national policy relating to the amount of assistance given to small school heads is required.

The arguments that a small school headship has advantages in providing opportunities to 'lead by example' are not entirely convincing. It is possible to imagine a head teaching successfully in her own classroom but having little overall influence in her school.

HMI (Welsh Office, 1985) reported one small school head who had 'effectively set the tone' of her school. It was a warm and friendly place with an acceptable standard of achievement. However, because of the lack of an evaluation mechanism and 'whole school policies for the curriculum' the pupils in some cases had inappropriate learning experiences. The report commented that: 'The good practice of the head is not emulated.'

The lack of guidelines may well be due, in this and other schools, to the lack of the time needed for their adequate formulation. There is a limit to which good practice will permeate from the headteacher's classroom without strong supportive strategies.

A final point to be made is that as the teaching duties of a headteacher rise, it is very likely that the amount of secretarial and ancillary help to her school will decrease (Walsh *et al.*, 1984). The head then, has to attempt to organise an administrative system which keeps interruptions to her classroom duties to a minimum. She could decide, for example, to restrict incoming telephone calls, unless urgent, to convenient times and insist that visitors have an appointment made in advance. Nonetheless, we are well aware that interruptions will continue, and that the suggestions given above may generate, in turn, their own problems. All these matters are presently being compounded by the additional and increasing administrative loads expected of primary headteachers due to such factors as devolution and appraisal systems. In fact, Meikle (1986b) has suggested that some local authorities are facing a recruitment crisis of a new kind – filling vacancies for the headships of small primary schools. The position has been exacerbated because deputies in larger schools are increasingly reluctant to apply for the top job because they may have to take a pay cut or only gain a small rise in salary. The biggest problem is for schools with under 250 pupils, and the number of these has grown rapidly with the decline in the child population. Meikle indicated that in 1986 Kent County Council was having to advertise headships up to four times. Ealing was sometimes advertising five times to get short-lists worth considering. Meikle quoted Mrs Jeanne Leeke, President of the National Association of Head Teachers, who said that the crisis was worrying because 'many people cannot afford to drop money for the status of headship'.

The deputy head in the small school

Though traditionally seen as a grooming for eventual headship, the post of deputy headteacher in the primary school has been called 'a position without a role' (Bush, 1981). According to the literature, there is little apparent agreement on what the deputy headteacher should actually do because the job description is largely dictated by the head. The only measure of agreement appears to be that it would be appropriate, 'for the deputy to act in an administrative capacity on the head's behalf' (Coulson, 1976). The deputy normally takes over when the head is absent and, in general, performs some minor administrative duties. Apart from these her everyday work, 'appears to be similar to that of other primary school teachers' (Coulson, 1976). HMI (Welsh Office, 1985) found that:

It is regrettable that in most schools the job of deputy attracts a clutter of mundane tasks such as organising infrequent school trips, or preparing pupils for church services, school concerts and confirmation, despite the fact that most deputies have the qualifications and experience to be curriculum leaders.

In practice, in some schools, the duties of the deputy are less demanding than those of some curriculum leaders. Bush (1981) explores some reasons for this, and proposes an interesting alternative:

> a senior teacher in smaller schools be given responsibility for the deputy's one tangible duty, that of deputising for the head in his absence.

Some schools are so small that they do not have deputies anyway. Responsibility in the head's absence is 'assumed by a scale post holder or, where there are no scale posts, by the remaining senior teacher'. Perhaps this demonstrates the need for a re-think of the role of the deputy head in larger primary schools. Clearly, the management and organisation of a small school requires an established sharing of responsibilities amongst staff. Where a deputy exists she should be given a 'suitably challenging and stimulating leadership role' (Welsh Office, 1985).

Staff in the small primary school

The appointment of any member of staff to any primary school is always extremely important. In the small primary school it is crucial. We would maintain that at a time when appraisal of teachers already in post dominates thinking, equally serious consideration ought to be given to appointment systems. The vital nature of appointments to small schools was highlighted in the West Glamorgan Institute of Higher Education Teaching Fellowship Report (Hopkins, Delyth, 1985). In this study headteachers of small schools considered that any profession has its less competent practitioners. However, they were adamant that strenuous efforts should be made to avoid appointing poorer staff to smaller schools, since not only might the added challenge of

having to cope with many children of different ages prove too much of a burden, but also as the Gittins Report (DES, 1967a) pointed out, one weak member of staff could have a disproportionate effect on the whole school. In fact, all the headteachers agreed that a weak teacher in a small school could be disastrous.

In a small school, one child may be taught by the same teacher for a long period of time. Personality clashes may occur or exposure to poor teaching be unduly extended:

> Since children must stay with the same teacher for more than one year, not only might a clash of personalities between a child and the teacher have a detrimental effect on that child's progress, but also a weak teacher could have serious repercussions on both the entire class and the whole school (Hopkins, Delyth, 1985).

Staff appointed are required to have a particular flexibility. Hopkins suggests that in small schools teachers need to be competent 'all rounders', who are committed to tackling the difficulties of smaller schools and who are able to provide suitable experiences for children of different ages and abilities. This inevitably involves an awareness of individual needs, a considerable amount of systematic planning, an efficient class organisation and a flexible teaching style, which most educators agree are the hallmarks of an effective teacher.

Even after careful appointments, one of the problems facing the headteacher of the small school is that of providing a broad curriculum, given the small number of staff and their necessarily limited curriculum expertise. A similar difficulty has to be faced in contracting schools, when staff with particular expertise leave and are not replaced.

The challenge for headteachers in the organisation of small schools is to develop strategies which will provide as broadly-based curriculum as possible. Not an easy task, given her limited resources, for several reasons.

In the first instance, it is important that the expertise and interests of all staff are fully utilised. Indeed, it could be argued that one professional advantage for class teachers within small schools is the opportunity for broadening curricular responsibility and leadership which may not present itself in a larger school. However, rather surprisingly, there is evidence of failure to make full use of available staff potential:

In general, insufficient use is made in small schools of the potential for leadership embodied in the interests and expertise of class teachers. As small schools face particular difficulties in providing a broad, balanced curriculum, failure to fully exploit expertise among staff is particularly detrimental to the school's aims. (Welsh Office, 1985)

Second, this identification and successful use of individual staff expertise requires the formulation of whole-school policies. In the small school, it is sometimes too easily assumed that meaningful discussion takes place on a regular basis between colleagues on professional, curricular and organisational matters. People tend to think that very small size makes for informality of leadership and easy communication. This is not always the case. Therefore, there is a need for definite structures of communication and consultation to exist between the head and her staff. A brief conversation in the school corridor between teacher and teacher should not be assumed to fulfil this purpose, no matter how frequent.

As we have already demonstrated, as heads assume more and more teaching responsibilities in may schools, the 'time' available for consultation and direction becomes more difficult to find.

Third, broadening curricular expertise by attendance at courses is made difficult for the small school by the need to arrange supply 'cover' for classes and in the case of rural schools, by distance from course centres. This could be partially offset by the use of school-based staff development strategies.

Recognising such problems, some local authorities have now begun to implement strategies for the 'clustering' or 'federation' of isolated small schools, so that a larger pool of mutual expertise becomes available. A con-

sequence of these moves is a reconceptualisation of school 'autonomy'.

For clustering or federation to help broaden the curriculum, staff and heads have to evaluate their own strategies and weaknesses:

It takes courages and a sense of dedication to expose one's difficulties and problems to the informed scrutiny of another professional. (Cave and Cave, 1982)

One of the benefits of clustering (see Chapter 9) may be to relieve the sense of loneliness felt by teachers in rural small schools where opportunity for the exchange of ideas with a wider cross-section of colleagues is limited. For this reason, visits to other schools to see good practice is part of the active support strategy of one local education authority for its small schools (West Glamorgan, 1985).

Sadly, a teacher may feel professionally isolated for other reasons. HMI (Welsh Office, 1985) report one small (two-teacher) school where contact between the head and the assistant teacher is:

limited to informal talk, and a sense of professional isolation is engendered by the lack of systematic consultation and the practice of holding separate class assemblies.

'Clustering' may also be supported by the provision of an extra 'shared' teacher who operates within the group of schools by spending time at each and by a financial arrangement which enables capitation allowances to be used for joint purchases (West Glamorgan, 1985). These strategies in turn have organisational implications. They require, for example, a lot of discussion, meetings and phone calls taking place on a regular basis between schools participating in the scheme (Roberts, 1987).

Mixed-age classes

A mixed-age range class is defined as one that contains at least one child who does not belong to the same year group as the other pupils in the class, although usually there are several children in this category (Hopkins, Delyth, 1985). In a larger school, where mixed-age grouping has been introduced through choice, all classes may contain pupils of different ages and the age range within each class may span two or three years. In larger schools, where mixed-age classes have been introduced by necessity, only one or two classes may contain pupils of different ages and the age range usually spans only two years. In the smaller school the variety of ages in each class depends very much on the size of the school and the number of teachers. Generally, the smaller the school the wider the age range in each form. Thus such grouping can vary considerably not only between schools, but even between individual classes. It is difficult to generalise about this phenomenon, since some problems and dilemmas may be relevant only to particular situations. Many authoritative statements on mixed age range teaching, such as the HMI Primary Survey (DES, 1978b), have tended to disregard differences in class composition.

As school rolls fall, the number of classes containing children of more than one age grouping has increased. Of course, such groupings have already been the norm in small schools and accepted as such. We would wish to draw a distinction, therefore, between those schools who have traditionally had mixed-aged classes and those for whom the experience is a new one. We do so because we believe the predisposition of staff appointed to a small school who are presumably sympathetic to mixed-age group teaching may be very different from that of staff who find themselves teaching a mixed-age class for the first time in a contracting school (Bennett et al., 1983). The same could be said for teaching heads. There are those who have been appointed to and wish for a teaching headship, and those who find themselves having class teaching responsibilities for the first time after a number of years.

The decision to 'go mixed-age' is frequently dictated by circumstances beyond the control of the school. The findings of Bennett et al., (1983) suggest that although teachers in this situation accept the new class structure, more difficulty is found in adapting the organisation of resources and pedagogical styles of teaching to this new situation.

The problem of 'match' of work to children's abilities in such classes has been well-documented (DES, 1978b; DES, 1982a; DES, 1982c). Organisational strategies to offset such difficulties have been suggested. HMI (DES, 1982a, para 4:16) recorded the fact that:

In times of falling rolls more classes with mixed-age groups will occur. This survey added to the evidence that mixed-age classes present difficulties for a substantial number of teachers. In this survey it was noticed that both the more and less able within the class might suffer some neglect. Where mixed-age classes most occur thought needs to be given how to minimise some of the problems. It may be necessary that ancillary or peripatetic help should be directed to these classes, or that heads should give them more than an equal share of their own time. Attention should be given to the in-service training needs of teachers who have such classes.

Existing evidence suggests that such help is often not available.

The advantages of mixed-age classes in the larger school are those which would be claimed by teachers in the small schools. These include: earlier opportunities for younger children to take classroom responsibilities; greater continuity in teaching; and, a greater concentration on the child as an individual. As we have indicated, there are also disadvantages, not only in 'match', but also in aggravating the effects of weak teaching (see also Chapter 7).

The organisation of mixed-age range classes requires sound long-term planning to ensure that the child's experience of the curriculum is sufficiently broad and avoids needless duplication of work (Welsh Office, 1985). Although comparatively little research has been undertaken specifically on mixed-age range classes, the dilemmas of smaller primary schools, especially those in rural areas, have been investigated and discussed for several years. Much of this discussion, however, has centred on financial and political expediencies.

By the 1960s, many questions were being raised about the viability of smaller schools. For example, both the Gittins Report (DES, 1967) and the Plowden Report (DES, 1967b) appreciated that the implementation of more sophisticated objectives and methods, based on experimental learning and a more open-ended child-centred approach, could pose problems for smaller schools where resources were limited. As the Gittins Report pointed out:

> Evidence offered by rural education authorities underlines the difficulties experienced in providing a suitable range of activities in small schools to meet the wide range of age and ability ... The small school may not provide children with the social stimulation provided by an age group. It can also be difficult in a one teacher school to ensure that the younger children are getting appropriate experience and attention.

Gittins also noted the possible disadvantages of children being taught by one teacher for too long:

> Outstanding work in one class of a two or three teacher school might be neutralised by indifferent or inadequate teaching in another. The personality of an individual teacher can have a disproportionate effect on children who remain in the same environment throughout their primary school education.

The Plowden Report stated similar fears, but it also emphasised some of the advantages of smaller schools:

> The National Survey showed that beginners settle easily ... children quickly assimilate the established traditions of learning and behaviour. Yet the older children ... may lack the stimulus of their peers ... it is for each headteacher in consultation with her staff to balance the gain and loss of classes containing more than one age group. No evidence is available to show whether a double age group is advantageous in the junior school.

Plowden concluded that a one- or two-teacher school was too small to be educationally viable and that every school needed to contain at least three teachers and 60 pupils. Research undertaken by Aston University in 1981, though, questioned the wisdom of this assumption and reported that there was no evidence to indicate that small schools, whatever their size, disadvantaged children:

> We had several well-founded reports that secondary schools found them (pupils from small rural schools) not only as well prepared academically as pupils from other schools, but that they generally had a better attitude to work. Having been accustomed to working for much of their time on their own, they could be given more responsibility for the organisation of their work. (Aston University, 1981)

After the Gittins and Plowden Reports, local education authorities were encouraged to investigate their smaller schools, and between 1974 and 1975 the Schools Council carried out a study involving 65 schools in a number of LEAs. This research commented on the concern shown by many authorities for their smaller schools and reported on some schemes which had been introduced to provide support in areas of need. It concluded that:

> ... good small schools performed useful, sometimes essential, social and educational functions ... Certainly all that the team saw in small schools was not of the highest quality in terms of organisation and curriculum, but this would be true of any random group of educational institutions. (Schools Council, 1975)

In January 1976, The Centre for Educational Research and Innovation of the Organisation for Economic Cooperation and Development (OECD) initiated research into issues surrounding the nature and provision of educational services in sparsely populated areas. Eleven countries, including Britain, took part in this project and as a result the Department of Education and Science instigated a further investigation to examine more deeply the educational problems of rural areas in England. The findings of the participating local authorities in this second enquiry were presented and discussed at a conference at Charlotte Mason College in Cumbria in March 1979.

Included in the presentations were reports on the 'Norfolk Cluster' and the Cheveley Federation School in Cambridgeshire, which was an amalgamation of four small primary schools into a main school with three annexes. Cambridgeshire was one of the first authorities to institute this type of 'area school', but unfortunately the project collapsed due to an unexpected decline in pupil numbers. However, much was learned about the difficulties and dilemmas of smaller schools while the Federation was in operation. In fact, a considerable amount of research into smaller schools was undertaken in Cambridgeshire and the authority published several papers recommending strategies for supporting these institutions. One of these studies, which examined curriculum provision in 18 schools, concluded:

. . . headteachers can feel secure that there is no evidence to support the view that small schools are any less educationally viable than large schools. The main problem lies in the fact that they are more expensive to run. Larger and larger units may be more financially viable, but they are not necessarily educationally better and do not take into account individual needs and differences. (Howells, 1982)

The HMI Surveys of both primary education (DES, 1978b) and first schools (DES, 1982a) commented on various aspects of the smaller school and suggested that many teachers found it difficult to teach classes of more than 25 children when their ages spread over two or more years. The primary survey, for example, stated that, '. . . there is evidence from the survey that the performance of children in these circumstances (mixed-age range classes) can suffer'. However, some of the evidence came from larger schools with falling rolls and in the same report the Inspectorate did point out that a school's location was more likely to affect pupil achievement than either school size or age range.

It is possible, therefore, that in some smaller schools inappropriate practices and teaching methods rather than mixed-age range classes *per se* are a cause of disadvantage. Clearly, too much formal traditional teaching will not make sufficient allowance for the wide differences in age and ability within a class. In fact, recent research by Barker-Lunn for the National Foundation for Educational Research (NFER) confirmed that smaller schools could be extremely successful if they adopted teaching methods that relied less on whole class instruction:

The smaller schools showed interesting differences. Responses showed they had less whole class teaching and more teaching in groups plus more individual teaching than the larger schools. In terms of organisation and curriculum they had more practical and modern maths, less English grammar, slightly more project work, more 'free choice' periods and more school visits and field trips. (Barker-Lunn, 1984)

Additionally, there have been numerous other investigations and articles concerned with the smaller school and mixed-age range teaching. For example, the following recommendations are adapted from the findings of Delyth Hopkins (1985):

(a) Selection procedures for teachers should be carefully considered and only those who are most suitably qualified and adaptable to the demands of mixed-age range teaching should be appointed to smaller schools or those schools which have mixed-age classes.

(b) All teachers in smaller schools and mixed-age range classes should ensure that their pedagogical methods and class organisation are appropriate and relevant to the needs and abilities of their pupils. They should adopt flexible strategies and base their approach mainly on individual or small group activities rather than on class lessons. The establishment of a caring and co-operative rather than a competitive class climate would also appear to be beneficial. In small schools and mixed-age range classes it is essential that philosophies and practices are congruent with circumstances.

(c) All teachers in small schools and mixed-age range classes should also continually evaluate their practices and procedures. Where mixed-age grouping is being introduced for the first time, either by necessity or choice, a school staff as a whole should adopt an agreed and carefully considered policy, re-examine their teaching strategies and keep parents fully informed of the impending changes and developments.

(d) Teachers of mixed-age range classes should also keep efficient and effective records to ensure that every child is progressing according to their abilities and stage of development.

(e) Parents should be encouraged to participate in smaller schools and in mixed-age range classes and there should be close liaison between parents and staff.

The research undertaken by the Research and Development Centre at Lancaster University in seven LEAs in the north-west of England, suggests that mixed-age range arrangements are far more complex and have far wider implications than many previous studies considered.

In conclusion, therefore, the literature on smaller schools and mixed-age range teaching indicates that although there is little hard evidence to support the view that small schools are any less educationally viable, LEAs recognise that developmental work in these establishments needs to be supported. Due to the significance of these findings and the rapid increase of mixed-age range teaching through both necessity and choice, it is perhaps inevitable that the dilemmas and strategies of the smaller school are a topic of much debate.

The community

The small primary school is often a focus for its local community. Research undertaken in Scotland emphasises that smaller schools should be considered in this wider context. In the report, 'The Rural Community and the Small School' (Forsythe, 1983), the research team concludes that: 'The primary school is part of a constellation of services to the rural community and it needs to be viewed in that way by the community itself.' The actual or impending closure of the local school can have disastrous effects upon a village for a whole host of reasons, including preventing families from buying property in the district.

One of the strategies available to the small school head is to widen the resource expertise at her disposal by enlisting help from parents or members of the community. One small school, for example, was delighted to share the enthusiasm of a parent for railway construction while, in another, the skills of a professional soccer player were utilised.

The West Glamorgan Working Party Report (1985) on *Resourcing the Small School* comments that in such schools:

The incidence of parental involvement, either officially or unofficially, was high. 50% of schools reported involvement in an ancillary capacity ... 17% of schools reflected a more direct involvement by parents in the education of children, e.g. listening to reading, helping with gardening, DIY, art and craft.

This high level of parental interest is generally welcomed by schools. However, as well as a reflection on parental attitudes, it can also be a tribute to headteachers' skills in overcoming their real shortage of ancillary help and curricular expertise.

As is pointed out in Chapter 12, close community involvement places its own particular burdens on members of staff. In addition to teaching duties, they may well hold other community positions and be expected to attend local functions such as dances, fêtes and official gatherings on a more regular basis than colleagues in larger schools who may be able to share such duties around.

A clustering experiment

In their report, HMI (Welsh Office, 1984) make specific references to the new educational challenges facing schools at a time of fluctuating rolls. One of these is that of providing appropriate educational experiences. To achieve this aim, a well-balanced curriculum is considered essential. While HMI admit that the realisation of such an aim is especially difficult to attain in establishments which have experienced drastic reductions in teaching staff levels, they maintain that schools which extend links already made in the sporting context into the more formal arena of curriculum innovation are the ones most likely to succeed.

Cave and Cave (1982) suggest that an exchange of teachers between schools, bringing classes together and generally planning as a group of schools rather than as isolated units can help alleviate some of the disadvantages inherent in small schools. This is one aspect of the clustering described earlier.

In his overview of the Small Schools in Concert Project (Schools Council, 1982) Mr M J F Wynn, HMI, notes that one of the major disadvantages of small schools is peer group isolation and he suggests that it is best overcome when schools begin to share a wide range of activities.

He notes that: 'This sense of wider identity could significantly enhance the living and learning of pupils in small schools.'

Much of the literature and research conducted into small schools supports the view that smallness in general terms could lead to certain deficiencies in curricular provision, thus making it difficult to cater for the needs of children today. The disadvantages of the small school are well-documented, the main areas at risk being: (a) lack of resources, both human and physical; (b) lack of, or limited social interaction for both staff and children, and (c) limited range and quality of learning experience.

It was these disadvantages and others that prompted the headteachers and staffs of two small neighbouring schools to meet and discuss the possibilities of co-operating on a school based project aimed at alleviating some of their common disadvantages.

The two schools

The two schools serve villages approximately five miles apart. When the project started there were 50 in one school and 30 in the other. These figures included the children receiving part-time nursery education. Staffing for both schools was identical and consisted of headteacher and one full-time assistant: 0.5 nursery and 0.3 headteacher relief. There was also weekly remedial provision. Both schools had a full-time nursery assistant and part-time secretarial help. On the face of it, this represents a relatively generous level of staffing.

Initially, the staff of the two schools met separately in order that their own individual needs might be identified and discussed. In the combined meetings which followed, it soon became apparent that the needs of the two schools were similar.

Both schools, despite having always been in the small schools category, were reducing in number and thus were experiencing some of the side effects associated with contraction.

Redeployment had taken place and the limited breadth of curriculum was narrowed further. The per capita system of allocating capitation resulted in a drastic reduction in official funding for both establishments. This meant that the purchasing, updating and maintenance of resources became more difficult.

Geographically, both schools are isolated, thus maintaining any contact with colleagues was difficult and the opportunities for widening professional horizons diminished.

It had become apparent during discussion that there were serious fundamental weaknesses in the schools' total curricula and it was felt that these two small units in isolation could not provide the children with the learning experiences necessary to comply with HMI's view of a broad, relevant and balanced curriculum.

Initially, the project was to last for as long as it would take to fulfil the intended outcomes which were arrived at during the discussion and early planning stage, namely:

(a) to increase pupil contact with other adults and children, thus helping to alleviate pupil isolation;

(b) establishing of local INSET, thus helping to alleviate teacher isolation;

(c) sharing of resources to include jointly produced material and, where appropriate, curriculum guidelines;

(d) to include the wider community into the venture;

(e) increased involvement through inviting other interested teachers and schools into the cluster.

At the very start of the venture, the two schools were extremely fortunate to be offered a week's residential course at one of the authority's education centres situated on the nearby coast. This afforded an excellent opportunity for all to meet socially outside their school environment. As was hoped, the extension of the peer group and the addition of other adults increased social interaction to a degree never before experienced by the children. The friendships and relationships which were established during this week continued to flourish during the year ahead. This proved beneficial for two girls in particular. They were the only children in their fourth year and when at the beginning of the following year they entered the local comprehensive for the first time, they met up with seven children from the other school's fourth year. As a direct result of the cluster the initial peer group of two was effectively extended to nine.

Both schools were combined for sporting activities. The larger numbers have enabled teams to be formed and matches have been played against other schools, thus extending the peer group further.

There has been a distinct improvement in their swimming, and because both schools amalgamate for the weekly session they have been receiving one hour's tuition instead of half an hour. The teacher responsible for swimming has commented on the improvement and believes that the larger peer group has introduced an element of healthy competition which was not there previously.

Throughout the first year of the project, many trips and excursions were undertaken to such places as the theatre, museums, art galleries and the seaside. As part of the Christmas festivities, a joint concert was produced and performed in both schools. This was an excellent opportunity for showing parents and governors the achievement of the group's first term activities.

Although it was never intended that major organisational changes should take place, a teacher exchange rota was established, thus spreading staff expertise and interest between the two schools. The headteachers began the rota by exchanging classes for one morning per week. Their areas of interest were language development and computer-assisted learning. Significantly, these two areas were identified at the planning stage as being particularly weak in one or other of the schools. As a direct result of these visits, joint curriculum guidelines were produced. Exchanges involving other teachers followed and areas such as environmental studies, art, music and PE were covered. The teaching sessions were reinforced with visits to centres associated with these areas: woodland, zoos, museums and art galleries. In-service workshops for the teachers were also established as a direct result of these visits.

Throughout the first year, resources were

shared, photocopying and general repro-graphic facilities, art and craft materials, library stock and many other teacher produced packs were made available. Through deploying and sharing existing resources the schools were able to make more effective use of their relatively small capitation allowances.

On reflection, the staff of both schools feel that the original aims were met and fulfilled. However, continuation of any innovation has its problems. The single most powerful factor which will influence the continuation of this venture is that of staff turbulence. To date, one of the headteachers has moved schools on promotion, the other is presently on second-ment for one year and one of the teachers has retired from the profession. Despite all this, the clustering arrangement continues to flourish, possibly due to the fact that the three replacement teachers are committed to the small school philosophy.

It is hoped that staff stability will be restored in the near future and one more additional school will join the cluster, thus making the joint venture a triangular one. By doing so the educational provision available to all – both staff and children – will be extended even further.

9 Looking at the primary school curriculum

As aspects relating to the organisation of the primary school curriculum permeate the book, we have deliberately limited the scope of this chapter to three issues. The first is a brief description and overview of the curriculum. The second is an analysis of good practice in one aspect of the primary school curriculum. We use this as an examplar and have chosen to write about primary art. We conclude the chapter with some in-depth findings obtained from a study of quality in primary schools (Morris, 1985). These data were collected between 1985 and 1986, and the findings used here are purely illustrative, to illuminate real primary schools in action.

Background

How we choose to organise learning in the primary school depends upon our values and beliefs. In fact, it has been suggested that any educational theory cannot avoid implicit expressions of value in its statements of aims, its view of the nature of children, and its view of the nature of knowledge and how children learn (Lawton, 1981b).

For example, if it is believed that children are naturally evil and therefore must be disciplined for their own good, the resultant educational system is likely to be rather different from one based on the view that children are naturally innocent and good and therefore to be protected and encouraged to grow like a delicate plant (Lawton, 1981c).

Similarly, the content of the curriculum is problematic and subject to debate. Different ways of looking at and describing the curriculum also reflect alternative views of knowledge, children and their learning (Blenkin and Kelly, 1983, 1987; Schools Council, 1983; Alexander, 1984; Kelly, 1986).

Organising the curriculum

Many primary schools have timetables. Sometimes they are used to allocate the use of shared resources, such as the hall, television or computer. On other occasions they are used to allocate subject areas and remain in operation throughout a school year.

The ILEA junior school study (1986) found that children in classes where the teacher followed a timetable did not appear to progress any more than children in classes where work was planned for the day, the week or even longer. What is important is what goes on during the prescribed time allocations. The Thomas Report (ILEA, 1985) was critical of primary school timetables, arguing that such divisions as 'English' erect boundaries which imply that, for example, it is only in the slot marked 'English' that any serious language work is undertaken. Clearly, language is used across the curriculum and children's use of language is to be encouraged wherever the situation arises.

Describing the curriculum

There are many ways of describing the curriculum, though it is doubtful if any one single way will be entirely satisfactory (ILEA, 1985).

Schools Council Working Paper 75 (1983) suggests several possibilities.

(a) *Subjects*

The curriculum may be described under traditional subject labels such as Mathematics or History. Though these titles are readily recognisable to parents and others, they are much more problematic than is usually realised.

The Schools Council (1983) suggests that such labels indicating adult attempts to organise and classify knowledge have little application in the primary school, where a child needs to be exposed to many varied experiences before he can come to understand these adult classifications.

Lawton (1981b) while agreeing that the child needs some structure to his learning, reminds us that such divisions of knowledge may help in decisions of content, but not in decisions on children's learning. For example, a logical division of knowledge into mathematics, science and so on does not mean that they have to be taught separately. There may well be sound arguments, supported by theories of children's learning, which would indicate the need for an integrated or thematic approach.

(b) *Process*

The process approach describes the curriculum not in terms of knowledge to be acquired, but rather as skills and qualities to be developed in the learner. These may be study skills, practical skills or the personal qualities necessary to work co-operatively with others. The model is usually associated with the work

of Lawrence Stenhouse (1975). It is based on the teacher encouraging children's exploration. The teacher is regarded as a researcher; the classroom rather like a laboratory. The model is very strong in developing the professional skills of the teacher but that same strength is paradoxically its weakness. It is only as strong or as weak as the classroom teacher (Stenhouse, 1975).

(c) *As problems*

This way of looking at the curriculum takes as a starting point 'the pressing issues of the twenty-first century'. Therefore, such issues as multicultural education would be included in the experiences of the pupils.

(d) *As forms or areas of knowledge*

There have been numerous attempts to divide knowledge into distinct areas. One of the best known is that of Hirst (1965). He logically defines several 'forms' of knowledge, according to their propositions and tests for truth. Some would regard these divisions as problematic (Young *et al.*, 1971). Nevertheless a structure of some kind is required in children's learning and such a basis may be used to facilitate planning (Lawton, 1975). HMI (DES, 1985b) distinguish nine areas of experience which may assist teachers when considering the school curriculum. These are:

1 aesthetic and creative
2 human and social
3 linguistic and literary
4 mathematical
5 moral
6 physical
7 scientific
8 spiritual
9 technological.

It is suggested that these areas could form a 'planning tool' to help schools, for example, to identify particular areas of weakness (Richards, 1986). The child's view and experience of the curriculum of course may not necessarily coincide with that of the teacher.

Good practice in primary art education

A number of surveys conducted during the last decade (for example, DES, 1978b; 1980; 1982a; 1983a; Welsh Office, 1984) have been helpful in identifying those elements of primary school art teaching which contribute towards good practice. What follows is a summary of these constituent elements.

The importance of direct, sensory experiences

It was noted in these surveys that drawing or modelling from direct experience was rarely encouraged in the primary classroom. It was far more common to see drawing done from second-hand sources, often provided by the teacher in the form of book illustrations or photographs. A more appropriate provision would:

- engage children in the close and careful observation of the 'real' world;
- encourage them to collect objects from that world – both natural and man-made – to handle them, display them, discuss them, classify them, look at them and draw/paint/model them.

Children's 'careful' drawings can run parallel with their more schematic, imaginative work, with perhaps the proportion of 'careful' drawing increasing as children get older and need more visual support. If children's looking is focused in this way, from nursery onwards, it is less likely that they will ever say: 'I can't draw.'

Sensory experiences in art are not confined to the sense of sight (looking); the other senses too are accommodated, particular the sense of touch. Giving children plenty of opportunities to handle materials is crucial in helping them to make a 'bridge' between themselves and the physical world in which they live.

Sustained experiences with materials and techniques

Eisner (1972) identifies a tendency amongst some teachers to:

> . . . work on the assumptions that the more materials [they use] the better and often tend to equate a rich art programme with one that provides the widest array of art material.

However, he warns that the lack of opportunity for children to achieve any kind of mastery with materials can lead to a feeling of general incompetence which in turn can cause loss of confidence. As Lowenfeld and Lambert-Brittain (1982) put it, creativity is not promoted by a 'smorgasbord of art products'. Instead, children need time for a sustained experience in specific techniques and material areas if they are to develop the skills they need to express themselves appropriately. The sort of material areas one might hope to find in a primary curriculum could include:

- drawing;
- painting;
- printing;
- textiles (for example, weaving, needlecraft, tie and dye, batik);
- 3-dimensional work (modelling, carving, constructing).

A balanced and well-planned provision of these material areas throughout the school, from nursery to top infants, would help children to achieve a high level of skill and a certain amount of self-esteem.

It is not being suggested that nursery aged children are ready for needlecraft, for example, but certainly a great deal of preliminary work can be done. Children can learn to understand about the 'feel' of different kinds of fabric by handling lengths found in the dressing-up box. They can examine a piece of coarse hessian under a magnifying glass, and unravel it to see how it is made. They can do simple weaving using a home-made loom with widely-spaced threads and wide strips of paper, long grasses, strips of

The proportion of 'careful' drawing and painting increases as children get older

Giving children plenty of opportunities to handle material is crucial

fabric: materials sympathetic to little fingers. These sensory experiences provide a rich stimulus for language development, in the hands of a creative teacher.

A balance between participation and appreciation

There needs to be time for dialogue between teacher and child in the art activity: time to reflect on what has been done, to discuss it and to look at other people's work. There is a tendency, not only in the primary school, but also in the secondary, to overemphasise the productive aspects ('making') at the expense of those aspects associated with 'appreciation'. This becomes more apparent if we examine the use of 'realised form' in the other arts (for example, poetry, music, drama, writing that has already been created). For instance, it would be unlikely for a teacher to expect children to compose a piece of music or write a poem without also providing them with opportunities to listen to music or hear a poem being read. Why, then, is there a reluctance to introduce children from an early age to art that is already in existence? It may be in an art gallery, or it may be the work of older students in a local school or college. It may even be in the form of reproductions, viewed in the classroom.

If we are enabling children, as the Warnock Report shows, to become responsible contributors and active participants in society, then part of our responsibility is to prepare them to be consumers as well as makers. The Gulbenkian Report (1982) and HMI (Welsh Office, 1984) suggest that appreciation and participation should be 'complementary strands' in a balanced arts curriculum.

The need to evaluate and assess

Appreciation also implies that children learn to appraise, not only the art of galleries and museums, but also their own work and that of their peers. Children may like to consider the following:

- how does my present piece of work compare with my previous work?
- how does it compare with the work of the others in my class?
- how might it be improved/modified?
- what would I do differently next time?

In this way, children make formative assessments which can be used by the teacher to suggest the way ahead for future work. It also helps teachers to assess their own practice.

Gentle (1985) has suggested that an effective way for the teacher to begin to formulate criteria for assessment is probably by looking at the drawings of a group of children of the same age. Careful scrutiny of these will enhance the teacher's understanding; certain issues may be drawn out and used as categories for a simple record card. Gentle (1985) gives some useful examples in his chapter on assessment and evaluation, which is practical and well worth reading. Some suggestions for 'check-lists' or lists of aims/goals for primary art education can also be found in Schools Council Working Paper 75 (1983), the Gulbenkian Report (1982, para 69) and Lancaster, J. (ed.) (1986, para 7).

Lack of planning in primary art education

According to some surveys of primary art practice (for example, Kleinberg and Crozier, 1979), there is little attention to planning on anything other than a short-term basis. Often lessons are organised in an *ad hoc* way, using the calendar as the starting point for curriculum content (Hallowe'en, Harvest, Christmas, etc.). Poor organisation and planning in project work and also in large-scale group work was also highlighted (DES, 1978b). In many cases there was little scope for all pupils to benefit from similar learning opportunities. HMI (DES, 1978b) stressed that care should be taken to ensure that sufficient demands were made on individual children and that work did not become purely mechanical and repetitive.

Teachers need help and support in planning their work, and this can be provided, at least in part, by a whole-school policy. There is a limit to what any individual teacher can accomplish: only a school policy can provide children with sequence and continuity in their art, craft and design activities. It is crucial that this policy should be arrived at democratically, so that there is a shared philosophy, a common vocabulary and a feeling of genuine 'ownership'.

The ethos of the school

The rich and stimulating environment that is established by good display can make a significant contribution to the ethos of a school. It should be understood that display is not just so much 'wallpaper' – a pretty background to cover the walls. It should reflect the curriculum of the school. It can be evaluative ('look – this is our project – this is what we have achieved'). It should inform and communicate to others (other children, other teachers, parents, visitors). It can also be the stimulus or the introduction to a project.

Good display might include:

- children's artwork, with any source material which inspired it;
- written work;
- maps;
- photographs;
- posters;
- visual resources – natural and man-made;
- focusing devices (for example, magnifying glass, viewfinder);
- reproductions of works of art;
- fabrics (for draping);
- boxes, bricks (for making arrangements at different levels).

Children's work should be carefully mounted on appropriately coloured card or paper. Older children can learn to do this for themselves and are capable of achieving a high standard of work.

Excellent advice and illustrations of good display can be found in Schools Council (1978 and 1981).

The foregoing has outlined the major points that might be considered in an examination of primary art practice. It may be apposite to conclude by mentioning that according to a number of commentators where there is good primary *art* practice to be found, then more often than not there is good primary pratice *per se*.

We now move on to a consideration of quality in primary education based on an in-depth, small-scale empirical study.

The study

Schools visited

Twenty-nine diverse schools in eight local authorities were visited for half a day, a day or sometimes two days, over a period of eight weeks. They ranged from the small rural two-teacher schools to large inner city schools and included infant, junior, primary, 'clustered' and first schools. Therefore, the methodology mirrored the kind of experiences which pertain during many HMI visitations.

The aims and purposes of the study

(a) To evaluate, through observation and discussion of good practice that which is qualitively sound in our primary schools.
(b) To examine in some detail the process by which this quality is brought about.
(c) To examine leadership styles in relation to quality in a range of local authorities.
(d) To abstract general principles to develop in other schools.

The notion of quality

Any notion of quality is, to some extent, subjective. The notion of quality underlying this study relates closely to the hypothesis that quality learning is based upon a child's real experiences within his immediate environment coupled with a teacher's genuine desire to understand the stages of child development:

It involves the power to perceive the learning, sometimes to make it explicit and always to build on it. (Brearley, 1983)

Marsh (1970) recognises the difficulties in analysing notions of quality relating to learning but makes this important point:

The image in the mind and the actual object are not clearly differentiated in the young child and the almost obsessional concern of some adults with reason and intellectualising is not present in the young child to act as a barrier to the process of feeling and gaining pleasure from sensual experience. A child takes an element of our world and makes it his own. It is this personal relationship, this intermingling of self and experience so that it becomes difficult to differentiate the two, that is characteristic of the development of understanding in young children.

It is to be presumed then that an element of good practice would be the organisation of the experiences so as to bring about this intermingling process to which Marsh refers. Sybil Marshall (1963) claims that quality is bound up with the process of 'seeing, understanding and expressing'.

Methods of observation and assessment

To evaluate elements relating to quality in the primary school and to assess the effectiveness of schools in achieving these, the data was obtained both visually and through discussion. It was felt that the organisation of the immediate environment and display of children's work would be an important indication of deeper held attitudes among the teaching staffs and also of the depth and range of learning experiences involved in producing the finished pieces of work. The nature of the children's interaction with their teachers, fellow pupils and with their own learning tasks was also held to be highly pertinent to the notions of quality discussed above.

There is a world of difference between the situation where the child is personally involved and that where he is going through the motions. (Marsh, 1970)

This was found to be recognisable during periods of observation.

A pattern of observation

No formal questionnaire was used but a pattern of observation and discussion evolved during the course of the study. The following aspects were investigated during the school visits.

1 Was the environment, both indoor and outdoor, stimulating, enriching and appropriate to children's learning?
2 Were there plants, flowers, animals, fabrics, collections of objects (natural and man made) to stimulate curiosity? Were there pictures, books, attractively displayed for children to look at and use?
3 How effectively was space used to facilitate art, crafts, cooking, modelling, reading, writing and listening?
4 How much care was given to the display of children's work?
5 Was there a balance of teacher and pupil work?
6 Was there a handwriting style throughout?
7 Did the displayed work reflect a range of experiences interpreted through a variety of media?
8 Was there a fiction library containing a wide range of children's literature?
9 Was it possible for children to sit and browse in comfort?
10 Were there resource areas easily accessible to all children?
11 Were there resources for practical mathematics and science?
12 Did the displayed work reflect school journeys and links with the community?
13 Did the displayed work reflect a balance between direct experience and the world of fantasy and imagination?
14 Were the children actively involved?
15 Were the children working from books?

16 Where was the teacher's desk? Was there one?

17 Was the teacher enthusiastic about the current topic? Was there one?

18 Did the displayed work spill out into the corridor or areas beyond the classroom?

19 Was there a clear line drawn between basics and topic work?

20 Did the classroom organisation allow for discussion between pupil and pupil, teacher and pupil?

21 Were the children happily and profitably occupied?

22 Were there opportunities for drama, dance and making music?

23 Were the children's activities of the kind and variety which allow them to use and develop a range of skills?

Findings

At best, schools visited were happy welcoming places. School reception areas and head-teachers' rooms were more attractive, less formal places than in the past. In all schools there was a willingness to share experiences and thoughts in a concern to improve the quality of primary provision and practice.

Physical provision

Opportunities and circumstances are unequal especially with regard to physical provision. It appears that the small rural schools with their open fires and outdoor lavatories will soon disappear to become part of the new area schools, but some of the older school buildings were seen to be in need of much more care and updating to ensure equality with the more modern open plan buildings which can support teachers in direct experience learning.

It would appear that all schools are becoming more and more dependant for their resources on parents. Consequently, while some schools in the more prosperous areas enjoy superb physical facilities such as well-equipped gymnasia, swimming pools, nature

reserves, others have less sophisticated resources.

School environment

In the majority of schools the environment, indoor and outdoor, reflected a high degree of care in the work children produced, as well as what the teachers produced. In many schools there were gardens, cultivated and unculti-vated, and ponds, providing valuable resource areas for environmental studies. There were also facilities, in many cases, for keeping animals and birds. At best, schools were rich in books, displays of materials, natural and man made, pottery, pictures, fabrics and arte-facts.

Children's work

Children's work was given special importance in some schools. The work was displayed attractively in various forms, reflecting a wide range of skills through a variety of media: paint, pastel, pencil, charcoal, clay, wool and fabric. The craft of bookmaking was seen in a number of schools. These books were usually treasure troves of children's real experiences, and permanent and aesthetic representations of discovery work in a topic over a period of time; sometimes a term, sometimes longer, reflecting, to good effect, the integrated nature of the learning process.

More emphasis was seen to be given to calligraphy, many schools giving time to the teaching and practice of handwriting. Some excellent examples of children's handwriting were frequently to be seen and these added considerably to the quality of visual displays. It was reassuring to see schools that are better places for children and adults to be in. There were some schools, not large in number, that celebrated children's work with them. Children were encouraged to observe keenly in order to discover or come to understand and to interpret their findings in as many ways as possible. There were opportunities for children:

to experience, appreciate and give expression through texture, tone, colour, shape, size, form and line (Plowden Report, DES, 1967b).

It was evident that infants can become capable of using a wide range of media and tools. Middle and top infants were not limited to large painting brushes. Given the small, finer kind they were seen to be producing quality observational work. Infants were also seen to be competent in: the mixing of colours, using suitable palettes to do so, and the use of needle and thread to produce beautiful examples of fabric work.

The care and respect given by the teachers in presenting children's work was reflected in the quality of work produced by the children, often the presentation of their own work. Infants were seen mounting their own drawings and paintings, even making books. From the very young to the oldest, they displayed mastery over tools such as sewing machines, spinning wheels, utensils, tools for printing, pottery and carpentry with such involvement and absorption so as to be almost oblivious of observers.

In many schools in Lincolnshire, Oxfordshire, Dorset and North Cambridgeshire the following crafts were taught and practised: spinning, dyeing, weaving, needlecraft, tie and dye, batik, printing, book-making, puppetry, pottery and enamelling.

Needlework for girls and craft for boys had become needlecraft for girls and boys in many schools. Some schools were developing the school curriculum to include schemes for craft, design and technology, and topics were frequently chosen to give more bias to science.

Literacy and numeracy

Work in the areas of literacy and numeracy was regarded in all schools to be of the highest importance. The almost universal use of topics provides breadth to the primary curriculum, but unfortunately in most cases learning within the range of the topic was seen to be distinct and separate from 'basic skills'. There was general agreement that the skills of

mathematics were learned efficiently when they were taught formally. A wide variety of schemes was used including: Peak Mathematics, Scottish Primary Mathematics, Nuffield Mathematics, Fletcher Mathematics, Hesse and Alpha Beta Mathematics. A topic frequently served to give a greater breadth of understanding of the nature of numbers and of the operations that can be performed with them. Generally, work was seen to be carefully structured to the needs of individual children, their attainments being monitored in a variety of ways. Infants were seen using calculators to test results and using computers with suitably modified programmes. In one school a project on their village, over the whole of the primary range, took in mapping, house plans, street plans, an illustrated plan of the village in two dimensions and three-dimensional scale models of some of the buildings. In a particularly illuminating school assembly, the deputy headteacher used symmetry as her theme. This was illustrated by use of natural objects, children's work through various media and finally by a group of children performing creative dance.

More than one reading scheme was used in most schools, ranging from phonic to individualised approaches and including *Breakthrough to Literacy*. In some schools within this authority and others, there was clear evidence that reading and writing have been given a boost from the new structured approaches introduced through the authority's in-service programme. Schools with a previous history of failure in reading and writing are producing anthologies of poetry, but it is even more exciting to see those children who were previously failing enjoying a wide range of quality literature and extending their own experience through doing so.

There are few more rewarding experiences in all English teaching than when teacher and pupil meet in the enjoyment of a poem. (The Bullock Report, DES, 1975)

Many schools in Wales have become involved with the 'Writers in Schools' scheme and much of the work children have produced is remarkable for its quality. We quote an example by a child of seven describing a stream having had the word metaphor explained: 'Its skin is the water and the stones are its bones' and this, about October, written by Timothy aged 8 years:

OCTOBER

I give you nuts in cloaks of green
I give you berries black and red
Conkers, polished bright and clean
Dropping down from overhead.
In the fields for you I grow
Mushrooms at the dawn of day
And on the hedges high and low
Old mans beard, soft and grey.
I give you leaves of red and gold
I bid the ivy spread its honey,
And though my nights are long and cold
My autumn days are sweet and sunny.

Personal and social interaction

In some schools the day began with a teacher/pupil discussion concerning that which the pupil needed to achieve during the course of the day. The pupil was then encouraged to decide how he wished to organise the work in relation to the time allowed. At the end of the day, time was given to evaluating that which had been accomplished, the pupil contributing to the appraisal. In these situations, children impressed by their independence and confidence. Equally successfully, groups of children were seen involved in corporate discussion and investigations, whether looking through magnifying lenses at the contents of owl pellets, testing to destruction the strength of a pyramid constructed in paper, measuring propulsion in air and water, or making a box camera.

School assemblies maintain their importance during the school day. Themes or content were seen to vary from a focus upon children's work, the results of a group scientific experiment, or a religious, historical, or musical topic.

In a move towards fostering attitudes of care towards others, a group of children, helped by a parent, prepared lunch once fortnightly for a group of senior citizens. The open-plan design of their school allowed them to entertain their guests in one of the learning bays in the teaching unit. This involved children not merely in the preparation and presentation of the meal, but also in other wider social skills. In many schools, members of the teaching staff chose to join the pupils at their dining tables for the midday meal.

Schools linked with their communities in a variety of ways, involving the local clergy in assemblies or retired teachers in curriculum development, using the neighbourhood and its members as a resource for topic work or in organising annual events such as festivals and fêtes.

Parental involvement

Parental involvement varied from school to school. Parents were seen to be involved within classrooms or within the school, providing valuable support to teaching staff by carrying out preparational tasks, organising school libraries or even offering skills in the teaching of crafts. In other schools where parents were involved only in a peripheral way, headteachers took positive steps to keep them informed of innovations or change either through meetings or printed newsletters. A small number of schools involved parents in reading support. Sadly, in some areas it was evident that teachers and headteachers were pressured into a counter-productive over-emphasis on the basic skills because of parental expectation.

Types of practice and classroom organisation

Overall, a very wide range of practice and classroom organisation was observed. Practice in most cases was a genuine response to the particular needs of the school or the children, and classroom organisation reflected this.

Although generally children were grouped according to age, occasionally they were grouped according to ability.

Whereas in some schools pupils were encouraged to organise their own work schedules, in others timetables were strictly adhered to. Children learned from books, from literature-centred experience or from direct experience. Children were seen to be working from textbooks, word cards or work-sheets. Pupils moved around freely from activity to activity exercising choice, but in some cases they sat in rows.

Many classrooms were seen to be organised almost as offices but, at best, classrooms were organised as corporate workshops, efficient, orderly, well-equipped workshops providing for the craftsman, the artist, the writer, the mathematician and the scientist. Where learning took place through the range of a topic, positive attempts were made to ensure balance in the curriculum by various methods: forecasting and evaluation, flow charts, regular and structured staff discussion.

Record keeping was considered to be of paramount importance in all schools and varied from checklists to pupil profiles or both. Many schools used graded tests.

Teachers

In spite of what is reported through the media, there exists a great deal of commitment within the teaching profession. In half the schools visited, teachers organised lunchtime and after school clubs involving a range of activities such as PE, rugby, soccer, chess, netball, hockey, folkdancing, choral singing, recorder playing and drama. Staff meetings and PTA meetings were held in their own time.

In some of the schools visited, staff and pupils were seen to be involved in various activities from 8.30 am onwards. The school bell was not used to remind anyone that school had begun.

Parent consultations sometimes extended over three weeks taking up a considerable amount of teachers' own time.

Many teachers took advantage of in-service training of some kind, sometimes in their own time, although many LEAs made provision for secondment.

Morale was highest where the commitment appeared to be greatest.

10 Resources

The organised class will usually promote superior learning. This is probably because the well-organised teacher is able to spend more time with children on activities likely to promote learning (Galton and Simon, 1980). Good organisation increases children's 'time on task' (Galton *et al.*, 1980) or 'engaged student time' (Denham and Lieberman, 1980) during which learning is much more likely to be taking place. For example, the most successful teachers identified by the Bennett survey (1976) were characterised by a high degree of classroom structure and organisation. A relative lack of organisation was associated with less successful teaching styles identified in the ORACLE study (Galton and Simon, 1980).

What are resources?

Everything which promotes learning experiences in the primary school may be regarded as a resource. To attempt to produce a single definitive catalogue applicable to all schools is an impossible task as each school has its own unique set of resources. However, it is possible to think about support for learning activities in a more general context by grouping resources into categories.

It is usual to classify resources in the following way:

1 Human
2 Material
3 Financial (Everard and Morris, 1985).

Some examples which may be included under these headings are given below:

1 Human:
   The people involved in the learning process: staff, pupils, parents, ancillary assistants, clerical help.
2 Materials:
   Buildings, furnishings, machines, classroom materials, books.
3 Financial:
   Capitation, Parents' Association Funds, Advisers' Funds.

The items deliberately include resources which may be found outside as well as inside the school. Clearly, the school community and the local environment have rich potential for learning experiences.

A policy for resource management

The selection, purchase and deployment of resources in schools reflects a particular view of the educational process. For example, Hamilton (1977) in a case study of a new Scottish open-plan school describes a deliberate policy to order less than the number of chairs required to match the number of children in the school. It was argued that at any one time a large number of children would be occupied in individual learning experiences, not all of which required a 'class seat'. This represents a particular view of pedagogy that is consciously seeking to break away from a sedentary class teaching model. Hamilton (1977) remarks:

> Superficially, the arguments and counter arguments are about the allocation of financial resources and the utilisation of available space. At a deeper level, however, they also interact with more fundamental concerns about the theory and practice of primary education. In short, discussions about tables and chairs are also discussions about methods and curricula.

From time to time many primary schools review aspects of the curriculum including, perhaps, policies for the teaching of mathematics. Before selecting new mathematics materials, important questions need to be asked, such as:

'What kind of mathematics do we wish to teach?'
'What view of mathematics do we hold?'

The answers will determine the choice of materials in a fundamental way. Some materials carry strong implications for styles of teaching and learning. They may require classroom organisation for individual or group work rather than whole-class teaching (Schools Council, 1983).

Learning materials may also promote a particular view of society. It is important in selecting resources to avoid stereotyping between the sexes and to have regard for people from ethnic, religious, cultural or social minorities.

A system of organisation is a priority in any school plan for resource usage. The secret of success is information (Schools Council, 1983). Information on people should locate potential abilities, strengths and skills. This can help to match teacher and class or identify expertise within the school community. Information on materials should ensure that all teachers know what is available and where to find it. This requires both an up-to-date inventory, and clear identification of responsibility for control and maintenance. Such information may help thinking about clearing out redundant materials and creating important storage space. Some items may best be located in a centrally situated resource area. Others, which are frequently required by individual teachers, may best be allocated to individual classrooms or bases. School premises may restrict opportunities for a central resource area, although classrooms made redundant by falling rolls are creating valuable extra space.

Information on finances may help to identify funding required for particular purposes. Schools also need to evaluate their expenditure to see if their financial investment in resources has produced the expected benefits (Everard and Morris, 1985).

Inefficient organisation of resources has been identified by teachers as a serious cause of frustration, inhibiting their professional work (Nias, 1980). Her study cited examples of 'broken, but unreported television sets . . . films not ordered as requested . . . sudden shortages of stock, expenditure which resulted in over-generous provision of resources in some subjects and too little in others'. In some cases, tragically, this inefficiency was reported by new entrants as a major reason for leaving the teaching profession. Time wasted and the thwarting of sound classroom planning by maladministration produced demoralised teachers who saw little point in preparing work in advance.

Human resources

The people who make up the primary school community are its most valuable resource. Frequently, however, teaching staff are merely regarded as a resource selected to fit the requirements of a particular position and individual class needs. In some ways, many headteachers appear to seek to develop, improve and adapt teacher performance to the needs of a school in the same way as they would a piece of machinery. They forget an important difference. People are 'thinking resources' (Everard and Morris, 1985). As such they have rights. They can, for example, choose to hinder or assist the learning function of the school. To a large extent, they can determine for themselves the amount of energy and skill they will invest in their work. Schools depend upon goodwill and satisfactory relationships between people to an extent not always fully appreciated.

The deployment of people is fundamental to resource organisation. The human resource may be inefficiently used, just as any other. For example, it could be questioned if the best use of teaching staff is being made when their time is taken up with routine office administration tasks. It may be that the purchase of a suitable machine or extra secretarial help would release their professional expertise for more profitable tasks (Everard and Morris, 1985). Similarly, organisational and administrative arrangements may have to be made to release a class teacher so that her particular expertise is more widely available.

Materials

Buildings

It is not surprising that:

> . . . some teachers tend to see the school building as a constraint in achieving their educational aims. Some schools lack important facilities, particularly for science and other practical work and very often for storage. Others lack proper accommodation for their library and this may make it difficult to initiate children into the system of classifying and arranging books. (Schools Council, 1983)

The conditions of buildings and premises in so far as they hinder the working of a school to an unacceptable degree is considered in school inspections by HMI. Commenting upon the implications of a sample of reports on schools, Clare (1987a) concludes that although Inspectors made criticisms of pedagogy and curriculum, they also drew attention to poor school environment. He suggests that improving standards in schools requires the provision of adequate plant resources.

Some schools have attempted to improve unpromising environments, often with the help of funds from parents. Alcoves and cloakrooms have been converted into libraries, bare corridors carpeted and painted. The school building, as well as housing resources, can be a learning resource in its own right. It may be used for all kinds of purposes:

> The school itself is a visual resource worth exploring. It contains forms which are coloured, patterned, textured, solid, transparent, reflecting soft, hard, warm, cold, noisy or quiet. Its people wear different clothes, have different shapes and different hairstyles. They move, play games and make funny faces. There are hundreds of exciting and interesting views in, from, through, around and out of a school. (Schools Council Art Committee, 1981, in Schools Council, 1983)

The use of buildings, as other resources, reflects the 'hidden curriculum' of the school. Teacher use of space in primary school buildings has been the subject of a study by Cooper (1982). He concludes that sometimes such space is used as a means of imposing order upon children. Immobility, the child being seated at a desk, was interpreted as work, while movement around the classroom, 'active, exploratory behaviour', was interpreted as 'non-work'. The 'non-working' child in this definition was disciplined by being rendered immobile.

Book resources

Organisation of book resources

(a) *Colour coding* is an increasingly common system of book organisation being adopted by

Some schools have been able to establish libraries and other resources with the help of funds from parents

primary schools for their classroom and general fiction stock. In recent years, attitudes have changed regarding children's reading. The rigid adherence to a reading scheme has given way to a view that reading is best promoted by access to a wide range of appropriate reading materials for each child. However, some kind of structuring of reading resources is required if this individualised reading is to help children to progress. One such system is to group reading materials by their 'readability', usually assessed by the application of a formula to a sample section of text. On this basis, the groupings are then allocated a colour signifying a particular reading level. Reading materials can then be organised by class teachers in accordance with school policy. The use of such formulae has been criticised, incidentally, on the grounds that factors such as the motivation of the child are ignored.

(b) *Dewey System* One way of classifying non-fiction book resources in a central library stock may be to use the basis of the Dewey System found in public libraries. The system divides books by main subject area, each being given a classification number. For example, information on Mary Tudor would be catalogued in the following way. Dewey general classification 900 (General Geography and History and their auxiliaries) would locate the broad subject area. This is then further refined to 940 (General History of Europe). In turn a further subsection 942 indicates British Isles History. 942.05 then identifies the Tudor Period and finally 942.054 locates Mary Tudor. It will be seen that the catalogue operates through a decimal point system, each figure allowing more precision. We have reproduced (Table 10.1) a version of the system using children's classification terms (Gordon, 1986).

Infant schools may, of course, seek to classify by means of colours. It is important, therefore, that any colour coding used in a linked junior school is identical (Gordon, 1986).

Adult terms	Children's terms	Colour	Dewey number
Reference books	Encyclopaedias Finding out	White	000
Religion	Bible stories Gods of other lands	Pink	220 290
Services	People who help us Jobs	Yellow	360
Communications	Cars, ships, trains Aircraft	Yellow	380
Language	ABC Words Dictionaries	White	420
Natural science	Our world Numbers Plants Animals	Green Black Green Green	500 510 580 590
Applied science	Machines Building	Purple	620 690
Arts Sports	Handicraft Music Sports	Pale Blue	740 780 790
Literature	Nursery rhymes Poetry Plays	Orange	 821 822
Geography	People in other countries	Brown	910 Exploration 912 Maps 940–99
History	People before us	Red	920–930

Table 10.1 *A table to show the link between simple colour coding and the Dewey Decimal Classification*

(SOURCE: Gordon (1986) *Resource Organisation in the Primary School*. Reproduced with permission of the Council for Educational Technology.)

Financial resources

Effective organisation of the school should be directed towards its aims. It may well be that a school could best achieve these ends by having the freedom to choose between using financial resources on people or on materials. At the moment, generally speaking, there is only limited room for manoeuvre within narrow local authority spending limits prescribed solely for materials. The option to purchase extra human resources was not open to many schools.

However, the post-1987 funding arrangements for in-service education of teachers may allow some freedom for schools in this direction depending on local education authority policy. Schools may well be able to 'purchase' supply cover, for example, so that staff development can take place (see Chapters 15 and 16).

Capitation

From within the total local authority education budget, a small amount of money is given to each school for its own particular use. This is known as the capitation allowance. It is allocated according to the age and number of pupils on a school roll. The size of capitation and degree of flexibility allowed in its usage vary considerably from area to area. One authority, for example, may allow a school £16 per head for junior aged pupils, but expect it to be spent only on basic stationery and general materials. Furniture and larger items would be purchased from a separate fund. Another authority may give a greater allowance but expect it to include the purchase of furniture. This makes comparison between local authority capitation figures very difficult (Sallis, 1985). Some time ago the Inner London Authority established an 'Alternative use of Resources Scheme' which gave enormous flexibility to schools. This allowed a choice to be made, for example, between using funds to increase staffing or to buy items of school equipment. It seems likely that, in line with the recommendations of the Taylor Committee, schools in general will increasingly be given more control over their spending. Small schools may receive an additional allowance so that their relatively tiny capitation may be supplemented. Contributions from parents are playing an increasingly important part in providing school resources.

Below, in Table 10.2, we provide an example of the capitation allowance for a Group 5 primary school as at 31 January, 1987.

Time is money

A teacher's time is an expensive school commodity. For example, the cost of a two-hour staff meeting for 20 teachers, if funded, assuming a salary of £10,000 a year, has been estimated to be between £400 and £600 (Everard and Morris, 1985).

Sometimes the purchase of recording or reprographic equipment is justified on the grounds that it will allow more flexible and profitable use of staff time. It may be claimed that the financial cost is outweighed by the amount of time saved. However, important questions need to be asked about the benefits of such purchases. Will the new-found freedom really improve teaching? Clearly, the whole exercise is pointless if the time released is badly organised and not used productively.

Cleaning material	= Area × £17.50 per 100 sq. metres with a min. allocation of £100. In addition an allowance is made to each unit with a Nursery Assistant.
Toilet requisites	= £1.00 per pupil
Furniture, Telephones, Postage	= £2.00 per pupil plus £2.00 per school.
Capitation	= £17.50 per pupil plus £600 per school with non-teaching head or £800 per school with a teaching head.

Table 10.2 *Capitation allowances for a Group 5 primary school in one LEA in 1986/7*

Theft prevention

Primary schools can go some way towards making things difficult for a potential thief. Prevention is better than cure. Teachers' general security consciousness should be encouraged. Valuable pieces of equipment must be removed from sight. Cassette recorders or calculators need not be left overnight on window sills in full public view. Door locks should be checked and key distribution limited. Broken windows should be repaired as quickly as possible. Storage rooms should be kept locked and signs removed which identify their contents. There is little point in publicising the location of an audio-visual store. Money collected from children should be paid into the school office and not left in the teacher's desk in the classroom overnight.

An up-to-date and accurate inventory of equipment is required by the local authority and must be kept. In the event of theft a list of stolen items can then easily be made. The inventory should include the make, serial number, model, colour and value of each item, a note to record whether it is on loan or purchased and an indication of its location in the school.

The storage and safekeeping of valuable items such as microcomputers is a problem in schools. Local authority guidelines should be followed as insurance claims may well be adversely affected by failure to comply with expected precautions in the event of theft. For example, storage of expensive audio-visual aid equipment in a locked, windowless store room may be required. The responsible officer of the authority will advise.

It is also worth checking the position of valuable items in transit, such as computers being taken home by staff for familiarisation purposes. Some local authorities provide cover for this purpose.

Another major problem facing schools in some areas is vandalism. In South Wales alone, for example, approximately one million pounds worth of damage was done to school premises in 1986 and primary schools were a particular target in some regions (Reid, 1986).

Electronic resources

Microcomputers

Microcomputers can produce stimulating and exciting work but are an expensive resource in financial terms. The number in primary schools, therefore, is relatively small. In 1987 there was one computer for every 100 children compared with one for every 60 in secondary schools (Clare, 1987b). Clearly, then, if all pupils are to have meaningful 'hands on' experience the number will have to be increased.

Many schools timetable computer usage, allocating them to classrooms or groups in different ways. Primary schools are in a period of assimilation, allowing this powerful resource to find its place in the curriculum. It may be argued that the computer is radically different from the television, video or cassette player which have become accepted resources because of its wide-ranging functions and performance (Garland, 1980), and rich potential (Fletcher, 1983) and most of all because of its interactive nature.

Calculators

Calculators are to be found in increasing numbers in primary schools. They are a powerful resource in assisting calculation and extending pupils' work not only in mathematics but across the curriculum. *Mathematics from 5–16* (DES, 1985c) suggests the need for a school policy on the use of calculators, particularly in 'estimation, accuracy and interpretation of results', so that children are given 'clear guidance' in their use.

The full potential of calculators in primary schools has yet to be realised. Interestingly, they may well initiate an enormous change in the mathematics work of primary schools which has traditionally been number-skill dominated (NAHT, 1985).

Microcomputers can produce stimulating and exciting work

Listening centres

The availability of cassette recorders, headphones and junction boxes has led some primary schools to establish classroom listening centres, where a small group of children may listen to materials prepared by the class teacher or commercially produced. A useful guide to commercial cassettes called *Hear to Read* has been compiled by Rachel Redford (1986) and is obtainable from the National Book League.

Children in classroom organisation

Eliciting a large degree of help from children has many advantages. Most obviously it releases the teacher for more important tasks. But, also, encouraging children's contribu-

tion to the organisation of the class is beneficial to them in more direct ways. First, it will give children a sense of worth and of being of value to the group. Second, it will help children to feel that they belong in the class. Third, it is an opportunity for children to develop a degree of autonomy. Fourth, it should help to promote worthwhile skills of organisation. Fifth, it can help to engender a spirit of co-operation. In a very real sense, such participation in the running of the class can help to promote qualities of coping, competence and co-operation – three qualities, so often neglected by our traditional education system, identified as vital for the future by the 'Education for Capability' movement (Burgess, 1985). The fourth quality which Capability Education emphasises is creativity – not so obviously developed in the same way but not discouraged either.

If children are to help in organising and

moving equipment in the school or classroom it is important that any risk of accident is avoided. The extent to which the movement of PE apparatus by children, for example, is allowed is usually outlined in local authority physical education publications for schools.

11 External agencies

Headteachers and staff in primary schools are able to call upon the guidance, expertise and assistance of a number of professionals from within and outside the education service as and when required. Sometimes, visits take place which are not requested – as in the case of school visits undertaken by Her Majesty's Inspectorate. Nevertheless, it is important that teachers understand the role, function and purpose of these 'external agents'. This is what the chapter is about. In particular, it focuses upon aspects of the work carried out by advisers, advisory teachers, Her Majesty's Inspectorate, the Education Welfare Service, School Psychological Service, and the Child Guidance Service.

Advisers

Responsibilities for grass roots provision of the education system in England and Wales have devolved over many years from central to local government (Bennett and Martin, 1980). It has been accurately described as:

> . . . a national service which is locally provided and administered (Evans, 1985).

In order that the local authorities can carry out their statutory obligations, they are able to appoint officers whose special duties include helping teachers in their professional work and development. Figure 11.1 shows that the position of these officers in a local education structure lies at the interface of a school or college and the local education authority (Bennett and Martin, 1980). The power to inspect schools was originally given to the then new local authorities by Section 77(3) of the 1944 Education Act (NFER, 1985). To over-emphasise the inspectorial aspect of the present service however, is simplistic and unhelpful (Wilcox, 1985a). In more recent years, the focus of the service has moved from inspection to advice and support with the growing realisation that change and development in schools best take place through negotiation not command.

The ambiguous nature of the service is reflected in a sometimes confusing nomenclature. 'Inspectors', 'advisers' or occasionally 'organisers' are terms used in various parts of the country. We will use the term 'advisers' as it is perhaps the most widely used and understood (Becher et al., 1981).

The lack of cohesion in terminology reflects a similar lack of agreement about duties and responsibilities. The nature of the service, as well as its provision, varies widely from authority to authority, in keeping with the nature

111

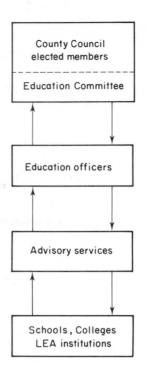

Figure 11.1 *The location of advisory services in a local education system*

of an education system based on a local authority centred structure.

Advisers are usually recruited from schools. Normally, they have had successful teaching experience and often held a senior position such as headteacher. In order to best examine their current work, we have included a typical job description (Figure 11.2) for a primary adviser which specifies the duties and responsibilities often required by local education authorities in making such an appointment.

Our examplar is for a general adviser as opposed to a subject specialist adviser, though clearly certain duties overlap. A general adviser would normally be responsible for a particular age range, for example nursery or primary schools, across the whole curriculum. The subject specialist adviser, on the other hand, is responsible for the promotion and development of a particular curriculum area such as physical education or music, usually, again, across the whole age range.

The two groups need to work closely together to provide a balanced curricular experience for all children from 3 to 16 years of age (ILEA, 1985).

Figure 11.2 *Appointment of General Adviser for East Blankshire*

BLANKSHIRE COUNTY COUNCIL

Appointment of General Adviser for Primary Education East Blankshire

Applications are invited from well-qualified and experienced men and women for this post. The County regards its Advisory Service as central to its concern to meet its curricular responsibilities under the terms of the Education Acts and the County Education Committee has established the following objectives:

(a) the need for the Authority to exercise a more positive role in relation to the curriculum;

(b) an acceptance of the Authority's accountability for educational standards;

(c) an acceptance that the Authority has *the* major responsibility for developing programmes of in-service education and training for teachers.

The main responsibilities include:

(a) establishing and maintaining a detailed knowledge of the working of assigned primary schools;
(b) advising the Director of Education on all aspects of curriculum, management, resources and standards relating to the assigned primary schools;
(c) liaising with architects and others in relation to any building programmes or re-equipping of the assigned schools as requested by the Chief Adviser;
(d) taking part in project group work;
(e) assisting with the survey and inspection of primary schools in whole or in part;
(f) providing first line contact between County and the assigned schools, including involvement in any information required on a regular basis for schools;
(g) providing advice to heads and other members of staff on the curriculum, management and organisation of the assigned schools, together with other pastoral support for any member of staff;
(h) assisting heads and governors of assigned schools with the appointment of members of staff and preparing reports at the request of the Director of Education on members of staff who are seeking promotion;
(i) assisting in the review and provision of the in-service training required by heads and staff in respect of the management, organisation and curriculum of primary education.

The job description shown in Figure 11.2 contains within it elements of the main aspects of the adviser's role as identified by Becher *et al.* (1981) and Wilcox (1985a). Wilcox (1985a), for example, sub-divides these functions into three broad headings: evaluation, curriculum development and change; systems maintenance and support. We will now consider each of these aspects in turn.

Evaluation

The evaluative aspect of the adviser's work is concerned with:

> ... assessing standards and trends and providing information on the performance of the education service. (Wilcox, 1985a)

In part, this is the traditional 'inspectorial' function, required when a formal judgement has to be made. On rare occasions, the local authority may well require a formal full inspection of a school which finds itself in serious difficulties (Becher *et al.*, 1981).

Most advisers themselves seem to play down their inspectorial role and give more emphasis to the establishment of good relationships with teachers as the cornerstone of their work. This may be due to their traditional recruitment from within teaching which, in turn, leads them to identify easily with teachers. Alternatively, it may be the result of a fear that an appearance of being too much like 'Big Brother' can alienate teaching colleagues and make their jobs more difficult to perform (Becher *et al.*, 1981).

The evaluative role of advisers seems to be becoming increasingly visible. Reasons are not hard to find. Demands for greater accountability, often of a crude cost-effective sort, have grown since the start of the 1980s. It is quite natural that the advisory services, which sometimes trail clouds of inspectorial glory, whatever their official title, should be seen as principal agents in satisfying such demands (Wilcox, 1985b).

The same decade has also seen development in evaluation methodologies and theories. There is much talk of teacher

113

and school self-evaluation and appraisal schemes.

Traditionally, the advisers' evaluative function has been carried out in a cumulative way, information on schools and teachers being built up over a series of visits. Local authorities, however, are now initiating varying evaluation schemes as part of authority-wide policies. While important, individual gathering of information cannot be sufficient in itself. Wilcox sees the adviser, therefore, adopting an increasingly managerial role within authority-wide systems which will incorporate various evaluative functions.

Change and development

The second function of the adviser is to encourage a response to changing curricular needs and demands (Wilcox, 1985a). He will, therefore, arrange in-service courses, initiate and encourage projects and disseminate good practice developed in schools.

As with so many aspects of the adviser's role, this seemingly straightforward function is not without paradox. Part of the demands for greater accountability from the education service by parents and others seems to require that local authorities visibly concern themselves with maintaining and improving standards in schools. Some advisers seem to feel that these requirements would be at least partly satisfied if the public at large knew more about their work. Others feel that to adopt a high profile might undermine important professional relationships with teachers (Becher *et al.*, 1981). We would see this as an example of the real need for role clarification. For example, cynics may regard a situation in which advisers are also expected to monitor those very same developments they have initiated as somewhat lacking in credibility.

Just as changes in evaluation approaches require a new response from advisers, so do impending changes in the provision of in-service education. The direction indicated by the funding arrangements begun in April 1987 is towards a local authority co-ordinated programme reflecting local needs and national priorities. The adviser who traditionally has worked as an individual agent of change may, as with evaluation, find himself involved in the management and co-ordination of LEA-wide INSET provision (Wilcox, 1985a). Therefore, the role of advisers is constantly changing, dependent upon local priorities and reflecting national policy.

Systems support and maintenance

Part of the function of advisers is to give guidance to the local authority. They may also give advice on teaching appointments and promotions to headteachers and governing bodies. Some would see this as problematic (Spooner, 1984). The adviser is sometimes used as a confidential counsel by a teacher experiencing frustration or difficulties within her own school situation. But he must adopt an altogether different perspective when he is a member of an appointment panel which may be interviewing that same teacher at a later date. Spooner controversially argues that the interviewing function of the adviser may best be filled by a professional administrative officer of the authority who has the advantage of remoteness and capacity for withdrawal from the school situation.

However, it is usual to involve an adviser in appointment interviews where his diplomatic wisdom can sometimes quell a heady atmosphere. A good adviser treats the unsuccessful candidates well and in so doing will enhance the reputation of his employing authority, engender goodwill towards it and assist in the future development of the unsuccessful candidates.

The adviser and the new teacher

After interview, the adviser's contact with a newly-appointed probationary teacher may take the form of classroom visits and assistance or a more formally organised induction programme (see Chapter 16). Often, this will involve release from teaching duties perhaps on a half-day-per-week basis. Probationers are then free to attend courses or visit other schools where good practice may be observed.

Sometimes an adviser is put in charge of a county-wide scheme of induction for probationary teachers. One particular adviser may be assigned to a probationer during the induction period and will be responsible for recommending that probation has been successfully completed and qualified teacher status achieved.

There still remains, unfortunately, a tendency on the part of some teachers, to over-emphasise the 'inspectorial' role of the adviser. As a result, a visit from the adviser is regarded with trepidation. This is unfortunate. After all, it is silly for new teachers not to make the best use of this source of professional expertise and assistance (Bennett and Martin, 1980). Certainly, if teaching difficulties are being experienced it is as well that they are discussed and a programme of remedial action drawn up between teacher, headteacher and adviser, sooner rather than later. Advisers, in fact, may spend a considerable amount of time, more than half their school term working days, helping probationary teachers according to one study (Becher *et al.*, 1981).

The work of Stillman and Grant

In a time of increasing demands for accountability, changing curriculum emphases, economic cuts and falling rolls, the tasks required of advisers are in need of clarification (Winkley, 1985; NFER, 1985). At the moment their position and the duties expected vary widely from authority to authority. In order to discover the overall position of advisers and to provide all local authorities with information on the workings of the advisory services, a National Foundation for Education Research project took place between 1985 and 1987 organised by Stillman and Grant.

The project's principal aims were to study the roles, management and practices of the LEA advisory services in England and Wales.

(a) *Findings*

In looking at the issues of change within the LEA advisory services it would seem reasonable to set out to describe the current situation first. Unfortunately, any description of LEA advisers and their advisory services is fraught with problems and it is probably fair to say that with the 104 mainland LEAs in England and Wales there are 104 different systems. Despite this it would still seem desirable to be able to describe a few of the more obvious commonalities.

Stillman and Grant suggest that advisers in general are engaged in at least some of the following tasks:

1 helping teachers in the classroom;
2 inspecting colleges, schools and teachers;
3 providing INSET for lecturers, teachers and support staff;
4 helping and assessing probationers;
5 offering subject advice to subject teachers, heads of departments, head teachers and officers;
6 offering school management advice to heads of departments, headteachers and officers; and,
7 interviewing heads and teachers.

The amount of time advisers spend in classrooms varies enormously from authority to authority. There is one LEA which claims that its advisers spend in excess of 65 per cent of their time in classrooms during lesson time, whereas in a number of other authorities the figure would be nearer 10 per cent or less. The problem is that the '65 per cent' authority is actually trying to increase that figure while the '10 per cent' authority is trying its hardest to get the advisers to spend even more time in the office and in meetings. Different authorities are setting very different targets for their advisers and in considering adviser performance we must be aware of what is being aimed at.

The same problem arises with inspection, where Stillman and Grant found four stereotypes:

1 authorities which claim to inspect and which actually spend a considerable time doing so;
2 authorities which claim to inspect but have

not done so for several years and currently spend little or no time on it;

3 authorities which claim not to inspect but which in practice tend to carry out a fair amount of inspection under one heading or another; and finally

4 authorities which claim not to inspect, and which do not inspect.

Stillman and Grant pondered whether the labels 'inspector' or 'adviser' make any difference to the actual inspection undertaken. What after all is meant by 'inspection'? When is an 'inspection' not an 'inspection' but just a visit from a number of advisers? What is the real difference between a 'review' and an 'inspection', if any? What is the link between 'inspection' and LEA standards?

On a different level, one of the more serious problems with the whole 'inspection' issue is that it focuses attention one one of a considerable range of methods actually employed by advisers in monitoring educational establishments and their personnel. In doing so it may produce an invalid polarisation between 'inspecting' and 'non-inspecting' LEAs. To describe an LEA as being an inspecting LEA may not tell us much about what really goes on. The same cautions apply to the other features on the list of advisers' tasks, i.e. the advisers' work with INSET, probationers, subject or management specialisms and involvement in interviewing. In essence, the activities on the list might be better thought of as being necessary within any LEA; but the ways they are executed could vary widely and they may not all be undertaken always by the advisers. Here, most clearly, the adviser's role can be seen as being part of a larger canvas of activities undertaken by the larger organisation – the LEA. The variation from advisory service to advisory service is influenced by two factors: the extent to which an activity is taken on board by the LEA, and the extent to which it is the advisers who are given it.

Apart from contextual differences between the roles of advisers, the research also suggests that individual advisers' aspirations and attitudes change with time and experience in advising, and that there might well be patterns in these changes. Therefore, to talk of the 'average' adviser may be misleading. Instead, Stillman and Grant are interested in what causes differences and in looking at questions such as whether there is a certain length of service as a subject-specialist beyond which the generalist approach looks more appealing to an adviser, and whether certain roles make professional change easier to cope with.

(b) *Four major changes in the adviser's role*

It seems clear from the research of Stillman and Grant that there have been four major changes in the adviser's role since the mid-seventies:

1 First, if there ever used to be a clear distinction between the 'adviser' and 'officer' roles, it now seems to have been eroded. Changing circumstances and new initiatives, as described elsewhere, are making more demands on LEAs. As a result, in many cases the adviser has acquired various parts of the conventional officer role. It is perhaps notable, however, that attitudes do not seem to have changed to the same extent, and that we can find few cases of the added responsibilities which have been given to advisers being accompanied by any greater involvement in LEA policy-making.

2 Within the conventional adviser's job it is frequently reported that there is now a greater emphasis on the 'generalist' role. Stricter financial accounting, curriculum-led staffing and a greater focus on schools being managed all require more adviser involvement. The current enthusiasm for accountability, coupled with the day-to-day management of the new initiatives are both reported as encouraging a more generalist orientation.

3 Over the past few years there has been a greater emphasis on technological subjects and continued moves towards a degree of curriculum integration. Thus, advisers have had to make efforts to update their

knowledge in these areas and be prepared to demonstrate cross-curricular expertise.

4 Accompanying these initiatives there appears recently to have been a small growth in the number of advisers and a much larger growth in the number of advisory–teachers. As a result, the adviser of the late 1980s is spending more time bidding for and managing the work of advisory–teachers, while at the same time a number of curriculum and professional areas that used to be covered by the adviser are looked after by the advisory teacher – particularly school-based work and probationer support. But as the adviser's role changes because of these new entrants into the service, Stillman and Grant find chief advisers claiming that this growth in their advisory services is making their communications more problematic just when the changing nature of the adviser's job makes good communications most necessary.

It would seem that the job of advising is now so different from that of the competent classroom teacher that it can no longer be regarded as a simple extension of it. One facet of this is seen in their research where several chief advisers have described problems in maintaining and/or developing their services because they feel they cannot attract advisers with sufficient width of experience or calibre for the new and complex tasks now required. If the job of advising is to be developed, the service needs to both develop the levels of experience in the pool of potential applicants and to offer a realistic programme of induction training.

It seems sensible to question whether the structure and organisation of advisory services as constituted some time ago are still appropriate? Do they encourage the necessary communication, internal guidance, and effective training? Do they encourage fresh ideas within the service? Do they deliberately, usefully and purposefully enhance the adviser's experience over time? Do they offer growth in a career while also meeting the LEA's needs?

But the advisory service and its work cannot really be considered in isolation from the work of others in the authority. Along with a number of CEOs (Chief Education Officers) and chief Advisers, Stillman and Grant are now asking whether the advisory service should be a separate entity from the administrative and executive branches of the LEA. A number of LEAs are currently implementing a form of 'education office integration' (i.e. overlapping the roles of advisers and Education Officers), in many ways a most exciting development. At the same time, there are those who are trying to maintain a distinction between these activities. Given the variety of needs, demands and characteristics of different LEAs, could it be that both systems are right? Unfortunately, questions such as this which arise out of the enormous rate of change in education at the moment, will require much more work before they are resolved, but even so, they offer some indication of the potential scope for future development within LEAs.

The role of the local adviser, because of its ill-defined and potentially conflicting duties, has been called 'perhaps the least rewarding job in the whole education field' (Spooner, 1984). Nevertheless, good advisers can have considerable positive influence within an authority, as they see many schools and are able to disseminate and encourage good practice. We would suggest that role clarification may not only tidy up the responsibilities of advisers but by the same token remove some important flexibility (Pearce, 1979). Whatever the outcome of this debate, according to Spooner (1984) the best adviser will always aim to do good by stealth.

Advisory teachers

Advisory teachers work closely with local authority advisers. However, unlike advisers, they have a minimal judgemental function (Bennett and Martin, 1980). Their role is predominantly with classroom teachers in schools, providing practical assistance in curriculum development and dissemination of good practice.

The advisory teacher is usually a subject specialist of some kind. How the position is used and the numbers of such teachers available seems to vary from authority to authority. Examples of their function may be assisting a newly appointed primary headteacher in promoting a school mathematics policy or helping a postholder to develop approaches to language work. She may visit the school on a one or two days per week basis for this purpose, or even undertake after school work, according to local policy.

HM Inspectors

We began discussion of the work of advisers by emphasising the responsibilities of local authories in our system of educational provision. However, the local authorities, in their turn, must operate within a national framework of law and policy (DES, 1983b). Just as advisers form a link between a local authority and its schools and colleges, so in this wider national context, Her Majesty's Inspectors link the Department of Education and Science or Welsh Office with educational institutions (Bennett and Martin, 1980).

The Inspectorate's work began in 1839, but the legal basis for its current role lies in Section 77 of the 1944 Education Act which requires the Secretary of State to cause inspections of educational establishments at appropriate intervals (DES, 1986b). In January 1984 there were 388 full-time HMIs in England and Wales, usually recruited from successful teachers or lecturers. Expansion to 490 is planned by 1988 (DES, 1986b). These numbers are small compared with the 28,000 maintained and independent schools and more than 1,000 institutions of further and higher education which they inspect. The Welsh Office in Cardiff has its own Permanent Secretary for Education and Inspectorate, which helps to promote the use of the Welsh language (Evans, 1985).

Since January 1983 formal reports produced by HMI on schools have been available to the public. In addition to inspectorial work, HMI is also involved in in-service training and publishing.

The functions, based on inspection, are three-fold:

1 to assess 'standards and trends and advise the Secretary of State on the performance of the system nationally';
2 to identify and make known more widely 'good practice and promising developments and draw attention to weaknesses requiring attention';
3 to provide 'advice and assistance to those with responsibilities for or in the institutions in the system through its day-to-day contacts, its contributions to training and its publications' (DES, 1983c).

They have the legal right to inspect nearly all educational establishments; amongst the exceptions are universities and religious education in some denominational schools (DES, 1986b). However, many university departments now 'invite' inspections by HMI; at least in a professional capacity as, for example, in the case of those departments seeking teacher accreditation through the CATE exercise (Reid, 1985b; Taylor, 1985).

The Inspectors have no powers of enforcement and 'no function which is independent of that of the Secretary of State' (DES, 1986b). Their strength lies in the widespread recognition of the value of their professional judgements and independence from Government, local authorities or teachers (Browne, 1979). Some have argued that this traditional independence is now being eroded (Salter and Tapper, 1981). Certainly it is true that the Inspectorate in recent times has been urged to move from an advising role and to increasingly exert its inspectorial authority.

Recent attacks on standards in State schools (Scruton, 1986) have included demands that an independent enquiry be set up to examine the work of HM Inspectorate (Meikle, 1987), the implication being that the Inspectorate ought to have exerted its watchdog role and given early warning of this alleged downward spiral. The Hillgate Group (1987), an educational pressure group, suggests that HMI is:

... as likely as any other section of the educational establishment to be subverted by bureaucratic self-interest and fashionable ideology.

A counter to this charge advocated reasserting the traditional independence of HMI. It appeared in the *Guardian* (6 January, 1987). The writer, an ex-HMI, and therefore still subject to the Official Secrets Act, recalled his appointment to the Inspectorate and the words of his boss at the time:

Your duty is not to the Authority, nor to the Headmaster nor to the Government but to the children and your own conscience.

The Times Educational Supplement in an editorial (2 January, 1987) also deplored attacks on HMI, warning of the damage that attempts to undermine Inspectorial independence may do:

It would destroy something which could never be recreated. As external ideology changes so too does the Inspectorate's ideology, but heaven forbid that HMIs should be instructed in these matters by the temporary incumbent of Elizabeth House.

The independence of the Inspectorate remains strong. For instance, in its report on *The Effects of Local Authority Expenditure Policies on the Education Service of England – 1984* (DES, 1985d) it commented that financial cuts by central government were adversely affecting educational provision (Evans, 1985).

The class teacher is unlikely to see very much of the Inspectorate in school as school inspections are rare and usually tend to last for around only a week except in abnormal circumstances. However, their influence may well be felt through courses and documents which are circulated to schools on matters of educational policy and development, such as the recent *Matters for Discussion* series on the curriculum from 5–16. These could usefully form the basis of whole staff discussions and reflection on school policy.

External referrals for difficult or needy pupils

School assessments of troubled pupils tend to place the blame for problems firmly on the child rather than on the teachers or the institutions. Consequently, most school initiatives are directed towards making deviant pupils conform to the rules and regulations of the institution, for example, by promoting regular attendance and good behaviour as defined by the school. The opposite approach – schools changing and conforming to the needs and demands of their pupils – is rarely tried (Reid, 1987a,b).

Apart from formulating their own policies to overcome disaffected or troubled conduct, schools have the option of consulting a number of outside agencies to assist them in their diagnosis and treatment of 'abnormal' behaviour. These include the Education Welfare Service, School Psychological Service, Child Guidance Service and the Social Services. Normally, the Education Welfare Service is only involved in non-attendance cases, although the complexity of these cases varies considerably. The School Psychological Service, Child Guidance Service and Social Services Departments may all be involved, collectively or individually, in cases involving non-attendance, disruptive behaviour, under-achievement and other problems depending on the circumstances.

Although these services exist to help schools, resources for realising their full potential (including staff) are distributed unevenly across Britain, which sometimes leads to delay in diagnosis and treatment. Hence, some non-conformist pupils tend to experience longer periods of what has been termed 'institutional hassle' than others before their cases are investigated by the appropriate service (Fitzherbert, 1977). What this means in practice is that some deviants tend to be dealt with only punitively by schools, whereas others, in different areas, are subjected to a host of highly imaginative schemes under the aegis of well-qualified and skilled professional staff. A great deal depends upon need, individual circumstances, staff availability and local resources.

Education Welfare Service

The Education Welfare (Social Work) Service is a much misunderstood profession. Currently, the service is administered by local education authorities. Some recent publications, however, have suggested that the profession would be better located within the social services (Ralphs Report, DES, 1974; Macmillan, 1977; Webb, 1980; Wood, 1981).

The service is also much maligned by pupils (the 'board-man' image), parents, educationalists and social workers for different reasons. Pupils, especially non-conformers, dislike the deterrent role of Education Welfare Officers. Parents of disaffected children tend to object to the punitive aspects of EWOs' role such as their involvement in court proceedings. Regrettably, some teachers look down on EWOs whom they regard as being less well qualified and intellectually informed than they are themselves. Finally, some social workers often see EWOs as rivals operating different codes of practice with different aims and objectives. In one sense, all these views are understandable as the main functions of EWOs include checking on pupils' attendance, instigating court proceedings for non-attendance, checking on child employment, investigating neglect and advising on clothing and free school meals (Davies, 1976). It can be seen, therefore, that the nature of EWOs' role often places them in invidious positions as they attempt to reconcile their dual functions of welfare and control (Pedley, 1975).

The operation of EWOs in schools is dependent upon a number of factors. These include the personality, preferences, determination and ability of the EWOs, their previous background, experience and training (if any), as well as the school's policy for referring and dealing with cases of non-attendance; all of which vary considerably. Non-attendance cases are generally referred to EWOs by headteachers, deputies, heads of year, school counsellors, form tutors, parents and a host of other sources, depending on the age and needs of the pupils and other individual circumstances. In many schools EWOs do their own 'checking' in registers and thereafter make their own decisions about which pupils to follow up (Wood, 1981). Research indicates that approximately one in four or one in five persistent absentees and truants begin their histories of non-attendance at the primary school stage (Reid, 1985a). Up to the age of around seven, 95 per cent of all absenteeism is for illness or for parent-instigated reasons.

Strategies adopted by EWOs for dealing with non-attendance cases also tend to differ by school and authority. Some schools, for example, instigate early court proceedings as a deterrent; others see them as the final option. In some LEAs, EWOs are spending two-fifths of their time on 'escort duties' for pupils in residential care.

Since the Ralphs Report in 1973, which recommended that Education Welfare Officers should have social work qualifications, an increasing number of authorities have regarded them as social workers with specific responsibilities for schools. Apart from enhanced professional status, EWOs stand to gain better salaries if they are recognised as social workers. Education Welfare Officers with social work duties are paid on social work grades, earning considerably more than ordinary Education Welfare Officers; a source of professional bitterness. However, the reluctance of EWOs to give up their social work role is more than unwillingness to lose hard-won professional benefits. Many believe that the punitive approach to non-attendance, which is evident in Circular 2/86, is ineffective in the long term. While parents and children may be temporarily shocked by a court case, the effects soon wear off and, generally speaking, non-attendance soon sets in again. In Avon, for example, only 62 out of some 7,500 non-attendance cases were brought to court in 1985 (Kirkman, 1986), which puts the issue into perspective.

The education welfare service is a divided profession. Some of its members prefer the preventative social work approach. Officers following this approach tend to pick out children with poor attendance records as early as possible so that they can counsel pupils and parents. Some authorities, such as Avon, produce socially orientated booklets, like the one entitled *Is Your Child Happy at School?*, which encourage parents to contact an Education Welfare Officer if their child is reluctant to go to school.

Conversely, in other authorities, Education Welfare Officers are still regarded and treated as attendance 'policemen'. They continue to spend much of their time browsing through attendance registers and making home visits and court referrals. Many continue to be treated as second class, non-professional citizens by teachers.

This professional ambivalence as to whether EWOs are really policemen or social workers is compounded by their training backgrounds. Some EWOs are completely untrained. Others are partially trained, while still others are fully trained, holding professional and/or academic qualifications.

These professional variations provide a massive handicap to the status of Education Welfare Officers in the eyes of employers, social workers, teachers, colleagues and other professionals. They make very little sense and, in effect, mean that absentees may be more or less fortunate with the attendance officer who is dealing with their case. Some Education Welfare Officers, being socially orientated, tend to be sympathetic to their clients. By contrast, others are punitively inclined, wishing only to see a pupil return to school, irrespective of the nature or cause of the absence. Being absent is regarded as illegal and the aim is to ensure a speedy return backed by whatever threats are necessary.

Debates on the role of Education Welfare Officers are backed by new arguments about whether or not non-attendance is a growing problem. Evidence suggests that attendance rates in Inner London, for instance, are no higher than 10 years ago, or for that matter what they were decades ago (Rubinstein, 1969; ILEA, 1981; Reid, 1985a). In fact, a National Association of Social Workers in Education survey of attendance rates in 1985, reported:

(a) a slight decrease in attendances in nine LEAs;
(b) a slight improvement in five;
(c) relative stability in attendance rates between 1980 and 1985 in the rest. (Kirkman, 1986)

In spite of the evidence, perhaps as a sign of the times, the Conservative Party chairman, Norman Tebbit, was able to claim in 1986 that London teachers were driving children to truancy by teaching 'anti-sexist, anti-racist, gay, lesbian, CND rubbish'.

At present there is very little evidence on whether trained Education Welfare Officers achieve more in non-attendance cases than their untrained colleagues – whatever 'achieve' may mean. Neither is there a great deal of evidence as to whether socially-orientated Education Welfare Officers perform better than their less enlightened peers. Therefore, an in-depth empirical study into the effectiveness of the education welfare service seems long overdue. That way, as Eric Blyth and Judith Milner (1987) argue, politicians and policy-makers in the DHSS and DES will have some evidence on which to base their decision-making and guidelines. Moreover, Education Welfare Officers on the shop floor will have a basis in fact on the best approaches to casework. It is quite ridiculous that the profession of education welfare has been operating in the dark for so long. It is not only stupid but a waste of time and money that so many people are employed without any real idea of their effectiveness.

The education welfare service has been given too low a status for much too long. One way of combating school absenteeism is to attract better qualified, trained and keen people into the profession. Perhaps another would be for bonus payments by results. In France, for example, parents whose children miss school lose out on family allowances. If parents in this country, whose children truanted or missed school without good reason, received reduced child benefit, the resultant effects might be fairly startling in some cases. The money saved in this way could be used to advance the profession of Education Welfare Officers by providing funding for training courses and increased bonuses. Explicitly, Education Welfare Officers who improved attendance rates in their schools by, say three or four per cent, could be paid a bonus of so many pounds for that year. If the figure improved above this, a further bonus would be paid. If the figure dropped below the level of attendance at the point the Education Welfare Officer took over, no bonuses would be forthcoming. Who knows, administrators, policy-makers, parents and others, may find this one of the most potentially effective ways of combating absenteeism ever suggested. It might just be worth a try.

School Psychological Service

In contrast to the Education Welfare Service, the School Psychological Service is regarded in awe by many parents, teachers and social workers. Nevertheless, conclusions reached by educational psychologists do not always find favour with every party and are often misunderstood by teachers (Topping, 1978; Wright and Payne, 1979).

The role of the educational psychology service has also become increasingly contentious because many schools seek instant diagnoses and 'cures' for their difficult and underachieving pupils. This is often nigh on impossible for educational psychologists to achieve given their terms and conditions of employment, their caseloads and lack of refined and precise instruments for use with pupils. Teachers sometimes fail to comprehend that educational psychologists are not solely employed to give further backing to schools' own internal assesments and require-

ments. Educational psychologists have to stand back and take a broader view of the problem. This frequently means making judgements on the quality of parental–child relationships, parental–teacher relationships, pupil–pupil and teacher–pupil relationships as well as the social, psychological and educational circumstances surrounding each case.

The School Psychological Service is normally staffed by 'qualified' educational psychologists, although, once again, regional variations in organisation abound (Wedell and Lambourne, 1980), including those concerned with channels of communication between schools and the SPS. The traditional role of the educational psychologist is one of accepting referrals from schools and, thereafter, undertaking cognitive and personality assessments of children's emotional and educational needs. Based on results obtained from standardised 'tests', reports supplied by other professionals, their own observations, pupil interviews and school performance records, educational psychologists generally make recommendations concerning the future handling or placement of children.

More recently, a considerable debate within the profession has begun as many psychologists increasingly question the wisdom of their conventional role. Many psychologists now believe that they would achieve greater success and recognition if they were encouraged to undertake more school-based therapeutic work alongside teachers and pupils both in and out of the classroom, more along the lines of community and clinical psychologists (Ravenette, 1972; Upton and Gobell, 1980). For instance, some highly successful teaching strategies such as the Derbyshire paired teaching scheme (Morgan and Lyon, 1979) and the West Glamorgan home-based 'Children and Parents Enjoying Reading' Scheme (CAPER) (Branston and Provis, 1986) have been initiated by school psychological services.

Child Guidance Service

The Child Guidance Service is little understood by many teachers and parents. Leaving regional variations to one side (Brunel Institute of Organisation and Social Services, 1977; CRC, 1980), the CGS is often comprised of interdisciplinary teams made up of psychiatrists, psychiatric social workers, non-medical psychotherapists and educational psychologists.

The value of the CGS is difficult to gauge accurately as no national survey of its role and school liaison policies exists. Nevertheless, it is clear that the CGS is a contentious service. Criticisms of its operating processes, effectiveness and quality abound in the literature. The CGS has been criticised for irrelevance, professional distance, ineffectiveness, under-staffing, poor communication, sending incomprehensible reports and overuse of technical language. Others have vigorously defended its work and achievements, given its function within the welfare network (Davie *et al*., 1972; Tizard, 1973; Mead and Mead, 1975; Fawcett, 1979).

According to the little evidence which exists on the interaction of the CGS with schools, it appears that the service mainly concentrates on the diagnosis and treatment of disturbed children and their families, often focusing on younger, primary school age pupils. Treating cases of school refusal is one speciality. In general, typical cases of absenteeism, disruptive behaviour and underachievement rarely require the intervention of the CGS unless there are extenuating or difficult family circumstances surrounding the case to warrant referral.

Social service departments are frequently involved in casework with families of school children without the knowledge of schools owing to particular domestic circumstances such as unemployment, deprivation and other social needs. Schools normally refer needy or disaffected pupils to social service departments because their personal, social or home backgrounds warrant it or because specialist provision is required as in the case of pupils with handicaps. Inevitably, a high proportion of social workers is involved in cases of persistent school absenteeism (Reid, 1985a) because of the adverse home backgrounds of these pupils.

Schools and industry

During the 1980s policy-makers have emphasised the need for schools to be made more aware of the requirements of industry and commerce. Previously, the emphasis had been placed on secondary school–industry links. According to the 1986 Education Act, 'Governors have a duty to provide links if none exists between the school and the business community'.

12 Parents and primary schools

Why should a book about primary school organisation have a chapter on parents? The simple reason is that direct and indirect parental involvement in primary schools is a fact of life, and it is increasing. By 1976, parents helped teachers in nearly one-third of seven-year-old classes (DES, 1978b). Expectations for parental involvement are increasing amongst parents and teachers, and also amongst many politicians and professionals. Increasing parental involvement is almost universally agreed to be desirable.

It is therefore becoming inevitable that schools will have to consider their attitudes and policies towards parents and they may eventually have to produce written policy guidelines. In short, parental involvement is becoming another aspect of primary school life which will benefit from good organisation.

This chapter assumes that schools believe in the value of parental participation, so there is only a brief discussion of the claimed benefits. Furthermore, it is assumed that because parents are inevitably involved with their offsprings' primary school, headteachers wish to make the communication network between themselves and the parents as effective as possible.

The chapter begins with a short historical survey. It then goes on to outline certain aspects of the legal position involving parents and schools. The benefits of involving parents in primary schools are then discussed. Finally, the chapter ends with a consideration of relevant research. During the discussion, the commonest forms of parental involvement are described, along with suggestions on the most effective ways of organising parental involvement.

In most primary schools the overwhelming majority of parents who make direct contact with school are mothers. Fathers also have contact with the school, but usually on a lesser scale. There is also a small minority of children who are not cared for by natural parents. Such children may have step, foster or adoptive parents, or be in the care of a relative (grandparent, aunt, older sister) or, occasionally, an institution such as a children's home. All people with parental responsibilities are considered to be parents for the purposes of the discussion.

Historical perspective

Parents have always been involved with primary schools. They do, after all, provide the children and even years ago would usually have some sort of interview with the head before their child entered the school. In small communities the teacher or teachers would frequently be well-regarded members of the community, known personally to the parents.

Many parents come into school to help with the teaching of reading

This is often still the case in small schools although improving transport has meant that teachers are now less likely to live in the community within which they work. Furthermore, the tendency is towards LEAs closing small schools in favour of sending children to the nearest school of a 'cost-effective size' (see Chapter 8).

A watershed in home–school relations was undoubtedly the publication of the Plowden Report (DES, 1967b). The Report was quite unequivocal in its recommendation of a real partnership between parents and teachers. Part of the reason for this was the identification of apparent class differences in parents' attitudes towards and contacts with schools, and the effects these appeared to have on children's attainment. While the analysis, assumptions and conclusions in the Report now seem rather naive (Roberts, 1980; Demaine, 1980), it did give new impetus to the whole idea of parental involvement – an impetus which has never subsequently been entirely lost.

The basic recommendations of the Report were that: parents should be welcomed into schools; they should regularly meet teachers; they should receive relevant information about the school and about their child's progress. By the standards of some of our modern primary schools in places such as Derbyshire, Cambridgeshire and Leicestershire, these proposals now seem modest indeed.

Since Plowden was published, there has been a plethora of other reports, studies, discussion documents, projects, DES publications and, recently, legislation relating to parents and schools. All of these are reviewed briefly by Wolfendale (1983) who points out that practical progress has been 'slow, tentative and conservative'. Post-Wolfendale there has been the 1986 Education Act which legislates on the composition of school governing bodies, giving parent–governors representation alongside that of teachers, LEA nominees and representatives from the community at large.

There is little doubt that there is a wide consensus on the fact that parents should – and indeed must – become involved with their children's schools much more than in the past. However, the type, range and extent of parental involvement can vary enormously from area to area, school to school and even class to class in the same school. Before discussing the commonest forms of involvement we shall consider first the legal position, then the claimed benefits of involving parents in primary schools. This information is supplementary to the evidence which is discussed in Chapter 13 on primary teachers and the law.

Parents' Rights

Most recent legislation has the intention, at least in part, of increasing schools' involvement with parents. And as more rights are given to parents, so the burden on schools increases. Although parents have always had certain rights, as we will now see, these have recently been extended and consolidated within the Education Acts of 1980 and 1986.

Parent governors

Following the Taylor Report (DES, 1977b), Section Two of the 1980 Act requires all state schools to have parents and teachers as elected representatives on the governing body. The Taylor Report had envisaged that the role of parents and teachers on the governing body should extend beyond representation to encompass effective partnership and co-operation between the groups concerned.

The 1986 Act consolidates parental participation in school government and the representation of the four parties: elected parents, elected teachers, local authority nominees and community representatives co-opted by the other three parties. Headteachers can choose

to be governors if they so wish. The Act attempts to produce non-political governing bodies with a genuine balance of interests by giving no overall majority to any one section of the co-opting body – parents and teachers together outnumber LEA nominees for example. Previously, the LEA 'invited' community representatives and could, in principle, appoint as many governors as they wished, thereby retaining political control of governing bodies (Fowler, 1980). There is now no reason, in principle, for any governing body to be politicised in this way. Parents have an influential voice on governing bodies and an increased choice of representatives to approach with their queries or problems. According to Sallis (1987), the seeds have been sown for a genuine dialogue and partnership. In voluntary controlled schools, foundation governors are the biggest *single* group while in voluntary aided schools foundation governors form an overall majority and retain effective control.

Choice of schools

The 1980 Education Act obliges local education authorities to 'make arrangements for enabling the parent . . . to express a preference as to the school at which he wishes education to be provided for this child . . .'. It should be noted that the wording enables parents to 'express a preference', not 'make a choice'. Indeed, at the 1985 meeting of the National Confederation of Parent-Teacher Associations in London, the then Secretary of State, Sir Keith Joseph stated bluntly: 'There is no parental choice, there is the right of parents to express a preference.'

However, it is the duty of a local education authority to comply with parents' stated preferences unless to do so '. . . would prejudice the provision of efficient education or the efficient use of resources'. (Different arrangements apply to aided schools or when recognised selection procedures are involved.) This means that there are various cases – over-subscribed schools, for example – when LEAs need not comply. However, LEAs must have an appeal procedure, which necessitates making public their reasons for refusing a preference and, in principle, enables everyone to see whether justice is being done.

In practice, about one-third of all appeals heard are granted (Garner, 1986). It remains to be seen what long-term effects this will have on schools. At the very least, LEAs will need to think carefully about their allocation procedures and parents will sometimes have to consider with equal care their reasons for preferring one school over another. And schools will have to consider the views, preferences and opinions of parents more seriously than they have in the past.

On the practical side, schools should ensure that they understand the whole preference and appeal procedure as well as considering carefully how they project themselves to parents (see next section). The Advisory Centre for Education (ACE) has published a guide for parents which is equally useful for schools (Taylor, 1981) and the book by Wragg and Partington (1985) can also be recommended.

Information

The right to a basic minimum of information about schools, and local educational provision generally, is built into Section 8 of the 1980 Education Act. A subsequent discussion paper put out by the Department of Education and Science set out the reasons for requiring basic information to be published and gave recommendations about what this information should cover (DES, 1980). Local education authorities have to publish their policies governing admission to schools, the arrangements whereby parents may express a preference, details of the appeal procedure and information on the availability of places in schools. Primary schools have to publish basic information including name, address and number on roll and also details of: the curriculum, organisation of teaching, options offered, pastoral care and discipline, school uniform, extra-curricular activities and arrangements for seeing the head.

The vast majority of schools now produce a school brochure containing the required information, which is given or sent to new parents. Most local authorities ask for copies of school brochures to check that they do, in fact, contain the minimum information required. A few authorities cover this minimum information by requiring all schools to fill in a standard proforma which is sent to all parents.

In practice, most schools give a good deal more information than the minimum required by law. There is evidence to suggest that the standard of school brochures is improving, although faults still exist (Bastiani, 1978). One common failure concerns the 'tone' of the brochure and how inviting/forbidding the school is made to seem. McGeeney (1980) gives some good examples of how it should, and should not, be done, while Taylor (1980) has prepared excellent guidelines for the Advisory Centre for Education.

The 1986 Act extends parents' access to information by giving them the right to see curriculum statements, syllabuses and schemes of work. It is to be hoped that primary schools will not be required to produce the kind of prescriptive 'syllabus' which some secondary schools have formulated.

Benefits of parental involvement

Obviously the ultimate reason for involving parents is the belief that it will benefit the children. And the main way in which most parties expect the benefit to be manifest is in improved pupil attainment (Wolfendale, 1983). At the same time, emotional and social benefits may be expected and in the case of certain children, for example those with behaviour problems, these benefits may be the more important ones.

However, although the children are intended to gain advantages from the involvement of their parents with the school, they are sometimes indirect beneficiaries; that is, the immediate effects of the closer contact are to the parents themselves, the teachers or the school.

Benefits to pupils

There is ample evidence that home factors are strongly associated with pupil attainment (Sharrock, 1980). According to several studies, the strongest association is between attainment and parental attitude towards and interest in the school (Cyster *et al.*, 1979). Although the definition and assessment of 'interest' is problematic, it seems reasonable that an attempt to stimulate and sustain parental interest and to engender favourable attitudes will eventually bear fruit in improved pupil attainment. One of the main reasons for involving parents, therefore, is to increase parental interest in the school, and to encourage positive attitudes, although the mechanisms by which these influence attainment are not very well understood (Reid, 1986; Brown, 1987). It has even been pointed out that the 'direction' of the influence is far from certain (Cyster *et al.*, 1979). It may be that pupil achievements encourage parental interest and favourable attitudes towards education rather than the other way round.

Benefits to parents

While it is implicitly assumed that greater parental contact with schools will improve parental attitudes and increase their interest in their children's schooling there are, at the same time, and inextricably linked with these, other benefits. First, contact with the school will give parents direct information about the school, the curriculum, the task of the teacher and 'how things work' generally. Second, parents will have access to advice on how to help children with their learning. Third, it is possible that the school could become the vehicle for satisfying personal needs in some parents – the need for acceptance, for regard, for feelings of 'worthwhileness' as well as opportunities to meet other people.

Benefits to teachers and schools

Changes in attitudes are not all one-sided. Greater contact with parents should make teachers more understanding of parents and children, with mutually beneficial effects on the relationships. At a more practical level, as well as having parents who are generally more co-operative and supportive, the school has available a huge pool of talent and help to call on. Parents can be utilised directly in their children's learning and also in a myriad of ways to aid the school and lighten the teacher's load as described later. And, of course, there is always the omnipresent fund-raising.

To sum up, closer contacts between parents and schools should increase mutual understanding, information flow and support of all kinds, to the ultimate benefit of the children. However, it is also worth bearing in mind that the benefits of increased parental involvement are not cost-free. As Cyster *et al.* (1979) put it:

> What is certain is that ambitious and comprehensive attempts to involve parents in school involve increased effort on the part of head teachers and staff, who are often required to work outside the designated school hours.

There are also potential problems associated with increased parental contact which Cyster *et al.* summarise. Teachers and schools looking to develop parental involvement must bear these things in mind. They should also consider the fact that almost all schools which have made efforts to involve parents have thought the effort well worthwhile.

Types of parental involvement

The range of ways in which parents are involved with their primary schools is enormous. What follows is an extensive although not exhaustive outline of different types of involvement adapted mainly from three studies (Cyster *et al.*, 1979; Wolfendale, 1983; West Glamorgan, 1986) supplemented from the authors' own experiences. We hope this discussion will prove useful to those schools who wish to develop their home–school links by alerting them to a range of possibilities which they could choose to promote or make use of if they so wish.

The following discussion deals with all home–school links including communication and active parental involvement. For convenience, home–school links are generally classified into two broad categories: 'written communication' and 'school-based activities'. There are, however, some activities which are not strictly classifiable.

Written communication

Written communications between home and school are important because they are almost universal and they are often the first home–school contact. Schools wishing to promote home–school links are advised to adopt an easy, welcoming style in school–home communications (McGeeney, 1980). Some experts, local education authorities and schools are now beginning to send out to parents general details on primary education as well as on particular primary schools.

School brochures

School brochures need to contain the minimum information already indicated but most schools use the opportunity to welcome new parents and give an overall picture of the school including its ethos and philosophy.

School reports

There are many types and styles of school reports (although half the schools in Cyster's 1979 survey did not send home any written report). The traditional type of school report contains a mark or grade for reading, maths and English, plus a space or spaces for comments. In addition, it is commonplace to have grades for effort, behaviour and attendance. Some primary schools still have fairly formal exams at regular intervals with the marks or grades indicated separately on the report.

Fortunately, many schools are moving towards more informative and open-ended ways of reporting. These are often called profiles and are designed to be more positive, informative and wide ranging, emphasising pupils' achievements rather than deficiencies and avoiding rank orderings of pupils one against the other. The majority of people much prefer this sort of approach in the contemporary primary school.

A newsletter

Many schools publish a regular (monthly, bi-termly) newsletter with all sorts of useful information – coming events, innovations in teaching, school visits, class activities, teachers' in-service commitments, children's work, advertisments, recent achievements, etc.

A noticeboard

A noticeboard is useful for more up-to-the-minute information. It can also be used to display a changing kaleidoscope of children's work and projects.

Anthologies

Anthologies of children's work are always popular at home and there is no reason why aspects of topic work, field work and maths and science investigations cannot be included alongside the more traditional stories, poems and pictures. Many a parent, for example, would be more than grateful to read the suitably tabulated results of a pocket-money survey!

Miscellaneous

All sorts of notes, instructions, invitations and requests go home in writing. Make sure they communicate the information you want the parents to have! And if sent by pupil mail, check that they reach their destination!

School-based parental involvement

Arguably, school-based parental involvement is the most important of all since very often it entails parents being included in or exposed to the day-to-day working of the school and, crucially, to children learning. Nothing is more likely to change attitudes favourably than for parents to see children working hard and enthusiastically on manifestly valuable tasks, children enjoying learning, children relating to one another and to their teachers. And this is what happens in the majority of primary schools.

According to Day *et al.* (1985), there are basically three good reasons for getting parents into school. First, parents gain knowledge and understanding of their child's school and of their child in a learning environment. Second, parents can offer a wide range of skills, interests and plain practical help (hands on deck). Third, involved parents almost always become more supportive of the school as Cleave *et al.* (1982) and the teachers surveyed by Cyster *et al.* (1979) confirm.

From their study of 1,400 primary schools for the NFER, Cyster *et al.* (1979) have compiled a list of the commonest forms of help which schools elicit from parents. Table 12.1 shows this list and the proportions of surveyed schools making use of each. The activities listed vary considerably in the extent to which they expose parents directly to the learning situation; very little, for example, when transporting children to and from school matches. But even at the level of 'extra help for the school' they represent a significant resource, as well as achieving other desirable results as outlined above.

In addition to the forms of help outlined, many schools bring parents into contact with teachers and pupils in other ways. The commonest ways identified by Cyster *et al.* (1979) are outlined below. The percentage of sample schools undertaking each activity is indicated.

Schools make provision for parents to discuss children's work or problems by appointment. (98%)

New parents are invited to visit the school before children start to attend. (92%)

Parents permitted or encouraged to meet teachers informally before and after school. (91%)

Parents invited to harvest festival/Christmas activity. (90%)

Type of involvement	Schools, %
Parents help on school visits and outings	78
Parents do sewing (for example, costumes for Christmas play) and minor repairs to school equipment	65
Parents provide transport for football, etc., matches at other schools	54
Parents with specialist knowledge, for example, local policeman, fireman, give talks to children	45
Parents help with craft work, cooking, music, etc., under supervision of teacher	36
Parents help in school library, covering books, etc.	29
Parents hear children read under supervision of teacher	26
Parents help with football, after school clubs, etc.	22
Parents help dress children after PE or swimming	20
Parents help generally in classroom, putting out materials, cleaning up at end of day, etc.	19
Parents do major repairs and/or alterations to school building (for example, turn cloakrooms into classrooms)	10
Parents run or help with holiday play scheme	7
Parents run a library scheme for the school	4

Table 12.1 *Parental help in school-based activities* (adapted from Cyster *et al.*, 1979)

Parents have formal discussions with teachers about children's school work on open day/evening. (87%)

Parents attend/help with summer fetes/ sports days. (85%)

Parents see exhibitions of project work. (53%)

Parents are invited into classrooms to see children at work. (43%)

Parents attend prize days. (10%)

All these activities are tried and tested over the years and it is pleasing to see the relatively large proportion of schools (43%) inviting parents to see children working in the class-room. This is one of the main ways in which parents can get a genuine insight into how children learn in primary school, which is still one of the areas of greatest ignorance and prejudice. The fact that some teachers seem to share parents' ignorance and prejudices about how children learn is a different prob-lem.

Many people would be pleased to see the relatively low number of primary schools still holding formal 'prize days', the rationale for such events having been widely questioned over recent years. Surprisingly, Cyster *et al.* found that only 35% of primary schools surveyed had a formal Parent Teacher Asso-ciation or other formal parent association, although a further 26% had some sort of less formal arrangement. This leaves nearly 40% without any obvious parent group. Bearing in mind figures like these, it would appear that there is scope for development here. How-ever, not everyone believes that a PTA is the best vehicle for improving home-school links. Certainly, the main function of most PTAs is seen to be fund-raising. At least this brings some parents and some teachers together in common cause. The (relatively) formal nature of most PTAs and the inevitable existence of a 'committee' are barriers to some parents. Broadening the appeal of a PTA and the range and scope of its activities can call for a lot of effort.

Well-developed PTAs which see their role extending beyond fund-raising often arrange or instigate a variety of events – dances, parties, socials, coffee mornings, visits, visit-ing speakers, even classes such as yoga – designed to cement relations between the parents and between teachers and parents. As a spin-off such activities can add a dimension to the life of the whole community. Many of these activities are not school based of course, but they do have the intention of promoting home–school links. Despite all the initiatives, however, one of the biggest problems remains that of non-participating parents. After all, involvement is for all, not just the few. One way of combating this problem is for schools to reach out to the parents – with home-visiting, for example, as encouraged in Nottingham-shire – rather than simply encouraging parents into contact with school.

Another type of activity which many schools undertake is the curriculum workshop where schools put on events designed to explain and illustrate their teaching methods. This is especially useful when changes are envisaged. Many schools arrange to have children actual-ly engaged in typical activities, available to show and explain to parents what is happen-ing. Such workshops have proved a popular way of introducing parents to the possibilities of the microcomputer. Parents have usually been much in favour of such events although care needs to be taken to ensure that com-munication is effective (not jargon-laden) and that parents' real concerns are addressed, rather than the concerns which teachers think parents have.

Parents and children learning together

Until quite recently, parents were thought to have little role to play in their children's school learning, aside from the discovered rela-tionships between parental interest and achievement. Lately, however, many initia-tives have taken place with schemes designed to involve parents much more directly in the learning process. Most of these have proved successful in promoting learning and make a reality of the idea of a partnership between parents and teachers.

Most of the schemes to date have involved parents with the reading process in various more or less structured ways. An almost universal feature of the schemes to date has been the effort to actually train parents in various low-key, motivating and unthreatening methods of encouraging reading in their children.

For example, Branston and Provis (1986) describe their CAPER scheme designed to foster collaborative reading between children and parents and the ways of instigating and fostering the scheme.

The majority of schemes are initiated by LEA advisers or the school psychological service, but use the school as a focus and involve teachers at all stages. There seems little doubt that such initiatives are destined to become more common and to spread to other subject areas – mathematics is a prime candidate in which some tentative work has been undertaken in Leicestershire.

Many of the successful schemes up to 1982 have been briefly reviewed by Wolfendale (1983) and further details are readily available from advisers, social psychologists or teacher training establishments. There is little doubt that such initiatives pay off for the pupils but, as always, they also demand extra commitment from schools and teachers.

Research

A national enquiry undertaken by Clift (1981) set out to investigate the ways and the extent to which primary schools had acted upon the recommendations for parental participation made in the Plowden Report (DES, 1967b). The research was conducted between 1976 and 1978 and its findings based on questionnaires returned by a national sample of 1,400 schools and on case studies of ten of these.

What is evident from this study is that the involvement of parents to any significant degree in the life of their children's school is no easy matter. It is hindered by a lack of enthusiasm on the part of many, mainly working-class parents, and by inherent architectural and organisational features of schools. For their part, teachers may perceive parents as an additional and avoidable complication in an already demanding professional life. They also fear that the broadening of their professional role evident in recent times, of which the 'counselling' of parents is a particular example, may lead to its dilution, with their energies expended in a variety of ways peripheral and debilitating to their main task – educating the children.

By contrast, the parents who were interviewed appeared to be far more concerned about whether their children were happy in school, whether they ate school dinners and whether they 'fitted in' with their classmates. There was little evidence of concern about the methods by which they were taught, methods that are so different these days from when they themselves were at school. Overall, 'the survey data suggests that primary schools have progressed cautiously towards a greater involvement of parents . . .' (Clift, 1981).

Becher *et al.* (1981) examined the extent of parental involvement in primary education through interviews with parents as part of the East Sussex Accountability Project. Their findings identified five broad groups of parents, each varying in the kind of relationship they have with their children's schools. These were:

1 Those who hesitated to question and who, often unsure of their own judgement, sought authoritative and unequivocal statements from the school.
2 Those who seemed reluctant to interact with teachers or to become involved in school life, preferring to seek external signs and indicators by which to appraise their children's progress (for example, noting a child's changing use of language at home).
3 Those who consciously exploited opportunities for being in school and conversations

with staff, to form their own independent opinions.

4 Those who judged their child's school, above all else, by the extent to which it subscribed to their own belief in the paramount virtues of work and discipline.

5 A relatively small group of those parents who showed familiarity and understanding which often came from some connection with the world of education.

The research also suggests that despite improvements in parent–school communication, misunderstandings and ignorance are still too prevalent. In this latter context, Golby (1981) argues that parent–school communication needs to be set in the larger context of school–community relationships. Golby seeks to redefine existing relationships in order to encourage schools to be more responsive to the cultural networks surrounding them. He writes:

It is a question of rendering the assumptions underlying the whole curriculum, to redress the balance in favour of the distinctiveness of the local community against the swamping forces of the mass produced, media saturated, instantly communicating, admass society.

Like work on pupils' perceptions, there have been comparatively few studies into parents' perspectives of their children's learning and behaviour at school, especially the latter. This is surprising considering the credence given to their role on governing bodies. Without such information, teachers are denied crucial insights into parents' values and requirements from the education service.

Perhaps the best-known study into parental perspectives of children's behaviour at school in Britain is the work of Newsom and Newsom (1983; 1984). Their longitudinal data derives from a long-term study of child rearing in the East Midlands, based on a social-class-stratified random sample of 700 children. We will now conclude the chapter with a brief consideration of their main findings.

(a) Children's behaviour in the primary school is seen by parents as something which the teacher ought to be able to control. It is also seen as part of a pattern which threatens the child's work and which exemplifies the teacher's inability to interest and persuade the child effectively. Parents have both admiration and sympathy for teachers but they are often critical on specific issues, usually relating to so-called 'new' education.

(b) One-third of the parents were unhappy about at least one of their child's friendships at school. Working-class mothers were more likely than middle-class mothers to worry about their children being led astray by their friends.

(c) Sixty-five per cent of mothers thought regular homework should be given in the final year at junior school. Only 3 per cent of the 11-year-old children received homework from their teachers at this time.

(d) The findings show that there is a striking link between pupils liking a teacher and being 'very happy' at school. Fourteen per cent of Social Class I and II children had specific difficulties with a teacher compared with 7 per cent for all other classes. Overall, 15 per cent of the parents did not like or had strong reservations about their children's J4 class teacher. The findings suggest that middle-class parents are less easy to please than others and may put more pressure on to their children than working-class parents.

(e) Some 60 per cent of the parents claimed that they normally react to their children's criticisms of teachers by supporting the member of staff. On the whole it takes extreme distress on the part of 11-year-olds to make mothers complain to schools or teachers. What parents seem to want from junior schools is 'effective organisation applied in a benevolent manner'.

13 The law

There are a number of sources of assistance in legal matters available to the teacher. An obvious source is the legal department of a professional association. Information is available to members on points of law affecting professional matters and legal representation may be provided by such an association. Local authorities also circulate to schools their own regulations and teachers are well advised to take careful note of such communications. These may range from local authority responses to national legislation to notes of

guidance on the correct use of PE apparatus. The mushrooming of laws, rules and regulations applicable to schools over recent years makes the area an important one for primary teachers. Readers should note that sections in other chapters also have relevance to the operation of the law.

Waters (1979) reminds us that: 'Ignorance of the law has never been regarded as an acceptable defence' by the courts. Nevertheless, it is probably unreasonable to expect every teacher, or headteacher, to have a knowledge of the minutiae of educational law. That is why we have begun this section by drawing attention to authoritative sources of guidance.

Nonetheless, teachers should possess a broad knowledge of those areas of the law likely to guide their everyday decisions and actions. It is the purpose of this brief chapter to outline some of these areas. More extensive and detailed reading may be found in Barrell (1978), Harrison and Bloy (1980) or Partington (1985).

The internal organisation and conduct of schools are the responsibility of the headteacher (Barrell, 1978). To carry out this responsibility effectively, she must establish and maintain a 'system' which facilitates the smooth running of the school. The establishment of a 'system' together with close monitoring of its efficiency may prove to be of crucial importance in matters of dispute which may arise, for example, when allegations of negligence are made after an accident in school (Barrell, 1978). The teacher is therefore strongly advised to adhere to the school 'system' and to familiarise herself with school procedures.

Attendance registers

The teacher may first encounter the law, perhaps surprisingly, as she marks an attendance register. Guidance for the completion of such registers is normally found printed in them. They are normally required to be retained in schools, 'for at least three years

from the date on which they were last used' (Barrell, 1978).

The school will usually have some internal arrangement for the storage and safekeeping of such registers. The document is an important one and may be used as evidence in a court of law. Indeed, it 'may be vital in a prosecution for failing to attend school regularly' (Barrell, 1978).

A teacher noticing a persistent pattern of absence on the part of a pupil should inform the headteacher. Detailed regulations governing the law on school attendance can be found in *Truancy and School Absenteeism* (Reid, 1985a).

Part of a school's Emergency Fire Drill will usually include the calling of the school roll. Therefore it is vital that the register is kept accurate and up to date in accordance with local authority instructions. This will form a part of the school 'system'. Failure to maintain the register is 'technically' grounds for the dismissal of a teacher and is breaking the law.

Supervision

Teachers should be familiar with the term *in loco parentis*:

> The law requires that every child should be in the charge of an adult person at all times. (Waters, 1979)

This responsibility is delegated by the parent or guardian to the teacher. He:

> . . . hands over his children to the part-time professional 'parent', and charges him with a share in the parental educational function. (Barrell, 1983)

The teacher is expected to act towards the child in the manner of a reasonable parent:

> The extent of this responsibility was defined by Mr Justice Care in the case of Williams *v* Eady (1893) when he decided that 'the duty of a schoolmaster is to take such care of his boys as a careful father would take of his boys'. (Waters, 1979)

It has been pointed out that such a situation may be a little unreal when applied to a teacher in charge of a class of 30 children (Harrison and Bloy, 1980) and that the duty is one of taking 'all reasonable and proper steps' to safeguard the well-being of pupils in school.

What is regarded as 'reasonable' will vary, of course, according to the ages of pupils and the nature of the activities in which they are engaged (Barrell, 1978).

Accidents

However 'reasonable' the supervision, accidents do happen. It would be both foolish and unhelpful in a section of this sort to offer more than the most general advice, as the circumstances surrounding accidents will vary so greatly. If an accident occurs to one child, and the rest of the class are still in some danger, clearly the teacher's responsibility in the first instance is to remove them to a place of safety.

The vast majority of accidents which concern teachers will happen to a single child in the playground or classroom. The 'system' of the school should provide for some emergency treatment and notification of parents or responsible adult. We would strongly advise that the teacher should err on the side of caution in such cases, 'unless the incident is manifestly trivial' (Barrell, 1978).

It is not unknown for a child to fall, complain of a pain in his arm, and be told that nothing is wrong and to 'go out and play'. Only later is it discovered that a serious injury, perhaps a fracture, has occurred. A telephone call to parents at the time of the incident outlining the school's concern at what may or may not be an injury requiring further treatment, is usually sufficient to set minds at rest and decide further action. Far better to avoid later accusations of negligence and discuss the matter with parents as soon as possible after the incident. Our experience has shown that parents are usually appreciative of this early contact.

When accidents occur the local authority will normally require that an accident report form be completed (see Figure 13.1).

Figure 13.1 *Accident report form*

BLANKSHIRE COUNTY COUNCIL
Accident Report
Education Department – Pupil/student

School .... Department ....

1 Name of injured pupil/student .... Date of Birth ....
   Address .... Telephone No: ....
   Occupation of Father/Guardian ....
   Name of the Father/Guardian ....

2 Resultant injury, as far as can be ascertained: ....
   Was he/she conveyed to hospital or medically attended: YES/NO*
   If YES, state: Name of hospital or Doctor ....

3 When did the Accident happen? On the .... day of .... 19....
   at .... am/pm

Where did it happen? ....
How did it happen, to what cause is it attributed? ....
....

---

4 If Accident is attributed to defect in your buildings, playgrounds, appliances, machinery, gates, guards, fencing or plant, state exact nature of defect:
....
....
If accident was caused through the negligence of any of your employees state:
Name: .... Occupation: ....

---

5 Names and Addresses of Witnesses of Accident:
   1 ....
   2 ....
   3 ....
   4 ....
   Names of teacher or other person who took particulars and if not a witness of Accident, state by whom, and on what date reported:
   ....

---

6 Was any complaint bearing on the cause of the Accident made prior to it? If so, when and to whom? ....
....
Has any indication of Claim been made in respect of the Accident?
....

---

7 What action has been taken by the Head of the establishment to reduce the likelihood of a similar Accident occurring?
....
....
....

Important
Any further information which the Teacher can furnish in reference to the Accident should be written on an additional sheet and submitted with this Form. The fullest information should be provided in order to prevent any misunderstanding.
Signed: .... Designation ....
Date: .... Time: .... Tel. No: ....

NB This Form should normally be signed by the Head of the Establishment concerned. Where, however, this is likely to cause unreasonable delay, it should be signed by the Head of Department, but in all cases the Head of Establishment must be informed of the Accident as soon as is reasonably practicable.

PLEASE GIVE FULL REPLIES TO ALL QUESTIONS

*Delete as appropriate

Barrell (1978) warns that in the event of an accident which looks as though 'it may lead to legal difficulties', the teacher is well advised to consult her professional association before completing such a form.

In practice, the teacher may feel more uneasy about approaches from parents. Barrell (1978) suggests:

> In the event of complaint by a parent about an accident, the teacher should take care not to admit liability in any way. The safest course is to express regret, and to say that the accident occured whilst the teacher was acting in accordance with general and approved practice.

Supervision before school

Teachers will come across the vexed question of children who arrive early to school for many reasons. Clearly, children arriving well before the start of school sessions cannot be turned away. A teacher who turned a child from the comparative shelter of the playground out on to a busy road would have difficulty, in case of accident, in maintaining that he had acted as a 'reasonable parent' (Barrell, 1978).

Headteachers and staff may adopt the approach of informing parents of a time from which they will accept responsibility for children arriving on school premises, say 10 or 15 minutes before the start of the morning session. Parents should be asked (in writing) not to send their children to school before this time (Barrell, 1978).

The case of a child who sustained injury before school in an unsupervised playground is discussed by Barrell (1978). Summing up:

> The judge did not think parents had any right to impose responsibility on teachers outside the ordinary school hours. Although many schools open their gates before the beginning of school, is that an implied acceptance of responsibility, or an act of grace offering the comparative safety of the playground as against the hazards of

the street? In this case the headmaster had not been negligent.

It may well be in some future discussion concerning teachers' duties that a definition of 'before school' supervision times will be included. Interestingly, the agreements on teachers' conditions of employment formulated at Coventry and Nottingham/London during 1986 between teachers' unions and their employers, the local education authorities, as well as the conditions of service outlined by Mr Kenneth Baker, Secretary of State for Education, mentioned the allocation of time for supervision before and after school as a part of teachers' duties. This may enable a much more uniform and defined system of supervision and responsibility than is the present case. Nonetheless, the time allocated per teacher, per week for supervision will not produce a great change in accepted practice of supervision commencing some 10 or 15 minutes before the start of morning school sessions and ceasing at about the same period after school.

The Secretary of State wrote to teachers in November 1986 outlining his salary offer and conditions of service. He included supervision within these conditions as follows:

> Ensure the safety and good order of pupils by carrying out an appropriate share of supervision on pupils' arrival at and departure from school, on dispersal and assembly at the beginning and end of the midday break, whenever pupils are authorised to be on school premises – with the exception of the midday break – and elsewhere when pupils are the responsibility of the school.

In the meantime the school should not imply willing acceptance of children brought to school early. Heads should frequently remind parents of a reasonable time of arrival (Barrell, 1978).

Collection after school

Our own experience is not so much of difficulties caused by children arriving early to school, but of those young children who are left at school, long after the other children have departed, because a responsible 'escort' has not arrived to take them home. Primary school teachers find this extremely annoying not when this happens on the rare understandable occasion, but when lateness becomes a matter of habit.

A number of points need to be made here. Parents should be informed (in writing) of the time that children are expected to leave the school premises. This has then established a 'system', delineating the point in time at which the school will cease to accept supervisory responsibility.

Barrell (1978) maintains that if the parent has been properly instructed and not arranged for the collection of a child at the appropriate time, he himself has brought about a failure in the 'system' of supervision, not the school, therefore:

> There is little likelihood that the courts will find against the school, even if a very young child has been released at the proper time into a potentially dangerous situation.

There are clearly many implications in this. In practice, we have yet to meet a teacher who would release a child in this way. As Barrell (1978) states, this is not particularly from a legal standpoint, but rather a 'moral and professional' one. Our experiences of waiting on cold, dark evenings for an hour or more with an increasingly distressed child have led us to accept the professional inevitability of these occurrences.

Leaving the school premises

Teachers are rightly concerned about the child who runs away out of school. This leaves the teacher with a dilemma; should she go in search of the child or not? Two points ought to be borne in mind. First, the remainder of the class, if left unsupervised in the classroom while a teacher goes off in search of a child, are themselves a source of potential hazard. The teacher must therefore make adequate arrangements for them, before undertaking any search. Second, the straying pupil, noticing that he is being followed, may panic and place himself in more danger than if he had not been followed (Barrell, 1978).

In case of an accident in such circumstances, we are brought back to the notion of the school 'system'. If the system of supervision is adequate and functioning properly, then schools ought to have nothing to fear. As Barrell (1978) reminds us:

> . . . schools are not – indeed, should not be – designed to resemble the high-security wings of prisons, and . . . teachers are not expected to emulate gaolers.

Every child knows he is expected to remain in school. If he leaves voluntarily, 'he does so in defiance of the school's requirements and his parents' wishes'. This would clearly be borne in mind by a court in the event of an attempt to substantiate a charge of negligence.

Physical education

Teachers are advised to become familiar with school and LEA policies regarding PE and sports activities. Provided these guidelines are followed and children are properly supervised, then the main sources of difficulty seem to lie in equipment itself. Part of the ever-vigilant role of the teacher, of foreseeing potential situations which may cause accident, is a prudent check of the sports and PE environment and equipment before sessions. Faulty equipment should be reported immediately. The Health and Safety at Work Act (1974) places particular responsbilities on the headteacher of the school in such matters. A useful summary is provided in Waters (1979).

The teacher is also warned of the dangers of using equipment in a manner contrary to that 'following general and approved practice'. Indeed, Barrell (1978) points out that a common defence against an action for negligence is (giving an example from physical education), 'The act causing harm was in accordance with general and approved practice'.

This is an important reason why the rules of games played in school must be strictly observed.

Control and discipline

An important part of the school 'system' is a policy for control and discipline in the school. The enforcement of such a policy is a collective responsibility, and therefore it should be the product of consultation, clearly understood by all concerned. Schools vary considerably in disciplinary codes of practice. As Waters (1979) points out, there are headteachers who encourage an authoritarian style of control and discipline and others who adopt a more liberal approach.

While the extremes of each approach may cause us to look with alarm, less extreme versions of either produce differing, but recognisably disciplined, situations. In other words, we are looking at 'safe and ordered' ways of organising the learning tasks of the school.

Before discussing issues concerning control and punishment, we would make two general points. If a teacher is experiencing classroom control difficulties, there is nothing to be gained by attempting to 'sweep it under the carpet'. Young or inexperienced teachers need support and should be entitled to receive it. There are many experienced teachers who can look back on their early classrooms experiences and point to problems they used to endure.

In the event of persistent or serious problems with pupils, the parents should be informed of the nature of the difficulties. Hopefully, a joint solution between home and school will subsequently ensue. Again, there is nothing to be gained by anything less than an open approach to such issues.

There are two further aspects of control which concern the primary teacher; those of detention and confiscation. The LEA may well have policies on sanctions in its schools, and these must be strictly observed.

In discussing detention, Harrison and Bloy (1980) draw attention to some of the factors to be considered when detaining a young child after school hours:

> . . . the seriousness of the offence, the age of the child, the distance he has to travel home and problems in reaching home if he cannot travel at the usual time.

As for any variation in the end of school session time, parents of primary age children should be warned in advance (in writing). The parents may object and can demand that their child be allowed home in the normal fashion. It will be both pragmatic and prudent to:

> . . . allow a child to go home if the parent so wishes, on the understanding that another form of punishment be substituted.

If another form of detention, say over lunchtime or break, is used, then children detained must be supervised.

Confiscation of objects causing distraction or nuisance in class is another form of sanction used by teachers. Barrell (1978) points out the importance of an early return of confiscated articles:

> . . . anyone who 'dishonestly appropriates property belonging to another with the intention of permanently depriving another of it' is is guilty of theft.

An early return of such property would obviate this risk. Some confiscated items, for example, knives, are clearly dangerous and should be returned directly to the parents. The teacher should ensure the safe keeping of confiscated goods.

Student teachers

The student in school on teaching practice is not an employee of the LEA and therefore cannot be considered with regard to the law in the same manner as fully-qualified appointed teachers. There does not appear to be a legal duty on the part of a LEA to accept responsibility for a student's actions while on school premises or engaged in school business.

Nevertheless, LEAs do accept such responsibility (Harrison and Bloy, 1980).

During teaching practice, responsibility for the safety of pupils in the care of a student rests with the experienced class teacher. The student is strongly advised to follow the guidance of the class teacher on all matters of discipline and control as well as adhering to school policy and LEA regulations.

The student teacher's position *in loco parentis* is questionable (Harrison and Bloy, 1980). Therefore:

> If the student ignores all advice and institutes his own methods and procedures he is placing himself at risk of being held personally responsible for any injury sustained by a pupil as a result of the student's negligence.

In most universities, polytechnics, institutes of higher education or colleges, student teachers are normally briefed on their legal position prior to teaching practice and generally advised to join a union of their own choice.

We have attempted to discuss a few of the points of law which a primary teacher may deal with in her everyday professional life. The key concepts we have emphasised throughout are the establishment and smooth running of a school 'system' and strict adherence to LEA regulations. Some LEAs in fact produce a school handbook which details procedures for school eventualities. But remember, the unexpected does happen.

14 INSET

This chapter focuses on aspects relating to the in-service training of primary teachers. In particular, it concentrates upon:

(a) the changing philosophy of INSET;
(b) the effects of the new funding arrangements in 1987 upon INSET provision;
(c) effective INSET;
(d) INSET and the school.

First, however, we should note that any organised education or training for teachers after they have qualified is normally referred to as 'in-service education and training'. This term is usually denoted by its acronym INSET. Initial training, in much the same way, is often shortened to IT. For the remainder of this chapter we will continue to use these labels in much the same way as teachers in staffrooms up and down the country use them during discussions over morning coffee.

At certain stages in this chapter it is necessary to refer to the secondary experience because the new INSET, post-1987, was piloted in secondary schools. Therefore, primary school staff can learn with the benefit of hindsight from the experiences of their secondary colleagues. As primary schools tend to be much smaller than their secondary counterparts, the key role of the staff development officer is much reduced.

The build-up to the implementation of a more responsive system of in-service training for teachers has taken two and a half decades. To many primary teachers it may feel as if it has come overnight. The scramble which in many areas has characterised the needs identification element of the compilation of the TVEI-Related In-Service Training (TRIST) bids and, even worse, the Local Education Authority (LEA) bids in response to Department of Education and Science (DES) circular 6/86 (GRIST: Grant-Related In-Service Training) has suggested that the volume of literature on the need for a 'new INSET' has gone relatively unheeded in many schools and, more importantly, in many LEAs. The hive of activity in county halls up and down the country in the summer of 1986 as advisers tried to devise systems for identifying needs within LEAs was reflected in schools as, at secondary level, structures were busily created to enable TRIST money to be spent and, at primary level, bewilderment as to how to identify and analyse needs and cost staff development programmes in the space of a few weeks (sometimes days!) presented new management problems.

Owing to the cutbacks in research activity, few studies exist which provide an in-depth analysis of school-based, or traditional INSET immediately prior to the new arrangements coming into force in April 1987. One exception is the Welsh Office sponsored project conducted by Clark and Reid (1986) on *The In-Service Training Needs of Primary Teachers in West Glamorgan* which provides illuminating quantitative and qualitative data on policy, planning, organisation and implementation of INSET, which is discussed in the next chapter.

This chapter attempts to anticipate the possible effects of the new arrangements for INSET by analysing the factors which have led to its development. It includes detailed discussion on policy and planning, regional and sub-regional co-ordination and the specifics of operating and eveluating INSET. The intention, therefore, is to review significant features in the background to the new INSET and, through them, to identify the key issues to be addressed in the coming years.

Developments in INSET

Literature on INSET in the late 1970s and early 1980s indicates a clear movement in philosophy away from seeing the teacher's role as either, on the one hand, mechanically being the recipient of INSET delivery or, on the other, acting as the human agent in transmission of ideas from predetermined curriculum packages. The concept of school-centred INSET is central to current thinking (Light, 1980). The conscious movement away from the word 'course'; the more acceptable accommodation by teachers of the need for evaluation; the increased profile of activities centred on the processes of learning and participation; and the fudging of the distinction between the terms 'education' and 'training' have all characterised INSET in the current decade.

Typically it has taken longer to get to this stage than earlier writers may have hoped. Cane's (1973) analysis of INSET requirements serve as an interesting historical documents of the 'traditional' INSET, the inadequacies of which had been identified in the early 1970s when Watkins (1973) commented that there was 'a great deal of irrelevant and idealistic nonsense masquerading as professional development'. Eraut (1972) and Hoyle

(1976) were both arguing that INSET/innovation should be institutionally rather than individually based. There was a lot of nodding at the recommendations of the James Report (DES, 1972a) (except by those who held the nation's purse strings) but it was not until six years later that ACSTT (1978) could state with any confidence that 'INSET is currently at take-off point in this country'. Even this, with hindsight, appears over-optimistic as the survey by Lynch and Burns (1984) on reasons for teachers' non-attendance on INSET courses shows.

A model to chart the development of INSET in schools in England and Wales might look like this:

Stage 1: Traditional INSET – predominance of courses, menu led, no overall strategy, individualistic, little evaluation or follow-up (Cooper, 1986).

Stage 2: Preconditions for take-off – the work of James, ACSTT 1974 and 1978, and the movement towards school-focused INSET. This stage would also include the build-up to TVEI since, characteristically, INSET was an afterthought in the gallop to get this initiative operational in schools.

Stage 3: Take-off – this can be more realistically associated (for the secondary and tertiary sectors) with the onset of TRIST in 1985 and, for the primary sector, with the rapid preparations to meet the requirements of DES circular 6/86.

Stage 4: The drive to maturity – this will be seen as a gradual process as LEAs and schools take on board the implications of implementing effective needs-identification, programme development and evaluation procedures.

Stage 5 The age of high mass consumption – will not be reached until needs of teachers as professional individuals and schools as organisations can be catered for, without resource conflict, in an INSET environment which accommodates the elements of both training and education.

The development of INSET to Stage three,

the take-off point, can be traced through two routes. The first of these falls clearly under the INSET label and has evolved from the award-bearing courses of the 1960s via the relationships with specific curriculum projects in the 1970s to the position of training related to a deficiency model of teaching whereby resources are channelled to INSET designed to remedy identified deficiencies at all levels in the education system (see DES circulars 3/83, 4/84, 6/86 and *Better Schools*, 1985a).

A second route can be identified in the development of links between action research and staff development. The encouragement of teachers to examine and record their own practice, evaluate teaching and learning strategies and develop a role as participant observers (collaboratively with each other and with external consultants) was stimulated by work carried out by Cooper and Ebbutt (1974) and developed further in projects such as the Ford Teaching Project (CARE, 1975), John Elliott's work with CARN and Schools Council Programme 2 (Elliott, 1978; 1981).

Furthermore, it is impossible to ignore two likely problems;

1 the question of 'ownership' of the INSET experience;
2 the relative importance and adaptability to change of the 'partners' in the new INSET arrangements (i.e. DES, LEAs, primary, secondary, tertiary and higher education institutions, and teachers).

On point one, it is almost certainly true to say that the balance of power has swung away from institutions (whether of higher education like universities or colleges or places of more modest pretensions such as teachers' centres) towards the school and the teachers. They are the ones who will articulate needs, set the agenda and even the venue. In these circumstances the question of ownership hardly arises. Ownership rests with teachers and the school.

Point two is more problematic. In a sense, everything must change – attitudes, values, habits, relationships, territories, even contracts. This, indeed, is the melting pot.

However, much of this will not impinge very directly on primary schools. But one thing no school will be able to side-step is the issue of 'needs analysis' itself and the nature of the new INSET which is required to begin to meet those needs as we shall discuss further in Chapter 15.

Policy and planning

One of the most important developments in INSET over the past 25 years has been a growth in the appreciation that provision can take many forms. INSET is no longer conceived solely as 'courses planned for teachers by those in higher education and elsewhere to take place in institutions apart from schools and leading to the award of a degree, diploma or certificate, but as a range of activities which can also be provided by teachers' centres, professional associations, subject associations, advisers, consultants or teachers themselves' (Skinner, 1981). It is also accepted that activities can be located in schools, teachers' centres, colleges or any other suitable venue and can take a variety of forms such as workshops, demonstrations, seminars, etc.

The expansion of types of provision and providing agencies has brought its own problems. As far back as the 1960s, Townsend (DES, 1970) and Cane (1969) highlighted the fact that while provision had expanded, it was both unbalanced and unco-ordinated. The availability of award-bearing courses depended on where you lived in relation to universities and colleges, and of short courses on the composition and strength of local advisory services. It is sobering to reflect that the 1984 ACSET report on INSET makes exactly the same point about the lack of balance and co-ordination in provision (DES, 1984a).

The fact that the expansion of INSET provision has not been accompanied by a more widespread impact on practice and performance in schools has also had a bearing on the issue of policy and planning. Many reasons for this limited effect have been proposed, of which the most compelling relates to the fact that INSET has not generally been directed towards the needs of the school but to those of individual teachers. It is now acknowledged that if schools are to be the main beneficiaries of INSET, then it is their needs that must be assessed. Schools must, from this perspective, assume responsibility for assessing their IN-SET needs, planning a programme to meet these and using whatever procedures exist to facilitate implementation. This shift in emphasis has important implications for existing relationships and channels of communication between schools, LEAs and providing agencies that will be explored further.

Another factor to be taken into account when considering policy and planning, is the role of the LEA itself in relation to INSET. Many consider that there has never been a greater need for INSET in the teaching profession. Fluctuating school rolls, static staffs with few promotion prospects, organisational adjustments consequent to the devolvement of more responsibilities to schools, curricular changes and new examinations, all have created situations in many schools that LEAs cannot ignore. Against this background, it is the responsibility of the LEA to ensure that national policy is implemented, that educational provision within its area is of a good standard and meets the needs of pupils and community and that the professional development needs of its teachers are met. INSET offers a means by which LEAs can meet all of these responsibilities.

The position outlined briefly above is presented in order that recommendations concerning policy and planning can be placed in context. The implications of the developments mentioned are that machinery and procedures must exist to ensure that:

1 existing provision is fairly distributed, that limited resources are maximally utilised and that no wasteful duplication occurs;
2 the INSET needs of teachers, schools and LEAs are articulated and incorporated into policy statements and planning decisions at the appropriate level;

3 plans are translated into action.

Levels of co-ordination

In a survey of INSET provision in the Oxfordshire area, Henderson identified three levels at which co-ordination of INSET can occur.

Level 1 Providing opportunities for those centrally involved in the various agencies making provision, to meet regularly and exchange ideas.

Level 2 Operating a 'clearing house' through which everyone involved in an area is made aware of needs, existing provision and resources.

Level 3 Meshing together of the resources available to produce the most effective and complete programme possible for the teachers in an area. (Henderson, 1975)

These levels present a useful model for conceptualising the structure in which the organisational needs of INSET, as outlined above, can be met. Levels 1 and 2 are more properly described as stages in co-operation and, as such, indicate the kind of flexible and responsive machinery required at sub-regional (LEA) level. The activities described at Level 3 represent true co-ordination and point to the kind of organisation deemed necessary at regional level.

Effective INSET

The paramount importance of INSET to the education service was recognised by the James Committee, which gave pride of place to the so-called 'third cycle' in its report, stating that 'to none of our recommendations do we attach greater importance' (DES, 1972a). The renewed enthusiasm for INSET that followed this report led to a rapid expansion in provision in the belief that INSET would be the most effective vehicle for promoting change and development within schools. The realisation that, on the whole, INSET has not had this effect has led many to look critically at what is being provided and for ways in which it can be improved.

Evidence from many sources, including surveys of teachers' perceptions of INSET, case studies of selected courses, large-scale assessments (usually American) of state INSET programmes and theories about change can be drawn on to obtain a picture of what appears to contribute to the effectiveness of INSET. Such sources can also be fruitful in highlighting what does not seem to work!

Teachers' surveys

Nearly all INSET has traditionally been offered in the form of external, award or non-award-bearing courses provided either by LEAs or institutions of higher education. Although the overall impact of such courses has been questioned, there is little doubt that teachers attach much importance to them. This is made clear by Rudduck who concludes that her study of short INSET courses:

> reveals the deep sense of professional isolation that many teachers still feel; this makes attendance at outside in-service meetings a crucial aspect of professional life and an important condition of professional development ... On the short outside course, teachers have access to ideas that they can explore in the company of professional colleagues whose reactions are likely to be less predictable than those of their own colleagues and whose experiences are likely to be less familiar. It seems important, therefore, to maintain a structure of opportunities that would allow teachers to engage in a professional dialogue with teachers from other schools and to work with them in a setting different from the familiar landscape of the staffroom. (Rudduck, 1981)

Teachers, through their responses to survey questionnaires, have indicated quite clearly what the strengths and weaknesses of courses are from their perspective. Although 80 per cent of the teachers in Cane's sample

declared a positive need for INSET, 50 per cent had severe reservations about the content, format and organisation of the courses provided. The topics that would attract the support of the majority of teachers related almost entirely to the professional concern of staff for improved practice and performance in the classroom. Topics like the pros and cons of new methods of school/class organisation, and the operation and applications of new approaches and equipment were typical of those selected as being important (Cane, 1969). Despite considerable educational and social changes since the survey by Cane, it would appear that primary teachers' preferences regarding course content have remained stable. For example, Bradley (1974) discovered the greatest demand to be for courses on teaching method and educational trends.

However, not only the content but also the type of activity provided on courses was regarded as important. The Gittins Report (DES, 1967a) had noted that:

> ... experience suggests that (in-service) courses are most successful when they avoid the classroom situation of passive listening and involve teachers in practical work, discussion and self-questioning. Too many local day and evening classes still depend exclusively on lectures which can be inspiring but leave little lasting trace on the work of the classroom.

This observation accurately reflects the opinions of teachers. Approval of 'methods allowing them a larger element of participation, such as working groups to explore topics and carry out practical trials, and lectures followed by an adequate period of questioning or comment' was given by a sizeable majority of Cane's respondents (Cane, 1969). The preferences of teachers from the East Midlands gave weight to this emphasis on teacher-participation in courses in that they selected 'to work with a group of teachers on a problem of professional interest' as the most attractive of five course format alternatives offered to them (Bradley, 1974).

The location, length and time of courses constitutes another aspect of course organisation on which teachers have commented. Once again, it is surprising how consistent teachers' views about these arrangements have remained over many years. A dislike of travel or inability to live away from home affected many teachers' attitudes towards participating in INSET. Also, difficulties in obtaining replacement staff and concern that children would be too disrupted influenced many teachers' decisions (Cane, 1969). A similar pattern of difficulties was mentioned by East Midlands teachers where over 50 per cent of women teachers were unable to live away from home and over 40 per cent were reliant on public transport for daily INSET activities. Cane concluded from his findings that the development of local provision was of prime importance. However, Lewis (1976) felt that the answer lay not in local but in flexible, provision. The INSET preferences of York teachers could most effectively be met by increasing flexibility in terms of:

(a) content – in any subject area a variety of alternative courses related to it should be designed;
(b) arrangements – in order not to interfere with teaching commitments;
(c) award patterns – making alternative arrangements for acquiring awards or credits;
(d) institutional base – necessitating the expansion of the variety of institutions involved in in-service provision. (Lewis, 1976)

Teachers' observations on courses have certainly influenced the pattern of provision. For example, it is now recognised that award-bearing courses can deal with subjects of direct interest and relevance to teachers and do not need to rely on themes geared to educational theory. Also, more part-time award-bearing courses have been developed which means that not only can teachers engage in a course without causing disruption to the children but also the course has direct access to and can address itself to a problem area of concern and relevance to the teacher. New INSET providers (Open University) and validators (CNAA) have contributed significantly to greater flexibility and diversification of levels of provision.

While such developments are welcome, it has become increasingly clear that no amount of change in content, format and organisation will be effective if it is not accompanied by a fundamental change in conceptions about the role of the course in INSET. In order to understand this role, models of in-service that have utilised findings in the areas of curriculum innovation and institutional change must be examined. Such models tend to conceptualise INSET in terms of stages and focus on how each stage can be made effective (Eraut, 1978; Rudduck, 1981; Schmuck, 1974; Stenhouse, 1980).

Stages in INSET

Eraut's (1978) model exemplifies the 'stage' approach in suggesting three functions for in-service education: the transmission of new knowledge, the facilitation of professional discussion among teachers and the promotion of innovation in response to educational problems. While the first of these functions has been dominant for some time in the form of courses, the third has been virtually ignored because it was assumed that the transmission of new knowledge to teachers and the facilitation of professional discussion would in themselves lead to a desirable level of innovation. In practice, the innovation function has, of course, failed to follow as a consequence of knowledge transmission. Eraut insists that this is because a significant proportion of the learning associated with any change in practice takes place in the context of use or conversely that ideas have to be used before they acquire any significant meaning for the user (Eraut, 1982). Any expansion of in-service provision must, therefore, concentrate on strengthening the innovatory function. A consultancy-based system of in-service is what is needed, in that it would not only maximise the innovatory potential of INSET

147

but would also make the other stages more meaningful to both teacher and school (Eraut, 1978).

Nowhere is more emphasis placed on the specific purpose of each stage in INSET than in the work of Rudduck (1981). She stresses that the in-service short course is only one episode in a process in which preparation and implementation constitute other equally important episodes. All three are essential; no one stage can be effective in isolation. For this reason, it would probably be more profitable to run fewer courses and to give more time to preparation, orientation and follow-through. Within this framework, the contribution that each stage can make should be precisely spelled out so that expectations of what it can achieve are realistic. 'It is important that a course is not having to carry more responsibility for implementation or development than it reasonably could be expected to' (Rudduck, 1981).

There is a need, therefore, for all those involved in in-service activities to recognise the distinctive potential of different kinds of events, so that expectations of what can be achieved are realistic in terms of the time and resources available. Courses differ widely in their aspirations and the kind of outcomes they make possible and it is against such criteria that their effectiveness must be measured.

A similar distinction between stages is made by Schmuck, who considers that the new demands made on schools will be met only if two strategies are employed. 'In-service training courses' are perceived as the first strategy as they are considered to be the most effective means of facilitating change in the individual. Courses will be successful in so far as they provide the necessary psychological and emotional support required by course members to cope with the stressful and threatening aspects of trying out new ideas. 'Organisation Development' is the label given to the second strategy which aims at dealing with changes in groups of personnel within the school, so that the necessary support and structure is provided for implementation of new ideas to occur. Unless sub-systems within the school are prepared to make adjustments, both attitudinal and organisational, to accommodate new ideas, then the fruits of successful in-service courses are likely to fall on barren ground. Once again, outside consultants are perceived as essential in that they are able to take a sufficiently objective view to persuade schools to make such modifications (Schmuck, 1974).

Effective courses

Bearing in mind that INSET is a continuous process marked by varying types of input and support at different stages, what specific contribution can courses be expected to make?

For many researchers some practical changes would enhance the value of courses. It is, for instance, extremely difficult to satisfy individual teacher needs in a situation where the course organisers do not have the knowledge of the teacher's specific problems. The fact that the teachers attending the group are likely to be a heterogeneous group with widely differing expectations simply exacerbates the difficulty. Inadequate descriptions of course content in advertising material and the unsystematic way in which teachers select courses also militate against course-member cohesion. However, if the following guidelines are borne in mind in the planning of courses, Rudduck suggests that there is a greatly increased likelihood that the course will be effective:

(a) more thought is given to strategies for recruiting course members;
(b) courses are efficiently managed and well prepared;
(c) courses use what the members have to offer;
(d) courses start with the concerns of teachers;
(e) courses gear the material presented to the teaching style;
(f) courses encourage participatory modes of enquiry;

(g) courses encourage members to attend as a team;

(h) course members are conscious of the need for evaluation (Rudduck, 1981).

A course will be even more effective if opportunities are provided for teachers to:

(a) experience cognitive, attitudinal and behavioural change;

(b) communicate with each other about their attitudes and feelings as to the new information and its implications for changes in their role;

(c) systematically plan how the new information might be implemented in the classroom;

(d) try out new behaviours in a 'safe' climate. (Schmuck, 1974)

The importance of establishing the objectives of an INSET course has already been stated. In an extremely useful study, Joyce and Showers suggest that one way of doing this is to distinguish between INSET directed at the 'fine tuning' of existing skills and that designed to promote the learning of new skills. Training orientated towards 'fine tuning' aims to consolidate existing competence and is easier to achieve than programmes which introduce a completely new approach. To master a new approach the teacher needs to explore and understand its rationale, develop the ability to carry out the new strategies and master fresh content. Different training approaches are necessary, depending on the hoped-for outcome. With the 'fine tuning'/ new approach distinction in mind, the effects of five derived components of training on four levels of impact are measured. The four levels of impact are: 1 awareness; 2 the acquisition of concepts and organised knowledge; 3 the learning of principles and skills; and 4 their application to problem-solving in the classroom. It is only when the fourth level is reached that it is reasonable to look for impact on pupil learning. The five components of training are:

1 presentation of theory or description of skill or strategy;

2 modelling or demonstration of skills or models or teaching;

3 practice in simulated and classroom settings;

4 structured and open-ended feedback;

5 coaching for application.

Based on a review of over 200 studies, the authors conclude that:

Where the fine-tuning of style is in focus, modelling, practice under simulated conditions and practice in the classroom combined with feedback, will probably result in considerable changes. Where the mastery of a new approach is the desired outcome, presentation and discussions of theory and coaching to application are probably necessary as well. ... The most effective training activities, then, will be those that combine theory, modelling, practice, feedback and coaching to application. The knowledge base seems firm enough that we can predict that if those components are in fact combined in in-service programmes, we can expect the outcomes to be considerable at all levels. (Joyce and Showers, 1984)

The implications of these conclusions are clear. Most pre-1987 INSET courses took the form of lectures, discussions and sometimes workshops. Modelling, practice and feedback were rarely included as course components and classroom coaching was even less likely. However, if all stages were to be incorporated into most INSET courses, the resource implications, both financial and structural, are considerable. Schools and providers would need to re-think their priorities and organise themselves in such a way that school and classroom-based INSET becomes an integral part of school life.

It is the strong belief of many involved in INSET that it is in the lack of structural/ organisational changes in schools and all agencies connected with in-service provision that the real problem lies. Minor adjustments to the way in which in-service is currently provided are unlikely to have much impact in isolation. It would seem that improvements in

149

in-service education or staff development are 'directly related to whether improvements in how schools are typically organised are made as well' (Howey and Joyce, 1979).

INSET and the school

If INSET courses are improved along the lines indicated, then there is a strong likelihood that individual teachers will embrace new ideas/techniques. The question then becomes: what else is necessary to ensure that these new behaviours are utilised by the teacher and disseminated in an effective way to colleagues?

If the notion of INSET as stages in a continuous process is persevered with, it is clear that the role of the school is important before and after any INSET activity. Once again, these stages will be discussed separately for purposes of clarity, though in practice, of course, schools are likely to be involved in every stage at any given time.

School-focused INSET

That much INSET has had limited impact within schools has been attributed partly to the fact that it has tended to be responsive to the needs of individual teachers rather than schools as a whole. It is now generally accepted that where the purpose of INSET is to help improve the quality of education in individual schools, then a school-focused approach has most chance of success (Bolam, 1982; Henderson, 1979; Henderson and Perry, 1981). Adopting a school-focused approach means planning and implementing an INSET programme which response directly to the specific needs of one particular school. This means that INSET activities are selected on the basis of their likely contribution to school needs rather than because of their interest to individual teachers (though it is expected that the wishes of individual teachers are also taken into account). The most important aspect of arranging an INSET

programme to meet school needs, however, lies in the method by which it is decided what these might be, for it is expected that heads will assess needs and establish priorities in full consultation with all staff and implement programmes with their complete co-operation. The pamphlet *Making INSET Work* distributed by the DES to all schools in 1978 encourages schools to:

1 identify the main INSET needs;
2 decide on and implement the general programme;
3 evaluate the effectiveness of the general programme;
4 follow-up the ideas gained. (DES, 1978a)

Concrete suggestions for achieving these objectives are included to assist schools developing such programmes. Particular emphasis is placed on the fact that the widest possible range of types of INSET provision must be used in planning programmes and that these can either be internal or external to the school.

Benefits of a school-focused approach to INSET

The most obvious benefit in adopting a school-focused approach to INSET is that priority is given to the specific needs of individual schools. This must be seen as an advantage because it counteracts the tendency which has so far predominated, to place the needs of individual teachers first. Most importantly, the basic tenets of the approach augur well for the organisational health of schools as institutions, in that schools are encouraged, with staff participation, to evaluate their policies and to look for constructive ways of dealing with problems. It has often been observed that where teachers are party to decisions, their commitment to the resultant activities increases considerably (McLaughlin and Marsh, 1978; Simmons, 1980). Also, staff morale is raised and sustained at a healthy level because:

... a strategy of INSET which has the

school as its starting point is likely to encourage groups of teachers to do things themselves; the initiative is theirs, the exercise becomes one of self-development and active participation rather than being sent on a course. (Sayer, 1979)

Finally, it is felt that school-focused approaches should encourage greater variety and flexibility in the kinds of INSET provided. While all existing provision has potential use in meeting schools' needs, it is regarded as likely that many more innovative activities will be developed in response to specific problems.

Many published accounts have elaborated the benefits that have accrued from a variety of types of school-focused INSET (Bolam, 1982b; Donoughue *et al.*, 1981; Henderson and Perry, 1978). Between 1978 and 1980 an action research project based at the University of Bristol, School of Education, monitored the progress of 50 schools engaged in designing and implementing their own INSET policies. Each school was requested to adopt a procedure which involved them in identifying IN-SET needs and priorities in relation to their own school's general policy, priorities and needs. LEAs involved in the scheme and local INSET agencies agreed to be supportive, provide resources and give priority to requests from project schools. Evidence suggested that school-focused programmes had the following broad effects within participating schools:

1 Increased awareness of INSET.

2 Increased contacts between staff within the school and between school and college lecturers about INSET.
3 An increased level of INSET activity.
4 An increase in school-based INSET activities, which was a new approach for some of the schools.
5 An increased involvement of college staff in school-based activities.
6 An increased amount of inter-school visits.
7 Particular school developments of curriculum materials, new syllabuses and different organisational methods to deal with INSET in a more participating manner.
8 Individual teacher gains in both knowledge and skills.
9 The introduction of changes in classroom teaching and an increased willingness to experiment.
10 Increased feelings of self-confidence among teachers and increased satisfaction with some of the things they were doing. (Baker *et al.*, 1982)

While the same kind of benefits are claimed in most of the published studies of school-focused programmes, it is of interest to note that the schools encountered similar difficulties. These difficulties, which are associated with how schools analyse needs, use outside consultants and organise their time, have implications which go beyond the school-focused issue. It is within this wider framework also, therefore, that the problems will be located and discussed in the ensuing chapter.

15 Analysis of needs

Three assumptions underpin the notion that schools are able to develop their own INSET policies and programmes. The first is that the school has clearly defined educational aims and objectives, agreed on and supported by all the staff, which can be maintained or modifed by a well-thought-out INSET policy. The second is that school staffs possess the skills necessary to be aware of and evaluate the needs of the whole school, functional groups within the school and specific needs of individual teachers in framing policy and negotiating priorities. The third is that the requisite amount of time is available for such activities. These three assumptions warrant closer attention.

In 1978 the DES publication *Making INSET Work* gave strong encouragement to schools to formulate their own INSET policy. A similar recommendation permeates the ACSET report on in-service (DES, 1984a). The committee considers that every school should have an agreed procedure for ensuring that the needs of individual teachers and groups within the school are regularly reviewed and that priorities are assessed in consultation with all interested parties. It is suggested that such reviews should be carried out annually by:

1 inviting individual teachers to consider their needs for training and professional development, with guidance as necessary (possibly based on a system of assessment) on priorities for INSET and the range of INSET opportunities available;
2 inviting groups of teachers to consider their needs as a whole;
3 inviting senior staff to review their own needs (e.g. for management training) and the needs of the school as a whole;
4 inviting the school governors to offer views on training needs in relation to the curricular objectives of the school. (DES, 1984a)

While useful in suggesting possible groupings for consultation purposes, the report offers little guidance on the more complicated issue of how such procedures might work. It has frequently been observed that consensus on goals and priorities is more easily attained in a small, cohesive primary school than a large, diffuse comprehensive (Baker, *et al.*, 1982).

Clearly, the complexity of the problem and the range of divergent interests present formidable obstacles to achieving consensus over INSET aims and objectives. Of greater significance, though, is the fact that the vast majority of teachers lack expertise in diagnosing problems, assessing priorities and planning programmes. This is not surprising as generally teachers are not equipped either during their initial training or by their subsequent work in the classroom in the evaluative and problem-solving skills necessary for needs assessment. If effective school-focused needs assessment requires the active participation of all teachers, the improvement of staff competence is an issue which will have to be tackled.

In general, few published accounts have not made clear how the hierarchical structure of schools affects the way in which decisions are actually taken (Price, 1985). What is presently required is close examination of the forms that participation takes when it is implemented in particular programmes of staff development and curriculum change. Are we, for instance, talking about 'paternalistic consultation' or 'radical staff democracy'? It is important that such alternative meanings of teacher participation are identified and examined in actual cases of educational change (Hargreaves, 1982). This will ensure that the concept of participation is not 'being used as a legitimating strategy for forms of social control, by securing the commitment of teachers to decisions they do not in fact make' (Hunter and Heighway, 1980).

Various methods of improving teachers' expertise in needs assessment have been suggested and tried. One approach is to develop an awareness of the demands of the task at the initial training level in such a way that the skill of the practising teachers and tutors involved in the training are enhanced at the same time.

The IT/INSET model provides a good example of this approach as it attempts to bring together initial training (IT) and in-service training (INSET) in a school-focused pattern. The scheme involves college tutors and students working co-operatively with teachers in their classroom for half or one day a week, ideally throughout the initial training period. The teacher is invited to select an area of curriculum for classroom work and this is then developed and implemented by the teacher/student/tutor team. The analysis which follows each session provides the basis for planning future work. In this way teacher, students and tutor engage in a cycle of

evaluation and development of that aspect of the curriculum (Ashton et al., 1981).

In both stages of teacher education (initial and in-service), the IT/INSET approach has an important purpose – the development of skills in reviewing the curriculum in co-operation with colleagues, so that the quality of education offered in schools is continuously improved. The skills requisite to this task are conceived as having six interrelated components:

1 analysing practice;
2 applying theory;
3 evaluating the curriculum;
4 developing the curriculum;
5 working as a team;
6 involving teachers in the school.

From a wider perspective it could be claimed that all classroom-based in-service education which attempts to help teachers become more reflective about their classroom practice in order to increase its effectiveness develops similar abilities (Day, 1981). It is indisputable that teachers possessing such skills are going to be better equipped to participate in more complex assessments relating to whole-school needs.

It is possible that classroom-centred approaches could help overcome two other problems associated with needs analysis. First, it has long been stated that the paradigm for INSET should be professional growth and not deficiency analysis (Henderson, 1979). This is a conceptualisation which can be realised only in a situation where teachers are fully aware of their own needs and are able to express these as equal partners. Secondly, the approach could help to ensure that needs are articulated at the required level of specificity. Many of the schools monitored by the SITE project identified areas of need (for example, mathematics, language) in such vague terms that effective INSET planning to meet them was virtually impossible (Baker et al., 1982). Such a situation should not arise if teachers are routinely evaluating and developing their work in the classroom.

Welsh Office INSET Project 1984–86

There have been comparatively few published studies on primary teachers' in-service needs. One exception is the large-scale research undertaken by Clark and Reid (1986) which reported on a Welsh Office sponsored project into the *In-Service Training Needs of Primary Teachers in West Glamorgan*. Owing to the dearth of information, a summary of the main findings is now presented. These data were obtained from headteachers, promoted and unpromoted teachers in 170 primary, junior and infant schools within the county. Clearly, individual findings will vary from region to region. Nevertheless, the value of the Report lies in its depth, the extent of the qualitative and quantitative data gathered, and the insights it provides in a county with a tradition for the in-service help which it maintains for its teachers. Given this background, the summary provides revealing insights into the state of in-service immediately prior to the 1987 regulations coming into force.

Summary of main findings

A *Policy, planning and organisation*

A.1 An extensive range of external course-based INSET is provided in the county. The LEA is active in encouraging teachers to participate in INSET and generous in providing financial support.

A2. The INSET programme has emerged in response to suggestions, initiatives and funding from a variety of sources and has lacked overall co-ordination.

A.3 There is no county INSET committee or policy-making body currently in existence. However, links between the LEA and providing agencies are being strengthened and proposals to cross the transbinary line (between university and LEA college provision) in delivering INSET are being considered.

B *Course provision 1983–86*

B.1 Most aspects of the primary curriculum with the exception of primary science are covered by longer award-bearing courses. There is currently no course dealing specifically with the infant/nursery stage. Level of provision remained steady between 1983–86.

B.2 Until the academic year 1985–86, primary science was also lacking from the shorter teachers' centre courses. There was also a significant diminution in the number of shorter courses offered by the LEA during this period due partly to the effects of teachers' sanctions.

B.3 Very few courses were offered in more general education-based areas during this period.

B.4 There is a lack of balance in courses in basic skills – many more hours are devoted to INSET courses in language and reading than mathematics.

C *INSET Needs of headteachers and teachers*

C.1 Headteachers would like to see more courses provided for their staff in primary science (69.4%), assessment and evaluation (64.5%) and classroom organisation (69.4%). Far fewer teachers expressed the need for more INSET provision though the areas identified were similar. For example, teachers also requested more courses in science (29.0%), assessment and evaluation (35.0%) and classroom organisation (25.0%).

C.2 Over a third of teachers (35.0%) find participation in INSET after school difficult due to domestic commitments, while a smaller proportion (15.0%) experience transport/time difficulties.

C.3 Almost half of all teachers (47.6%) are happy to attend courses which are provided partly in and partly out of school time.

C.4 The vast majority of teachers (73.2%) and heads (84.0%) are satisfied with existing provision for primary teachers in the county. However, under half (47.5%) of all heads are satisfied with existing provision for headteachers.

D *Extent of participation*

D.1 In the academic year 1983–84, over half of all teachers (51.6%) and two-thirds of heads (65.3%) stated that they participated in some form of INSET. Newer heads and heads of small schools participated more than experienced heads of large schools. However, in the case of the teachers, the least experienced and those from small schools participated less than fairly experienced teachers from large schools.

D.2 The whole range of formal course provision was well utilised. Degrees were pursued mainly by younger heads with the majority of teachers following curriculum-based, certificated courses.

D.3 Very few staff attended courses where the time was equally split inside and outside school hours.

D.4 School visits for INSET purposes were very infrequent for teachers.

E *Information*

E.1 Heads overwhelmingly insisted that they always pass on all information they receive about INSET to their staff.

E.2 The majority of teachers say that they obtain information about INSET from the LEA Course Handbook or Bulletin.

E.3 Most teachers do not consult anyone (for example, advisers or course organisers) nor are they approached by others when making choices about INSET, though a quarter say that they would discuss their choice with their headteacher.

E.4 Heads would most encourage the following types of teacher to participate in INSET:
  (i) post of responsibility holders (43.0%)
  (ii) active teachers who will disseminate new ideas in school (23.1%);
  (iii) teachers needing help either generally or specifically (39.7%).

F *Reasons for participating*

F.1 The majority of teachers say that they participate in INSET in order to 'update their knowledge' (78.6%). A similar proportion (80.0%) think that this should be a major purpose for INSET.

F.2 A third (33.0%) participate because they feel it might improve their career prospects. It is interesting to note that for 59.6% of all male teachers this is cited as a reason as compared with 26.0% of all female teachers.

F.3 Only 7.0% of teachers stated directly that they participated for the benefit of the school as a whole.

G *School INSET policy*

G.1 Over half of all teachers (52.0%) and a third of all heads considered that their school had an INSET policy.

G.2 Descriptions of policy were usually framed in terms of the schools' current practice (e.g. we send postholders on courses).

G.3 Over three-quarters of teachers (78.0%) think that their school should have an INSET policy and a similar proportion (74.0%) think that all staff should be involved in deciding the policy.

G.4 At present, decisions about INSET needs are taken by teachers individually (57.2%) or the headteacher alone (26.1%). In very few schools (14.3%) would the whole staff make these decisions.

G.5 Headteachers (41.0%) are far more likely than teachers (13.0%) to claim that INSET is provided within the school. This discrepancy relates to differential perceptions of the kind of activities which constitute school-based INSET.

H *Effective INSET*

H.1 Almost all teachers who had been involved in INSET mentioned an external course as the 'best' INSET activity they had attended (90.0%).

H.2 Half of the teachers who had participated in INSET stated that the best activity had been a practical course or workshop where materials had been produced for classroom use.

H.3 Half of the teachers complained about courses that were too theory based and tutored by unsuitable personnel.

H.4 Almost two-thirds of all teachers (63.8%) stated that the theory behind new ideas was sometimes clearly presented on courses while 58.0% stated that demonstration of the required skills was sometimes provided. However, two-thirds also stated that feedback was never given to a teacher about classroom performance following a course.

H.5 Regular, structured discussions with other staff (53.6%) and adequate resources in school (53.3%) were regarded by teachers as more helpful than workshop sessions (38.4%) or a course of lectures (21.8%) in attempting to implement new ideas in the classroom.

H.6 A good proportion of teachers (72.0%) and heads (69.0%) consider that teachers use new methods in the classroom some of the time following an INSET course. Very few teachers (3.7%) feel that they use new methods all of the time.

H.7 Less than a quarter of all teachers feel that attitudes or resources constitute barriers within their own school to implementing new ideas.

I *Dissemination in school*

I.1 More heads (29.8%) than teachers (14.9%) stated that an INSET course was *always* followed by a formal talk to a staff meeting.

I.2 Informal discussions with other staff constitute the most common form of dissemination following a course.

I.3 Working parties or demonstration lessons following an INSET course would only *sometimes* be used in less than a third of all schools.

I.4 Only a quarter of all teachers who had participated in INSET were asked to assist other teachers in their school following a course.

I.5 Almost three-quarters of all teachers (73.0%) would like to see scale postholders conduct more INSET sessions in schools.

INSET in school time

A pressing practical difficulty relates to the problems of finding time during the normal school day for thorough discussion of INSET needs. It has been suggested that each school which seeks to implement a policy of staff involvement must look to its priorities, manage its resources and adjust its commitments to find a solution, until such a time as some revision of national regulations may take account of the time necessary for staff consultation and planning.

Alternatively, it has been suggested that more school time could be made available for INSET if teachers ceased to equate their own hours with pupils' hours (Clark and Reid, 1986). Certainly this is a position which was debated in the 1987 review of the terms of teacher employment. The teachers' representatives described the LEAs' position in these negotiations as limited to a collective determination to deprive teachers of some of their existing conditions of service by demanding a contractual extension of the working day and a contractual reduction in the length of holidays while ensuring that teachers' salary levels are progressively depressed.

Use of consultants

Another approach which is often recommended, but rarely used, involves the use of consultants both in the process of needs analysis and programme implementation. In situations where consultants have been employed for these purposes there is evidence that schools have benefited considerably (Baker *et al.*, 1982; McLaughlin and Marsh, 1978; Sefton-Davies, 1982; Reynolds and Murgatroyd, 1984). That the consultancy system is not more widely used is not, however, surprising as neither the kind of relationship required, the nature of the task expected, nor the resource implications of this method have been adequately explored.

Eraut's (1972) model of school-focused in-service education links success in helping schools solve problems to the quality of the relationship which he sees as complex and problematic. He points to the possible 'power and authority gap between teachers and providers' related to their respective role positions; and also to an 'epistemological gap' between consultant and teacher which can itself be a major barrier to communication (Eraut, 1978).

While emphasising the importance of building a mutually supportive relationship with teachers based on the commitment of the consultant to serving the client needs, he develops a preliminary typology of consultants' roles which reflects the complexity of both purposes and processes of school-focused INSET:

1 the expert
2 the resource provider
3 the promoter (of an idea, etc.)

4 the career agent
5 the link agent
6 the inspector/evaluator
7 the legitimator
8 the ideas man
9 the process helper
10 the change agent.

Such a typology illustrates the range of consultancies that are potentially available to schools and teachers engaged in school-focused INSET.

In practice, it appears that teachers find some of these forms of consultancy more acceptable than others. Bolam (1982a) makes a broad but significant distinction between task and process consultancy and suggests that most successful consultancies have involved the former. The task consultant is usually invited into a school to help in a specified area (for example, aspects of mathematics teaching, assessment and record keeping). He thus works with highly specific problems which teachers have identified as areas of personal need. The key to successful task consultancy appears to rest in a consultant/client relationship which is based on mutual respect, equality of status, complementary skills and a wish to co-operate in the resolution of the problem (Sefton-Davies, 1982). The procedures employed by the IT/INSET scheme, already referred to, suggest one way of achieving this; another form could involve clinical supervision (Hopkins, 1982) of a teacher in the classroom, though this has to be carefully managed. Whatever the practical problems, teachers are more likely to be attracted to task consultancy because they believe their problems to be mainly of a curricular kind.

By contrast, the process consultant will be involved in helping the school with less obvious problems such as its underlying decision-making and problem-solving procedures. The area of concern in process consultancy would be 'departmental and school staff meetings, the way in which communication takes place in the school and ultimately the allocation of power and authority in the school' (Bolam, 1982a). The indications are that teachers find this kind of intervention unfamiliar and unwelcome (Sefton-Davies, 1982; Reynolds and Murgatroyd, 1984). However, despite its relative unpopularity, process consultancy offers a way of introducing organisation development into schools and for this reason has important implications for school-focused assessments and implementation.

Leaving aside the nature of the consultancy task, the question of who should act as a consultant to schools arises. Eraut (1978) considers that, excluding lay people:

> . . . a consultant is any external agent from within the educational system who involves himself in discussing the educational problems of a department or school with a view to improving the quality of teaching and learning.

In effect, such external agents tend to be either LEA advisers or college/institute lecturers. Queries about the suitability of these two groups for consultancy purposes are immediately raised; many teachers feel that advisers to some extent, and college lecturers in particular, are far too removed from the school situation to offer constructive help. In fact, many college lecturers have quite close relationships with schools through supervision of students on teaching practice and, increasingly, in other ways. However,

> unless teaching practice tutors are alert to the opportunities presented and trained in the stimulation of consciousness of needs, and unless the task of identification is given significance in timetabling and the organisation of teaching practice, this mode of identification can be formless and ineffective (Sefton-Davies, 1982).

Such a comment reflects the critical fact that, in general, neither college lecturers nor LEA advisers receive any training in the consultancy skills relating to clinical supervision or organisation development. There can be little doubt that, were such training avail-able, it would be taken up. A recent study of the role of LEA advisers in 14 English local authorities found that 70 per cent recognised that their position needed specific training, though only 15 per cent had received any (Bolam, Smith and Canter, 1979).

On a more practical level, the consultancy work of college lecturers can be limited because of the way in which it is financed and recognised. The present formulae for calculating staff/student ratios and the points count related to student hours, make it difficult for colleges to expend their efforts in short courses, school-focused INSET and consultancy. Such activities are very time-consuming compared with conventional courses and recognition of this is needed in the formulae. This recognition becomes more significant when it is appreciated that internal promotion is often based on the amount of higher-grade work (usually measured in terms of award-bearing courses) undertaken. The requirement that local authorities pay for any consultancy work done in their schools has also been recognised as an obstacle to further development. As a consequence, guidelines have been drawn up which have offered alternative forms of accountability for such work (DES, 1976a). These, unfortunately, have not been taken up and the latest ACSET proposals recommend a continuation of conventional financial arrangements (DES, 1984). The report expresses the hope that these arrangements will encourage the colleges to be more responsive to the specific needs of LEAs. However, in a time of contracting resources, it is possible that a curtailment of college activities in this direction will be the outcome.

This would be an unfortunate development as indications are emerging that college lecturers do have an important role to play in INSET. It has been noted, for example, that on occasions when lecturers have become involved in school INSET programmes, they have been found helpful (Donoughue et al., 1981). In their American survey of INSET programmes, Howey and Joyce concluded that on the basis of all the evidence:

... reward structure, available time and logistical problems were greater deterrents than lack of competence on the part of college lecturers, or their need to acquire credibility in the eyes of teachers. (Howey and Joyce, 1979)

Implementation of INSET

The evidence so far presented has stressed that in order to be effective INSET must:

(a) address the needs of school as well as those of individual teachers;
(b) be planned in full consultation with all staff;
(c) relate to specific, clearly defined objectives, perceived as priorities;
(d) utilise outside consultants.

In addition, opportunities must be given for the ideas and techniques derived from INSET to be developed in the school/classroom situation. How can this best be done? There are no simple answers to this question though the literature on INSET does suggest methods which are unlikely to be effective. Much has been learned in this area from the experience of the early national curriculum development projects. These projects demonstrated that, in most cases, curriculum changes were not instituted in schools even after teachers had been introduced to and familiarised with the new ideas and materials (either by lecture, workshop or demonstration). If implementation were to occur, then far more effort was required in terms of developing the materials to suit the particular class, individualising programmes, modifying attitudes, changing established patterns of work and organisation and supporting the teacher through unpredicted obstacles and problems. A distinction, therefore, had to be drawn between the dissemination and implementation phases of curriculum change.

Not only British but American experience has highlighted this distinction. Following a review of many large-scale surveys, Fullan (1979) concluded that if new curricula are to be effectively introduced into the classroom, then changes must occur in the materials used, the existing structural arrangements, teachers' comprehension of the underlying philosophy, teaching skills and prevailing assessment techniques. While much effort has been expended on developing and disseminating new materials, not enough attention has been paid to how change can be induced in teachers and structures.

In the United States, McLaughlin and Marsh (1978) looked specifically at the question of teacher change and found that various clusters of factors contributed in motivating teachers to acquire new skills and helping them to retain these.

1 Institutional leadership – a positive attitude of the principal and a supportive organisational environment proved essential.
2 Institutional motivation – collaborative planning between district administrators and school staff in combination with a complex and ambitious project (as opposed to a routine and limited one) elicited the highest degree of teacher commitment to change.
3 Project implementation strategies – found that skill-specific training was effective only in the short run and that staff support activities in the form of classroom assistance and use of outside consultants had much longer-term effects on teacher change.

The message seems to be that fewer courses but far more support services are needed.

Clearly, support in implementing change can come from many sources – course organisers, the advisory service, teachers' centre wardens, college lecturers – though the small numbers and restricted time available to these groups is bound to impose limits on their effectiveness. Many authorities have recently appointed advisory teachers or (probably a better title) curriculum support teachers, whose specific role is to help teachers in the school situation. Seconded teachers who then return to the classroom are often used in this capacity and for this reason they often have

159

credibility in the eyes of practising teachers (Brighouse, 1981).

It is becoming clear, though, that this supporting role is increasingly been seen as the responsibility of the curriculum leader within the school. Recent specifications of curriculum leaders, duties in government documents have indicated that their role is moving from a position of marginality in the curriculum to one of centrality. It is now recommended that curriculum leaders should play a more substantial curricular leadership role in order to influence the quality of work throughout the school (DES, 1978b).

In order to do this, such leaders need to possess:

(a) curricular skills which should incorporate knowledge of subject, ability to devise and implement a programme of work and ability to relate this programme to both the developmental stage of the child, and the resources available;
(b) interpersonal skills which should include the social skills necessary to work with colleagues, lead discussion groups, teach alongside colleagues and inspire confidence as well as representing the subject to outsiders.

A study (Campbell, 1984) has examined in some detail the role of postholders as curriculum developers in 10 primary schools and has provided useful empirical data on the potential and difficulties of the position. While in most schools the postholder was perceived as valuable and knowledgeable in guiding discussions and formulating curriculum policy, friction resulted when they attempted to monitor implementation of decisions and work alongside other colleagues. This was often perceived as inspectorial and threatening by colleagues and resulted in the postholder withdrawing from this role and settling for staff taking the initiative in seeking advice. This is an important finding as it suggests that it is not simply the perceived status of the person entering the classroom which is seen as threatening (for example, headteacher or adviser) but the activity itself. It also maybe

calls for some querying of teachers' claims that their most effective learning experiences are provided by colleagues.

Seven of the postholders also experienced some degree of uncertainty, ambiguity and conflict in their role arising from pressures:

(a) to simultaneously fulfil other roles (for example, as class teacher);
(b) to assume an authoritative role, while at the same time respecting the autonomy of the classroom teacher.

However, an overriding difficulty related to finding time for the work or the inflexibility imposed in situations where a limited amount of time was allocated at the same time each week. The study highlights the 'critical need for revised conceptions of the use of teacher time for in-school development' and that 'lack of time combined with inappropriate arrangements for curriculum analysis and discussion' must now be recognised as major obstacles to effective development (Campbell, 1984). Once again it appears that it is not lack of expertise but problems of structure and organisation that are paramount (Clark and Reid, 1986).

The last two chapters have looked at IN-SET from many perspectives and have presented evidence found in the literature concerning ways in which provision might be made more effective. The central message is that INSET has many purposes which extend from broadening the horizons or providing specific assistance to individual teachers, to tackling policy issues which could fundamentally influence the organisation or curriculum of the school as a whole. However, where the aim of the INSET is to improve the quality of education in individual schools, then a much closer match between needs and provision must be attained. The corollary is that schools must become responsible for assessing and articulating their needs and that providers must tailor their courses or services to meet their demands. A far more flexible pattern of provision which stimulates the development of INSET within schools is therefore needed (Clark and Reid, 1986).

16 The new teacher

Before new entrants into teaching receive qualified teacher status (often referred to as QTS), they have to successfully complete a probationary period. Despite a great deal of literature on the subject (Brinton and Watson, 1975; Hannam *et al.*, 1976), there remains a surprising degree of anxiety and ignorance about the topic. Much of this emanates from three sources: recent legislative changes; misunderstandings resulting from popular myths about the implications of probation; and new teachers having an incomplete understanding

of what is meant by the term 'probation'. The Baker proposals on education and the teachers' agreements reached in Coventry, Nottingham and London during 1986 and 1987, suggest that the length of probation will be extended from one to two years. Although the length of probation looks likely to increase, there is no existing body of research on the advantages or otherwise of the longer period. It is often asserted that the probationary period *per se* is at present inadequate (Reid, 1984b; 1985c).

Consequently, this chapter attempts to clarify the prevailing situation in the light of all the evidence. To achieve this aim, the chapter is subdivided into sections. Later sections will examine research findings on the induction of new teachers, including the influential HMI Report on *The New Teacher in School* (DES, 1982b) and data obtained from the respondents of the 1979/80 SPITE (Structure and Process of Initial Teacher Education within Universities) cohort of 4,350 postgraduate student teachers obtained near or at the end of their probationary period in 1981 (Reid and Patrick, 1980; Reid, Patrick and Bernbaum, 1981; Patrick, Bernbaum and Reid, 1983; Bernbaum, Patrick and Reid, 1983; 1985a,b); and make a number of constructive suggestions for professionals to follow.

First, however, it is important to dispel the myths, to describe the induction and assessment procedures and to provide a feel of new teachers' problems through some verbatim statements made at an 'induction' session.

Defining probation?

Schedule 11 of the School Regulations states that:

> The initial period of service of a teacher as a qualified teacher shall be a probationary period (which in the case of a full-time teacher who has satisfactorily completed any course of training other than a course outside the United Kingdom as mentioned in Regulation 16(2)(*a*) shall be one year and

in the case of any other teacher shall be two years) during which he may be required to satisfy the Secretary of State of his practical proficiency as a teacher, but in exceptional cases the Secretary of State may approve a probationary period which is less or more than one year (or as the case may be, two years), or dispense with it entirely.

Shorn of technicalities, what this means is that teachers who successfully completed an approved course of teacher training, or graduates of British universities who had also completed a course of professional training at a university department or college of education (PGCE), were required to do a one-year period of probation. All other entrants, such as teachers from overseas who had been granted qualified status by the Secretary of State, were required to do a two-year period of probation. This applied to all newly-qualified teachers employed in maintained primary, middle and secondary schools, maintained and non-maintained special schools and direct grant schools other than direct grant grammar schools in England and Wales.

The Baker Pay Deal imposed in 1987 makes it a condition of service that teachers should 'contribute to the selection for appointment and professional development of other teachers, including the assessment of probationary teachers', as directed by the headteacher. According to the 1986 Education Act, school governing bodies have to be consulted on whether to extend probation or not, and receive a report on candidates. Therefore, progression to qualified teacher status is subject to a more rigorous assessment than before. Moves may soon be afoot to extend the probationary period to two years. Local education authorites are now advised to produce a handbook for probationary teachers. Some have done this for years.

It should be noted that the probationary period in Scotland has always been two years. Likewise, the notion of a probationary period is not peculiar to Britain. It is normal practice in many other countries such as the United States.

The purpose of probation is partly to make sure that newly-qualified teachers are capable of making the crucial transition from trainees to teachers. This is well expressed in Article 39 of the UNESCO document on the status of teachers which states:

A probationary period on entry to teaching should be recognised both by teachers and employers as the opportunity for the encouragement and helpful initiation of the entrant and for the establishment and maintenance of proper professional standards as well as the teacher's own development of his practical teaching proficiency. The normal duration of probation should be known in advance and the conditions for its satisfactory completion should be strictly related to professional competence. If the teacher is failing to complete his probation satisfactorily, he should be informed of the reasons and should have the right to make representations.

Hence the probationary period is intended to discover whether the former student is capable of becoming, with further development and experience, a fully efficient teacher.

It is now virtually agreed by all parties involved in teacher education – the colleges and departments of education, the local education authorities, the DES, student and teacher unions, and probably a majority of teachers – that the completion of a course of training does not mean that the newly qualified teacher is fully equipped for the job. Neither is the newly trained doctor, dentist, solicitor, accountant or any other professional man or woman for that matter. Clearly, experience is a vital factor in any professional person's growing competence.

Thus the probationary period should be considered a necessary and significant stage in the continued professional development of the young teacher. No one should really expect that by the end of the probationary period the teacher will have reached perfection or anything like it. What is looked for is evidence of development on the right lines, showing ap-plication and the potential to become a good and fully competent teacher (DES, 1982b).

Probationary year myths

In the past a number of myths and misunderstandings surrounded the probationary year. Before proceeding further, therefore, it might be useful to clarify some of these popular misconceptions lest old myths become perpetuated in the new system.

First, probation starts from the moment a new teacher commences a full-time appointment as a qualified teacher in a maintained school in England and Wales. The probationary period, however, does not necessarily have to begin or follow on immediately upon the successful completion of an initial training course, or within any specified time. It is totally untrue that newly-qualified teachers have to undertake their probation within five years of qualification despite the persistent rumour to this effect. This popular misconception caused great concern to many newly qualified teachers who failed to obtain posts immediately after completing their BEd or PGCE courses.

Secondly, probation cannot be served abroad. If a newly-trained teacher goes abroad before undertaking or completing the probationary period, he or she will normally be subject to probation on returning to the UK to teach in a maintained school. There is only one exception. In certain limited circumstances, the Secretary of State may be prepared to recognise teaching service in the British Families Education Service in Germany, and in other British Service Schools Overseas. It is a moot point since, technically, probation cannot be served in these establishments. Nevertheless, in practice, the requirement may be waived if the teacher returns to this country with suitable recommendations from the Inspectorate. People contemplating voluntary service overseas, or taking other forms of short- or long-term employment overseas, have to make a personal decision about whether to go before or after completing their probationary year, bearing in mind the prevailing 'market' forces.

Thirdly, the power to dispense with probation, to shorten or extend it, is normally only exercised by the Secretary of State in exceptional cases, and not necessarily even then. Usually this applies only to teachers entering the maintained school system after good experience as teachers in the non-maintained sector. Such exceptions also depend on strong support from the employing authority. It is often not fully appreciated that the waiving or shortening of the probationary period for 'returners' from the independent sector is far from automatic.

Fourthly, since 1968 part-time teaching in maintained primary and secondary schools can be counted towards probation requirements. The appropriate period of probation for all teachers concerned is determined by the Secretary of State, but it is normally equivalent to the appropriate full-time requirement.

In this connection, 'supply' or 'relief' teaching is a thorny issue. The DES advises local authorities that it is particularly undesirable for a probationer to be placed on the supply staff of an authority if teaching in a number of different schools for short periods would be entailed. Teaching well in such circumstances is difficult enough even for experienced teachers. As a result, many authorities actually exclude the use of probationers in this role but policies vary between authorities throughout England and Wales. It is possible, however, to secure recognition of a continuous period of at least one term's teaching in the same school for probationary purposes. In practice, the degree of supervision exercised by the head and other colleagues during the supply teaching period is the critical factor. People who are unsure about their precise circumstances should ensure that the appropriate arrangements are made for them at the beginning of any fixed time which is likely to last at least a term, whether on supply or temporary appointment. New entrants on short-period fixed-term contracts should seek individual clarification from their authority on this matter because their position is more complicated than the norm. For example, under certain circumstances, if the larger part of the probationary period has been served, the authority may, exceptionally, recommend that probation has been satisfactorily completed. Periods of less than two terms' duration rarely qualify for this exemption.

Fifthly, primary and secondary trained teachers do not necessarily have to obtain employment in the stage of education for which they were trained. Those trained for the primary years can take a first appointment and serve their probationary period in a secondary school if they wish, and vice versa. People to whom this might apply should note, however, that the school and the local authority are asked by the DES to see that teachers are placed in conditions which give them the opportunity to demonstrate their professional competence. Clearly, some secondary trained teachers are more likely to struggle in a primary school than others.

Sixthly, all teachers in maintained schools should have completed an approved course of professional training. Graduate equivalent qualifications acquired after 31 December, 1973 are no longer sufficient for the achievement of qualified teacher status unless accompanied by professional training. Former regulations which entitled holders of science and maths degrees and certain other qualifications in the fields of art, handicraft, music, needlecraft and domestic subjects to enter teaching conditional only upon the successful completion of a two-year probationary period have recently been rescinded.

Finally, it is normally considered unwise to change posts during probation although if a second post is obtained in the first year, it does not interfere with probation provided the appointments are continuous and served in maintained schools. It is irrelevant whether the second post is with the same or a different local education authority.

Induction

Induction is the process by which new teachers receive structured professional support and guidance as they begin the practice of their work. At least, that is the theory.

A number of DES-funded projects (DES, 1977a; C. McCabe, 1978; Bolam, Baker and McMahon, 1979; Davis, 1979) and 'unsponsored' induction schemes in Avon, Clwyd, Cumbria, East Sussex, Gloucestershire, Leeds, Newcastle upon Tyne, Northamptonshire and elsewhere have explored structures and programmes for the induction of newly-qualified teachers. These have included release from a proportion of the school timetable for further training, with staff (usually supply teachers) made available to cover classes, and the use of experienced teachers, either on the school staff or acting in a peripatetic capacity, as supervisors for each new teacher. Although few of the pilot schemes were entirely successful, many authorities continue to make positive attempts to establish helpful local arrangements of various kinds (Hill, 1975; Baker, 1976; 1978), despite the financial constraints imposed on them in recent years.

Induction is the first stage of in-service training. Schemes are generally difficult to evaluate (Bolam, 1981) because they are dealing with the rather ill-defined areas of personal and professional development and with the long-term effects of these upon attitudes, teaching performance and benefits to schools and children. Whatever type of induction scheme is adopted, a reduced teaching load seems to be a critical element in its success, since without this facility, many useful induction activities cannot take place (Baker, 1978). Inexperienced teachers, for example, often take longer to complete 'chores' such as marking and preparation than experienced staff, which may only add to the problem if release time is not granted.

There is increasing evidence that courses which: are school-based; are run by 'internal' rather than 'external' staff; include probationers who are being 'fostered' by teacher tutors; have positive personalities and attitudes towards their work, stand the greatest chance of success. In this latter connection it is worth noting that there is some disagreement in the literature about the extent of teachers' attitude changes (measured on the liberal-traditional paradigm) in their first year (Morrison and McIntyre, 1967; C. McCabe, 1978; 1979; Richardson, 1981). While most writers agree that new teachers generally swing towards the traditional, rather than the liberal philosophy of their college or university days, exceptions do occur and it can be dangerous to generalise or put too much faith in these findings. Clearly, there is evidence that some schools are more liberal than others in their ethos. In any event, very little is known about how and why these changes occur (Lacey, 1977).

Case data

Case studies of probationary teachers are by no means unusual. Several short and long accounts of part of or the whole of the probationary period have been written, usually from autobiographical perspectives. For instance, Otty's (1972) anecdotal compilation of extracts from his probationary diary is probably the best known and most widely read with its insights into his traumas and the coping behaviour he adopted during his first year as a teacher.

For many probationers the first year oscillates between an ostensibly comfortable passage and a hassle. A lot of confident probationers carefully conceal their true feelings from colleagues. Extreme examples of self-doubt, loneliness, isolation and anger can be obtained from reading the relevant literature, as some new teachers despise the lack of help and information which is given to them at the start of their careers (Hannam et al., 1976). These facts are acknowledged by teachers' unions and the DES alike. One union official once called the probationary period 'a great strain', while an official document regards it as a 'test of survival' (DES, 1976b). Experienced teachers, therefore, should not take an outward sign of calm as necessarily meaning competence or inward strength. Being a new teacher in a school is an emotional experience in itself. Given the level of help currently on offer, it should come as no surprise to anyone when some probationers express feelings of disappointment and frustration and even enter into unnecessary conflict situations.

Early research

The probationary period has been extensively studied, probably because of interest in the relevance of initial teacher training and of extending training into this period. Lacey (1977) considers it unfortunate that:

> . . . the scatter of probationers in a variety of schools and the rather pragmatic focus of the investigations have given rise to a series of fact-finding questionnaire surveys that have contributed little to an understanding of the process of socialization of teachers. At the other end of the scale, there have been a number of publications incorporating highly impressionistic reports, many of them autobiographical from practising teachers (Hannam *et al.*, 1976) which are often vivid, but usually fall short of giving background information and are too idiosyncratic to give a reliable picture.

One of the best known of these studies is the work of Taylor and Dale (1971) who conduct a survey between 1966 and 1969 of 4,000 probationers and their headteachers. Their report subsequently served as a basis for future work in the United Kingdom with probationary teachers and provided a much-needed stimulus to the issue. Amongst their many findings, Taylor and Dale reported that extension rates for probationers are higher in secondary than primary schools in those schools with a higher than average intake of children from 'difficult' neighbourhoods. Probationers who taught in urban rather than rural schools, who were not invited to an induction programme and who were working in an authority which was not their first choice,

were also more likely to have their probation extended.

A considerable amount of early research into the probationary year concentrated on the continuity and relevance of training to the early teaching experience, in order to feed back information to training courses. These studies led to the reform of some initial teacher training programmes. For example, Rudd and Wiseman (1962) reported on the findings of a questionnaire issued to 590 teachers trained at the Manchester University School of Education. A low correlation was found between headteachers' ratings of probationary teachers, and their college grades. Early teacher dissatisfaction appeared to be more related to teaching factors than training aspects. The former included salaries, teaching loads, buildings, large classes and poor personal relationships.

Wiseman and Start (1965) undertook a follow-up study of 248 teachers nearly five years after training. Their findings showed little relationship between the continuity of grades obtained in training and 'success' (promotion) in the profession, satisfaction in teaching or even the headteachers' assessment of current work.

Less discontinuity was found in Clark and Nisbet's (1963) study of 242 teachers' experiences during their first two years of teaching and their attitudes to their courses of training. They reported a small positive correlation between teaching practice assessment and assessments made by inspectors nearly two years later (end of Scottish probation). But even in this sample there were signs of discord and discontinuity. Illustratively, a third of the probationers found teaching to be, at times, a strain on the health. Difficulties with discipline emerged as a major problem.

Cornwell *et al.* (1965) reported that one-third of a large sample of primary teachers did not have a syllabus made available to them before the beginning of their first term. Major discrepancies emerged between the perception of the probationers and their headteachers. For instance, 69 per cent of the headteachers stated that the probationers had major disciplinary problems. Conversely, only 22 per cent of the probationers shared their opinion. Overall, the headteachers' perception of probationers emerged as people who: lacked the ability to maintain order in the classroom; had problems with less able children due to inappropriate teaching methods; were prone to poor organisation and inadequate preparation. The probationary teachers' perspectives of their situation were that their problems were due to poor equipment, inadequate buildings, lack of books, bad discipline in the school and the lack of a coherent school policy. Hence there was a tendency for headteachers to blame the probationers themselves for their difficulties. By contrast, the new teachers tended to find fault with their schools, headteachers and the general lack of facilities – everything but themselves.

Interestingly, both Taylor and Dale (1971) and Cornwell *et al.* (1965) found that 'the headteacher' and 'an experienced colleague of our choice' were the people most consulted by probationers when they needed help and advice. In secondary schools, however, the head was considered to be more remote than in primary schools. Thus experienced colleagues and the informal staffroom discussion ranked above headteachers in these schools. Further work by Butcher (1965), Oliver and Butcher (1965; 1968), Cohen (1969), McLeish (1970) and Cope (1971) underline the importance of the discontinuity between training and the reality of teaching.

In one revealing experiment conducted in the United States, Edgar and Warren (1969) studied probationary teachers. They found that when new teachers were made aware of the person responsible for their evaluation, significant changes took place in their attitudes towards their evaluators. Cases were found of probationary teachers attempting to ape their assessors' teaching styles – presumably in the hope of creating the right sort of impression.

Previous research, therefore, seems to suggest that new teachers see their major problems arising from discipline and difficult teaching assignments – classroom-orientated problems. Probationers seem to depend for help mainly on the formal structure of the school, the headmaster, or senior colleagues. They may equally turn for advice and assistance to the friendly colleague and the person they like.

Newer research

In this section, the influential HMI Report on the *New Teacher in School* (DES, 1982b) is considered, as well as some findings from the SPITE Project (Bernbaum, Patrick and Reid, 1985a,b).

The New Teacher in School

HMI (DES, 1982) visited a sample of 294 schools in England and Wales in which newly qualified BEd and PGCE trained teachers were spending their first year of teaching. In each case one new teacher was observed at work. The specialism of the visiting HMI was matched to the age level and nature of the work with which the teacher was mainly concerned.

The overall picture presented by the survey is a very mixed one. For example, the report states that nearly one in four of the probationers was in some respects poorly equipped with the skills needed for teaching. Three out of ten of the new teachers met with conditions in schools unlikely to promote their professional development. Many of these teachers were receiving little support from headteachers or fellow staff. Many, in both primary and secondary schools, were engaged in teaching subjects in which they had little academic background.

By contrast, the findings showed that a majority of the probationers were well trained, appointed to suitable posts, given teaching tasks which called upon their skills and knowledge, and provided with support in those areas in which they needed help. A considerable amount of 'job satisfaction' was found, especially amongst primary school teachers. HMI reported that the effectiveness in the classroom of some newly-qualified teachers was impressive. Few showed serious weaknesses that were not in part attributable to inexperience and likely to be remediable, given suitable conditions for teaching.

It is worth recording that while HMI rated over three-quarters of the probationary teachers as adequately equipped or better for their posts, their headteachers thought an even higher proportion was well prepared for teaching. Conversely, it is very disturbing to find that approximately 25 per cent of the probationers were poorly equipped for teaching especially when far more teachers are trained than posts available. The report suggests that training institutions should weed out their weaker teachers and considers that the assessment of teaching practice may be less rigorous than it should be or it may be carried out in conditions of such artificiality as not to make it an adequate test. Finally, HMI found that the personal qualities of the teachers were in many cases the decisive factor in their effectiveness. Although the practical performances of the probationers were generally very good, a high proportion of them expressed dissatisfaction with some aspects of their initial training programme.

The report made a number of strong recommendations. Of these, six stand out.

(a) Training institutions should carry out a more effective process of 'quality control' to ensure that only those who have the qualities of personality and temperament as well as the academic and professional skills needed for teaching are awarded teaching qualifications.

(b) Those responsible for first appointments should take personal and temperamental factors into consideration as well as the academic and professional preparation of the candidates in determining their fitness to teach in a particular school.

(c) The appointments of teachers to schools should be the result of a thorough process of selection which seeks to ensure that the best possible match of qualifications and teaching tasks is achieved. This match is

particularly important in the case of first posts, both in the interests of the pupils and of the teachers themselves.

(d) There is a strong case to be made for the setting up of national guidelines which should indicate both the acceptable minimum and the desirable levels of support that should be available for all new teachers both from the schools and local authorities, taking account of good practice. In drawing up a detailed induction programme, schools and local education authorities should consider ways of providing help for probationers according to individual needs.

For instance, the report cites examples of new teachers being inadequately prepared for mixed ability teaching, assessment, the teaching of ethnic minorities and socially deprived children, and the matching of work to pupils' capacities. In this connection HMI generally found the probationers working under constraints which might have been avoided (inadequate resources, over-large classes, drab buildings). The Inspectorate considered that these factors often had a significant and bad effect upon the quality of the work which was taking place.

(e) Both induction and probation requirements should influence the planning of the new teachers' teaching programme. Perhaps, in the lower term, the possibility should be considered of separating the two processes and requiring a year's probation after the completion of an induction year.

HMI recognised that BEd and PGCE trained teachers require different induction schemes. As the PGCE is such a short course, the report suggests that these probationers need more mastery of a range of teaching skills. The report states that:

PGCE trained primary teachers require more emphasis on a wide range of curriculum areas in addition to a greater mastery of at least one part of the primary school curriculum. By contrast, BEd trained teachers seem to require courses which focus on the enhancement of their subjects rather than developing teaching skills.

(f) It is not a satisfactory condition either for induction or probation that new teachers be required to teach a subject in which they are not personally competent – nor is it likely to be a rewarding experience for the pupils in their classes. (DES, 1982b)

Further comment is necessary on some of these points. First, it is very difficult to accurately judge a potential trainee's temperament and personality at interview. Without adequate instruments for the purpose, most of these decisions are bound to be subjective. Hence errors of judgement are always likely to occur. How can you really tell if and when an 18- or 22-year-old is really suitable for teaching? Likewise, without really explicit testimonials and references, how can headteachers and their appointment panels be sure that a recently-qualified graduate teacher is the right person for the job and their school? A cross-section of popular gossip in staffrooms up and down the country would soon put anyone right on this matter. There are few schools up and down the country which are fortunate enough to have completely integrated and united staffrooms.

Secondly, it is highly unlikely that the length of initial training will be extended in any significant way during an era of constraint and cutback. Thus the notion of linking probation and initial training is presently a dead duck. The overall training period could be extended, however, by separating induction and probation, without a substantial cost to the exchequer. If such a scheme were introduced, a number of potential teething troubles would need sorting out. For example, as new teachers take up their appointments throughout Britain, it would be very difficult to link induction schemes with the original training establishment – unless a new teacher was forced to seek employment for a period in the same area as his or her college or department of education. This might not only prove unpopular but dramatically change national recruitment patterns.

Thirdly, there is every reason to suppose that the DES will draw up guidelines for more rigorous school-based induction programmes for all new teachers, to be carried out by local authorities. This should have been done a long time ago. The present situation whereby some new teachers are given induction programmes while others are not is ludicrous.

Fourthly, without a nationally agreed common core initial training curriculum, the content of induction schemes is unlikely to suit everybody. Surveys of the content of initial training courses (Patrick, Bernbaum and Reid, 1983a,b) have shown the remarkable diversity in practice between institutions, subjects and age ranges.

The SPITE project ascertained that new teachers working in primary and middle schools tended to get more help from the head or deputy head than is common in other phases of schooling. Local authority advisers were generally of more help to primary teachers than their secondary counterparts. Primary teachers, too, were more likely to have been on an 'induction' course of one sort or another than their peers in secondary schools. The types of induction courses varied considerably. Many were only of the adviser-talk variety or on ways of teaching individual subjects.

Two-fifths of the new teachers stated that their schools had made special arrangements for them when they started their work. This was less true in primary schools that others. Such arrangements generally took a variety of forms. Usually there was a senior member of staff with responsibility for all probationers in the school. Many probationers attended meetings specially arranged for new teachers. The survey found that some probationers were given fewer teaching periods than other members of staff or were relieved of tasks such as playground duties. Alternative arrangements mentioned were short courses in the school to introduce new teachers before the term began, opportunities to observe other new teachers at work and a requirement to submit lesson plans to the head before using them. Over 40 per cent (40.7%) of the cohort stated that they would have liked a course at the end of their first year to help them with their work.

Advice for professionals

Local authorities, headteachers and staff can do a great deal to ease the burden of new teachers through enlightened and empathetic policies. But first they need to be clear about a few points. They have to be able to distinguish between new teachers' initial and later anxieties. Explicitly, probationers' early concerns usually include finding their way around the school, having an appropriate syllabus and scheme of work, worry that they know less about the way things are done in school than their pupils, or that some of the pupils may be more able than themselves, worry over appropriate sanctions, what standard of work to accept and achieving a good standing in the eyes of their colleagues. Later, they may worry more about their overall school performance, pupil and teacher criticism (the first year can be a particularly sensitive time), and, especially, practical methods of dealing with classes (McCabe, 1978).

Probationers usually welcome all forms of positive support from their schools. Ideally, schools should adopt active induction programmes. In this respect, schools should appoint a wise, senior person to co-ordinate these in-house induction schemes. It should be remembered that new teachers generally prefer specific advice on aspects of their classroom performance to more general titbits. Although probationers are frequently reluctant to have their own teaching observed, most find this a helpful activity – particularly when the observer's comments are well articulated. Observers have a key role to play in this process. They should endeavour to be both critical and constructive. Praise can go a long way. Over a period of time, significant changes and improvements in teaching and managerial performance should be pointed out.

In view of the preference for school-based support, Baker *et al.*, (1982) suggest that LEAs could work through their advisers to encourage schools to implement their own planned induction support for probationers. This should be seen as a crucial part of the LEA's in-service training programme as well as part of an individual school's staff development policy. Local authorities and individual schools should ensure that appropriate booklets are provided for new staff about the running of the authority and their school.

Probationers themselves should endeavour to be active not passive in their work. It is essential that they are firm with pupils in their first few weeks of teaching. This is crucial for their success and survival. Although most students are repeatedly told this during their initial training, many young teachers continue to create long-term problems for themselves by trying too hard to be liked – especially by the pupils. Respect is won, not given freely. It is much simpler to ease-up on discipline than change direction in mid-stream. Students and new teachers who try too hard to be liked by their pupils often end up by being disliked by their colleagues as well. After all, they may be giving them more work.

All teachers nearing the end of their probationary period should ask their headteacher what the likely recommendation will be in their case. Don't be too shy. Although the local authority should automatically supply confirmation of successful completion, new teachers should be prepared to ask for their letter if they have not received it. Similarly, ask about the reasons for any extension period. Primary schools with good induction schemes will usually give this information without a request being made.

Under certain circumstances the LEA advisers or inspectors, the teacher's former college or department of education, teachers' unions and HMI can be approached. If something goes drastically wrong, union help can always be sought. For serious offences, such as striking a pupil (even if inadvertently), it is vital and common sense to obtain the correct advice, more especially if there is any chance of legal action being taken. If major personality or educational problems occur, arrangements can sometimes be made to make a fresh start in different surroundings.

Primary headteachers should ensure that new teachers in their school are well catered for and looked after, in terms of advice, information and professional assistance.

Sometimes a wide ranging, structured discussion between a recent appointee and the headteacher is one of the best ways of going about this process.

Despite all the work which has taken place, the probationary period remains an immensely personal and unique experience. How a new teacher starts is likely to determine much more than mere initial success – it is likely to shape his or her entire future.

17 Towards effective teaching in primary schools

Background issues

One of the difficulties in discussing the effective primary school lies in attempting to define exactly what 'effective' means. The label 'effective' is usually seen in terms of achieving a result of some sort, that is:

> It defines the interdependent relationships between purpose, effort and accomplishments. (Brodie, 1983)

Thus if you install double glazing into your home, you would expect an increase in warmth and a decrease in your heating bills. If this did not happen you would start complaining: 'It hasn't made the slightest difference.' In other words, you will judge the effectiveness of the product against its aims and by its outcomes. Therefore, effectiveness is linked to output.

Very few people would disagree with your laudable attempts at energy conservation as the outcome measures are easily discernible. This is not always possible. If, for example, you start considering an 'effective' colour scheme in your kitchen, how are you to measure the outcome? By juxtaposing the colours red and green perhaps? In this latter case your 'output measure' is based upon your own personal judgement. Indeed, your valuation could well differ significantly from that of other people like your next door neighbour. In

other words, the term 'effectiveness' can sometimes be used to describe outcomes which are recognisable but extremely difficult to define or measure in any quantitative sense.

Applying these notions to the complexities of the primary school, it soon becomes clear that in one sense the effective primary school 'gets results'. For instance, the school gets good results on measurable outcomes such as attendance, pupils' reading ages or attainment test scores. There are, however, many aspects of the process of primary education which do not lend themselves to such measurable outcomes. These include, for example, the sense of wonder in a child who observes a crystal under a microscope or the aesthetic quality of children's drawings which cannot be assessed in this way without severe distortion of the whole enterprise. Nevertheless, these non-cognitive outcomes are an indispensable part of the 'effective' primary school.

Part of the attraction of the idea of primary school effectiveness is the feeling that if only the 'Holy Grail' (a series of measurements and instruments of measurement) could be found then schools could be allocated 'effective' or 'ineffective' labels in total or in part and practice subsequently maintained or improved.

Many have hoped – and are still hoping – for blueprints of the 'effective' or 'high achieving' school or for clear visions of what makes the effective teacher, so that practice can be directly improved. (Reynolds, 1985a)

Any verdict on effectiveness is largely a matter of judgement. To make any sense at all, a prerequisite is that there must be a set of aims and objectives against which performances can be compared. We have already hinted at some of the problems in making this equation as the aims of primary education are in themselves problematic.

There is far from unanimity about what aims should be pursued and which are more important, even among teachers. (Ashton, 1978)

Hence effectiveness is linked to questions of value. Eisner (1974) raises this critical notion when judging schools. Speaking of the problems in defining the effectiveness of the Plowden-orientated English primary school he writes:

In the final analysis, the value perceived in such schools will be largely a function of the values that individual educators hold. And these values will themselves be influenced by political beliefs and by the vested professional interests that all of us possess.

Therefore, different professionals or pressure groups will judge the 'effectiveness' of a school in different ways.

Effectiveness is also context bound. What is judged effective in one situation may not be in another (Brodie, 1983). Outcomes cannot merely be seen as being produced by "effective' or 'ineffective' schools without consideration of other factors. These include an understanding of pupils' backgrounds, social circumstances and geographical and community influences (Reynolds, 1982). Thus a working-class child may reject school rules because of their predominantly middle-class nature.

Before leaving this introductory discussion of 'effectiveness', it is important to consider the related concept of 'efficiency'. Efficiency is concerned with maximising output from input, achieving maximum return for effort. Brodie (1983) uses the useful analogy of driving a motor car to distinguish the two ideas. Efficiency in driving is to do with speed, control and skill. One may be a very efficient driver, but be heading in totally the wrong direction, hence ineffective. A school may have an efficient headteacher, but be steering the wrong course. Effectiveness is to do with purpose and direction. So in discussing effectiveness we are considering how far we have travelled and in what direction. To extend the analogy further into primary education, we are concerned with the mode of travel; with means as well as ends.

For educational purposes teachers need to know in which direction they are being asked to steer. It is our contention that any effective primary school has at its heart this sense of purpose which is fundamental to all subsequent endeavour. This purpose is maintained by the headteacher and individual members of staff constantly asking such questions as 'What is school for?'

The good school keeps asking this question. If we don't really know, the school and its functionaries are without clear authority. The good school is an authority structure rather than a power system where survival is all. (Everard and Morris, 1985)

What is teaching?

Suffolk (1985) states that teaching can be thought of in four different ways. 'First, there is teaching as "labour" where teaching activities are planned and organised as a programme which can then be implemented in the classroom by means of standard, laid-down procedures. The planning is done by administrators and the teacher is expected to carry through the programme in the way prescribed. This system assumes that effective practice can be determined specifically: following the practices will bring about the necessary results.'

Secondly, ' "teaching" can be viewed as a

"craft" requiring the implementation of a range of skill–techniques. The teacher will be required to carry out the task as laid down with only indirect and informal evaluation. If the teacher has the requisite skills, all is well!'

Thirdly, ' "teaching" ' can be regarded as a 'professional activity' which means that in addition to the acquisition of skill–techniques, there is a specialist theoretical body of knowledge to be mastered. More important, the professional is required to exercise judgement as to when one, two or more of the range of skills should be applied.' In other words, the teacher 'takes responsibility for both strategy and tactics in the classroom'.

Finally, there is ' "teaching" as an art'. Here, teaching techniques may be 'highly personal' and could be 'unconventional' and 'improvisatory'. Thus, 'the shape and use of skill–techniques is not standardised. Gage (1978) argues that although teaching uses science it cannot be a science because the teaching environment (classroom) is shifting, changing and unpredictable. The teacher makes use not only of a body of professional knowledge and skill but also of personal resources which are possibly unique, and almost certainly uniquely expressed according to the teacher's personality and the interactions between her and individual pupils or whole classes. . . .'

Suffolk (1985) goes on to outline the broad agreement as to the 'effect' teachers should be having on their pupils. Pupils should be learning information, skills and attitudes. 'At the same time they should be helped to recognise their increasing competence, feel better about themselves as individuals, become better, more co-operative members of the community, develop more responsibility, increase in problem-solving ability, prepare for the world of work and develop independence. Much of this is difficult to measure.'

Suffolk continues, 'a great deal has been said and written about the possible "traits" which help make a teacher effective: punctuality, reliability, co-operative sense, an exemplar of school and LEA objectives, consistency, sensitivity to pupils' needs, sense of fairness, flexibility of approach, firmness when necessary, genuine interest in children, sense of humour (see also: Reid, Hopkins and Holly, 1987). This is by no means intended to be an exhaustive list. It is clearly possible to observe the traits listed above, but we question how far it is possible to measure many of them, although the research contends that given skills training and a heightened awareness, it is possible to gauge, in general terms, the presence or absence of some of the more intangible of them.

We will never have a set of (definitive) teaching skills. However, current research suggests that it is possible to determine, again in general terms, aspects of teacher action that contribute towards effective teaching in three areas.' These are:

(a) school climate;
(b) planning;
(c) management.

The Suffolk (1985) study adds to these three further aspects:

1 subject knowledge;
2 the act of teaching;
3 interpersonal relationships.

Effective teachers

We now move from the notion of teaching *per se* to the equally vexed notion of effective teaching. Again we recognise the inherent problem of making value judgements in issues revolving around good or effective practice. Nevertheless, we suggest that some teachers appear to be more successful and better than others. In rejecting an 'output' model which seeks to label a teacher 'effective' if her pupils achieve certain test scores, we are not saying that judgements are impossible. In fact, judgements on teachers and schools are being made all the time by parents, governors, advisers, colleagues, inspectors, pupils and many others. Rather we are suggesting that judgements should be made appropriately on a sound basis giving proper credence to the context and all the available evidence. This should include data relating to schools, teachers' and pupils' circumstances. That is, we are beginning to suggest that other criteria than simply 'cognitive outputs' are used.

One way of doing this may be to ask what a teacher is responsible for and answer it in professional terms. In other words, by looking at principles of professional procedure or competence which provide some kind of indication of the best kind of primary practice. There are various ways of doing this.

HMI (DES, 1986b) base their observations on an understanding of the best practice. Certain key indicators are identified:

> Satisfactory teaching, wherever it takes place, will have certain consistent indicators such as evidence that lessons are being planned and prepared in relation to a scheme of work, that teaching methods and resources used are varied and matched to the abilities of pupils, that there is evidence of appropriate pacing and the good use of time, and that pupils' work, in whatever form it is presented, is supportively and constructively assessed.

In evaluating the work in classrooms, HMI look at:

> ... whether the teachers' expectations of the pupils are appropriate; whether there is progression in work, whether the teaching stimulates interest, curiosity, enthusiasm, initiative and a responsibility on the part of the pupil for organising studies, in addition to a mastery of the content of the material being taught; whether the teaching methods, books and materials are suited to the age, aptitude and ability of the pupil; and whether the teaching is influenced by the condition and suitability of the accommodation, and the availability and quality of the equipment and materials. (DES, 1986b)

The kind of report and comments written by HMI following a school inspection are shown in the extracts now presented. These are taken from the sections in the report as identified below with the prior consent of the LEA and headteacher concerned and the approval of the Welsh office:

A – Introduction
B – Accommodation
C – Staffing and staff development
D – Organisation
E – Curriculum and standards of work
F – Assessment and Recording
G – Links (parents, etc.)

A The school was built in 1978 to replace an existing school some two miles away. The catchment, which is broad and includes many village-like communities, is mainly working-class with a measure of social disadvantage. Since opening, the number on roll has steadily increased to approximately 210 full-time and part-time pupils.

The environment can provide opportunities both for study ...

175

. . . and enjoyment

B The school is attractively built of red brick with a tiled pitched roof and occupies a commanding site with extensive views. Its position, overlooking what was once a heavily polluted industrial wasteland, which has in recent years been rehabilitated by coniferous tree planting and the establishment of new industrial areas together with an imposing sports arena, endows environmental studies with a potentially rich and challenging situation. The grounds include a playing field and a hard-surfaced playing area as well as other grassed areas planted with deciduous trees by the pupils.

The design inside is based upon 'open-plan' main areas with shared provision between classes. The nursery and reception classes occupy a large area separated by a moveable partition; off each section there is a withdrawal area where activities such as story-telling and singing may take place. The two infant classes occupy two main teaching areas with, between them, a shared practical space and a kiva (withdrawal area) capable of accommodating a whole class. Similar but more spacious accommodation is provided for junior classes; two main areas, each for two classes, and common practical areas, a kiva and basic skills withdrawal area. The junior and infant sections are separated by the hall, administrative offices, cloaks and WCs. The hall is used for a variety of purposes including drama, music, singing, PE, and assemblies. It is also used for dining and subsequently cannot be used for teaching for part of the day.

The teachers have adapted to the school design and manage the accommodation effectively. The children move within and between areas purposefully and maximum usage is obtained from spaces provided. Within each teaching space there are stimulating displays of children's work. These include teacher-designed, child-executed drawings and displays of writing and craft-work as well as painted murals. Throughout the school there are interesting artefacts and growing plants. The whole effect is to create a general ambience of care through an attractive and welcoming environment.

C The school has a teaching staff of 9, including the headteacher who does not have full-time charge of a class. Additional support is provided by a part-time remedial teacher and a peripatetic violin teacher. Further assistance includes a full-time nursery assistant, a part-time reception assistant and part-time clerical assistant. Student teachers from both the local University and Institute of Higher Education attend the school, together with NNEB and Child Care Course trainees. A significant feature is the extra help provided by visiting adults. Indeed, all visitors are made welcome and all staff share a common purpose in providing a safe, caring and stimulating environment for pupils.

Staff are appropriately trained for the primary age range with a balanced spread of main subject specialisms, including expertise in science and mathematics. The team is well qualified; six have degree qualifications and a seventh is currently completing studies for a degree. Curriculum studies undertaken in the course of work towards the degree directly contribute towards curriculum development within the school. Apart from his administrative duties, the headteacher is regularly involved in providing direct support for his colleagues inside and outside school and is first source of cover for absent staff. Well-established opportunities for consultation and discussion and clearly stated expectations of the deputy, scale postholders and other staff ensure a firm and effective style of leadership. This results in a strong corporate ethos and a general consensus on curriculum and other matters which contributes to a consistency and continuity in the approaches adopted throughout the school. In order to achieve this corporate approach to curricular planning, all the staff have agreed to a system of regular staff meetings. A lunchtime meeting of staff, conducted with varying degrees of formality, is held weekly and is the main forum for determining curricular policy and introducing innovation. These discussions have initially been logically sequenced according to the headteacher's perceptions of priorities, starting with a clarification of aims and objectives, proceeding to a review of the major curricular areas and, eventually, to a consideration of aspects of record keeping and assessment, including, for example, the introduction of graded objectives in mathematics. For all these meetings it is the normal procedure to maintain written records of transactions in order to chart the progress of important initiatives.

D Apart from the headteacher and deputy, three Scale 2 postholders also have designated functions and the remaining basic-scale teachers have also accepted specific responsibilities. With this approach the headteacher is able to share curricular leadership in broad areas together with providing appropriate attention to liaison between the nursing and reception, the infant and junior stages and to links with secondary schools. The scale postholders operate in a co-ordinating and consultative role and have played major parts in the preparation of guidelines and frameworks for curricular development. Opportunities are created to allow for these teachers to perform effectively in a co-ordinating capacity; groups of teachers meet together during assemblies to discuss proceedings before taking the findings back to the remainder of the staff in the weekly meetings; the headteacher provides cover for a co-ordinator to spend time with colleagues in the classroom to initiate change in a particular curricular area.

The staff have taken advantage of the opportunities offered by the school and the LEA, to attend in-service courses in order to update and extend their skills and knowledge. There is a match between the curriculum responsibilities of individuals and the courses attended and any remaining deficits are known. Feedback from any courses is facilitated through the practice of school-based in-service professional development. The success of certain dimensions of retaining nurtured within the school, for example a course in primary music for the whole staff conducted by a visiting advisory teacher, hastened the decision of the staff to become collectively involved in vigorous self-evaluation. The participation in the GRIDS (Guidelines for Review and Internal Development in Schools) process indicates unanimous commitment to a process generally accepted as one of the major strategies for improving professional practices.

Involvement in the GRIDS process for the past two years has placed extra demands on staff time and energy though it was possible to adapt the process to ensure that it complemented the school-based in-service tradition already in existence. Having made a collective decision to review a particular curricular area (Art, Craft and Design) a 'specific review' group of teachers was chosen to lead and direct the staff in the investigation. It was agreed from the beginning that the headteacher and the teaching team would be actively involved and would take seriously any recommendations made. Throughout the review, the information generated is controlled by those closely involved. Strengths, weaknesses and deficiencies are identified and plans for remediation offered. The collection and analysis of evidence in order to allow judgements to be made as to the school's effectiveness is a difficult task which has to be recognised by the staff. In order to accommodate this difficulty it is accepted that external help is desirable and so an outsider consultant (college lecturer, teachers' centre warden, advisory teacher) is involved to offer a different perspective to enable the school to see itself as others see it.

In formulating a school policy for the review area, many factors have to be taken into account, including: the values reflected in the overall aims of the school; the present 'climate for change' within the school; the availability of resources, time, space and materials; the integration with other curricular areas; and the use of the school grounds and the local environment for close investigation. The policy is considered a 'document for action' and not a final product. To ensure effective implementation, various strategies are employed: staff are encouraged to attend appropriate in-service courses and report back to colleagues; regular meetings are to continue; constant monitoring of resources; the specific review group have a responsibility to evaluate progress, to consult and offer advice if required. At the present time the staff, having worked enthusiastically to bring about change, are in some cases having to make changes in teaching style. With growing confidence and experience of school-based review the staff have involved parents, governors, LEA officers and advisers in workshop activities with outsider consultants so indicating a concern for the feelings and expectations of the wider community.

Presently the staff are involved in the review of another curricular area, namely science. Taking into account the experiences learned, adaptations have been made to the planning of strategies for future development. Various members of staff are involved in in-service courses and an advisory teacher for science regularly works with the teachers and children in implementing new ideas.

E Since the school is of open-plan design,

the classes are organised to take advantage of the shared accommodation and to encourage co-operation among teachers. As the intake into the school annually is approximately of one class size, classes are organised on a chronological basis. Organisation within classes is variable according to size, subject and type of activity. In the main, pupils work as individuals, in groups or as a whole class. The most usual form is the group within the class – the arrangement of the groups being flexible and variable; the group may be seen as a device to ensure that a range of activities is covered allowing teachers and pupils to make effective use of time, or as a means of encouraging the children to work together co-operatively. The arrangement of furniture and resources within the rooms enables this form of organisation to work effectively. When group work occurs small groups may be assisted by parent volunteers, for example in cooking or needlework with infant and junior classes; these activities are always teacher controlled. The rotation of groups among activities means that several different learning experiences occur at the same time. The intention is to provide a curriculum which is broad and balanced with appropriate differentiation according to the needs of the pupils. In all classes an appropriate use is made of class teaching. Class teaching is used to start a new topic; to explain the organisation and objectives for the group work; to recapitulate on work already started. Some individual teachers have identified pupils with special educational needs and planned suitable learning experiences especially for language and mathematics. A remedial teacher attends the school and arranges a programme of work for those pupils identified as needing extra help. The organisation of the remedial teacher involves withdrawal of children for reading as well as working in the classroom situation giving assistance in the class project, mathematics and computer work. The remedial teacher works closely with the class teacher in organising a varied programme of activities.

The school has prepared a statement of philosophy of primary education accompanied by a general statement on aims and objectives. These provide the basis for planning the range of curricular experiences including basic skills, empirical studies, aesthetics and the moral/religious aspects. These are not recognised as watertight compartments since they contain overlapping elements. Preliminary discussions among staff where ideas and the results of in-service training inputs are evaluated have led to the production of guidelines and schemes of work. The scale postholders have been offered the challenging role of playing a major part in curriculum planning and a significant feature of the organisation is the regular consultation between the headteacher, deputy, scale postholders and other staff.

In general, an agreed philosophy permeates the school and offers continuity and progression according to the differing needs of the pupils. Efforts are made to encourage cross-curricular activities with a variety of work including mathematics, language, science, drama, religion and art and craft.

F Assessment and recording of progress are seen as a vital part of curriculum planning. The school uses assessment and record keeping to ensure continuity and progression in pupils' learning. The nursery children are assessed by observing progress in a wide range of activities and dated samples of children's drawings and paintings are retained and 'pen pictures' describing children's needs and abilities are regularly prepared. Records are the basis for planned programmes of work and activities are appropriately matched to pupils' needs. The retaining of dated samples of work continues in the infant department and efforts are made to ensure smooth transfer of information from class to class. Due to an acute shortage of space and with only

179

one small store room for the whole school, practical difficulties are encountered in retaining samples of work. In an attempt to overcome these difficulties, continuity and progression is fostered by keeping a photographic record of much of the aesthetic and empirical experiences, by video recording activities and by arranging shared displays of the whole school's work. Advantage is taken of the video recordings and display to invite parents and other interested parties to share in the learning experience accompanied by their own children in the viewing process to allow for suitable discussion and sharing of opinions.

All the oldest infants are tested in reading, according to the LEA's policy, as part of a screening process to identify special education needs. Similarly, J4 pupils are tested in reading prior to secondary transfer. Additionally, the school has its own policy for assessing reading development, and standardised tests are used with all junior pupils. Results are entered on the official LEA record card which is updated annually and eventually transferred to the secondary schools in the Easter term preceding the transfer of pupils.

The assessment and recording of progress in reading is given priority throughout the school with note taken of related language skills, for example, literal, inferential, reorganisational and evaluative comprehension. The headteacher and language co-ordinator oversee the work and monitor the development of language skills by sample testing to verify progress.

Every class records progress in mathematics and number through the use of checklists devised within the school. These checklists indicate learning objectives, for example, matching numbers to corresponding sets in the case of younger children. The understanding, experience and practice of objectives for each individual is noted on the check-list in order to secure appropriate continuity and progression. Checklists for the older children are designed to complement the published schemes which are used but they also include objectives which have been discussed and agreed by staff. Children's understanding of mathematical concepts is regularly tested, the results serving as the basic for deciding new objectives.

General summaries of progress in spelling, number table tests, homework grades and 'pen pictures' of development over a period of time are kept thus helping to secure an appropriate match of learning to pupil ability. The staff, however, realise the need to obtain appropriate objectives in the wider curriculum. Through the continuing process of school-based in-service the staff have determined objectives for Art, Craft and Design, as mentioned earlier, and are in the process of determining activities matched with objectives for varying abilities in science.

G The statement of the school's educational philosophy specifically mentions a commitment to develop an open-partnership with parents and other interested people. It is in this way that good teacher/parent links are fostered so securing understanding and support for the school's aims and objectives and the methods by which these are attained. The parent–teacher association is very active in promoting the financial, social and educational life of the school. Educational events include 'open evenings', discussions on mathematics and reading. The school is involved in promoting the CAPER (Children and Parents Enjoying Reading) scheme which encourages parents to become more involved in the reading process through activity in the home.

Many parents and friends give assistance at the school in a variety of ways including: supervision of nursery children on the minibus provided by the school, practical aid throughout the school including colour coding of new books and by enriching the curriculum opportunities by assisting, through teacher direction, in such activities as cooking, fabric work, collage and training the chess team. In the context of community and environmental studies much is made of links with the wider community, including contacts with a naval ship.

Before transfer, arrangements are made to visit the secondary schools on a few occasions including a day where a range of lessons is experienced. Various teachers from the secondary school visit the upper junior pupils and monthly meetings are held between the headteachers of the 'feeder' primary schools and the secondary school. It is expected that curriculum transition links will be established to improving liaison in the future.

There are, of course, many other ways of looking at teachers and teaching and, indeed, of judging whether schools are effective. These include such systems as GRIDS I and II (Reid, Hopkins and Holly, 1987) as well as many others (Hopkins, 1987). Other researchers have sought to clarify specific aspects which are related to school and self-evaluation.

In a national study of a cohort of postgraduate trained student teachers, Reid, Bernbaum and Patrick (1981a) reported that the one aspect which the trainees feared was maintaining control and discipline in the classroom on teaching practice. The ability or inability to do so was considered the key issue which could make or break them. There is little doubt that similar judgements are made by headteachers, advisers and other teachers of their colleagues, although, in primary schools, a number of other aspects are considered important. These include relationships with pupils, voice projection and diction skills and the preparation of lessons and visual aids.

Elliott-Kemp and Rogers (1982) sought to identify some of the indicators of teaching performance within a three-fold framework of personal qualities, skills and knowledge. These three areas were perceived as forming a possible basis for a reflexive analysis of teachers' tasks utilising a self-assessment approach. In this system the teacher considers the requirements of her own professional knowledge (or subject area) as well as her situational knowledge of the organisation, pupils, school policies and environment. She considers her competence under such headings as lesson planning and using visual aids. Moreover, she questions whether she is updating her skills, in, for example, changing pedagogical styles. She also considers other non-cognitive aspects like her own values, respect for people and sympathetic understanding.

Ideas on self-assessment are presently in their infancy. Nevertheless, questions like those posed by Elliott-Kemp form some kind of framework for teachers to look honestly at their own practice and as such it would repay a much fuller and detailed study. Indeed, one of the most valuable qualities to be developed in student teachers, and those beginning a professional career and experienced teachers is that of reflectiveness; the ability to reflect critically on experiences.

Cowan (1984) reminds us that the White Paper *Teaching Quality* (DES, 1983d) outlined three broad criteria required for qualified teacher status:

1 Suitable personal qualities.
2 Appropriate academic standards.
3 Sufficient professional and practical knowledge and skills.

There is nothing particularly controversial about these. Nevertheless, it is interesting to note that in his research, Cowan goes on to demonstrate that deputy headteachers, when assessing potential appointees for a Scale 2 post using simulated references, rated personal qualities above professional skills.

Comparatively few references were made to evaluative skills, the quality of children's learning and contribution to curriculum planning and innovation, but participation in out-of-school activities merited a high priority although not directly related to the new post.

His research reflects the diversity of views about what may constitute a good primary school teacher. He warns us in an era of increasing accountability and impending appraisal that if the profession is unable to define its own criteria 'other outside bodies will be tempted to do so'.

This emphasis on subjective personal qualities was also critical in the findings obtained by Grace (1978) who examined the concept of the 'good' teacher in the urban secondary school.

> In only a minority of the schools was the emphasis in typification of good teachers strongly upon the quality of classroom teaching or pedagogic skill as such.

The evidence from research, therefore, suggests that presently, as with appointment panels, personal qualities are regarded more highly than or as highly as professional skills, perhaps because the latter are less easy to obtain, define or be certain about. Perhaps, too, it is because people are keen to have professionals on their staff with whom they can relate.

Yet, just what are these personal qualities which are so important? Cowan (1984) talks of 'character' (reliability, dress, punctuality) and such intrinsic values as contributing to the life of the school. These qualities are often seen as prerequisites to everything else in the primary school. That is, unless a teacher is able to work co-operatively with colleagues and has suitable personal qualities then everything else will suffer, including pedagogy. Here we are beginning to return to a notion of effectiveness being seen in, and influenced by, its context. Effectiveness requires in part a conducive environment.

The importance of personal qualities in assessing teachers appears again in *The New Teacher in School* (DES, 1982b) an HMI discussion document focusing on the probationary teacher. Paragraph 5.5 discusses the criteria by which probationers' performances were judged by schools. These included professional competences such as abilities in control, punctuality, good preparation, marking and so on. But personal qualities:

> . . . played a significant part in the school's assessment in two-thirds of the cases. Amongst those most commonly mentioned were: energy, enthusiasm, commitment (including willingness to participate in extracurricular activities), conscientiousness, confidence, imagination, resourcefulness, good relations with pupils and staff, willingness to seek advice and perceptiveness to advice when given. Adaptability and ability to 'fit in' were also stressed.

Paragraph 6.2 goes on to comment that:

> HMI found that the personal qualities of the teachers were in many cases the decisive factor in their effectiveness.

HMI go on to make the point that there were some entrants to the profession whose 'personal qualities were such as to make it difficult for them to be fully effective, however good their training and however well supported they were by other teachers in the school'.

HMI (DES, 1982b, para 5.41) found the constraints which affected the observed lessons given by the new entrants were several. These give some insight into the sources of classroom ineffectiveness in general. Most common were:

(a) Difficulty of classes often containing children of low ability and poor motivation and mixed ages.
(b) Limited expectations of the school. 'The dependence of some primary schools on "a work-card production line" or on a single set of undemanding text books . . .'
(c) Non-availability of teaching materials, such as shortages of suitable books.
(d) Absence of guidelines.
    Here we return to the notion of effectiveness requiring a sense of direction. Clear and helpful guidelines were needed together with support and leadership from the primary school headteacher.

HMI (paragraph 6.3) also point to the situational aspects of effectiveness:

There are teachers who would be able to work happily in a relaxed, supportive environment and thus develop into good teachers, but who have been appointed to schools where a rigid or authoritarian style of organisation exists. In consequence they are both unhappy and unsuccessful. The reverse can also be true. This is an element of 'match' which tends to be neglected.

The same is true of more experienced teachers. One such teacher comments:

I get on very well with my present head who leans towards the formal. And in that atmosphere, I thrive. (Huggett, 1986)

There is little doubt that many of the issues we have dealt with here are, and will remain, problematic. However, we are optimistic that now more attention is being given to them, they will become less problematic with time. There is no such thing as the perfect primary school; the 'Holy Grail' does not exist.

18 Effective primary schools

What is an effective primary school?

Having briefly considered some aspects of what an effective teacher may be in Chapter 17, we now turn to the notion of the effective primary school. We hold that an 'effective' teacher is linked with an 'effective' school; the effective school is the context in which an effective teacher will flourish. To recall for a moment the double glazing purchase with which we started the previous chapter, you will remember that one of your expectations on its installation was that it would make a difference to your heating costs. Another aspect of effectiveness then, concerns making a difference. To ask, 'Is a school effective?' is in some sense to ask 'Does it make a difference?' 'Does it change its pupils in some way?'

Until comparatively recently, research has concentrated on the view that success in the education system is predominantly determined by home background. The Plowden Report (DES, 1967b) found little relationship between outcomes and school characteristics, with the great majority of variance in attainment explicable by family background and parental attitudes.

As Reynolds and Reid (1985) have shown, research into school effectiveness is in its infancy partly due to a host of methodological problems. But there is another more significant reason. Early studies on school effectiveness suggested that school factors had few consequences on outcomes when compared with the stronger influences of home background, social class and environment (Reynolds, 1985a; Reid, Hopkins and Holly, 1987). We now know this is not true. These pioneer studies could not show school effects because they tended to exclude school variables from their analysis. Since then, important work by the school differences group (Reynolds, 1985a) has shown that schools can and do make differences to their pupils' performances to a significant extent. In fact, the studies by Rutter *et al.* (1979), Reynolds (1976) and ILEA (1986) have begun to suggest that a school need not be simply as good or as bad as its intake.

> We believe that teachers and headteachers have everywhere been encouraged to reduce their efforts to help the underachieving child by the growth of this climate of opinion. Children are not necessarily born to fail. What goes on in school between nine and five is an important determinant of the type of child that emerges at the end of the process. (Reynolds *et al.*, 1976)

A number of important questions now emerge such as: 1 On what basis can this claim be made? and, 2 What are the factors which seem to contribute to effectiveness?

The research so far seems to indicate that secondary schools may have an effect on academic development 'amounting probably to one and a half O level or CSE passes' (Reynolds, 1985b). Other measures used to indicate differences include attendance rates, future employment prospects of pupils and delinquency rates. One could argue of course that these 'outcomes' are measurable and easily comparable and that many other important aspects of school life cannot be measured in this way. It is, for example, comparatively easy to measure the quantity but not the quality of pupil–teacher interaction.

Rutter *et al.* (1979) discuss some of the reasons for their choice of indicators or 'outcome measures'. They argue that the five outcome measures chosen for their study: pupil behaviour, academic outcome, attendance, future employment prospects and delinquency, while not reflecting the whole range of school life, do provide indicators of 'crucial aspects of the outcome of the educational process'. For instance, attendance is included because, if a school is going to have a beneficial effect, a fair degree of attendance is necessary. In other words, these indicators reflect areas in which some degree of success is necessary if other broader and more nebulous aims are to be achieved (Rutter *et al.*, 1979). They set the context of the process.

More specifically related to the primary school is the ILEA Junior School Study. This four-year project began in April 1980. It was a longitudinal study, that is, the same group of pupils (an age cohort of approximately 2,000) were studied over their junior school career. The pupils entered junior school in September 1980 and transferred to secondary school in September 1984, and were drawn from 50 randomly selected Inner London Schools (Mortimore *et al.*, 1985).

Previous research had tended to focus on secondary school effectiveness in promoting pupils' progress in learning (Rutter *et al.*, 1979; Reynolds, 1982). No previous study of primary aged pupils had 'focused specifically on the question of school differences' (Mortimore *et al.*, 1985). The researchers hoped:

... to be able to establish whether differences remain between schools in average pupil attainment and development, once account has been taken of the variation in the pupils' backgrounds.

The 'cumulative effects of disadvantage' were recognised and 'taken into account'. Comprehensive information on children's backgrounds was obtained in order to avoid criticisms made of previous studies.

Measures of cognitive outcomes were used, but also measures of non-cognitive development in order:

... to do justice to the diverse aims and breadth of the curriculum of many primary schools.

Included, therefore, were measures of self-concept, classroom observations based on the instruments developed by the ORACLE team (Galton *et al.*, 1980), qualitative observations of pupil/teacher relationship and measures of home–school liaison. In addition, the researchers also examined attitudes to curriculum area such as the 'basic skills'. Similarly, while acknowledging the difficulties of developing measures in aesthetic areas such as drama, dance, music, art and craft, the research team 'felt it was important not to neglect these areas'. The study is an important one and would repay more detailed analysis. It has attempted not to distort the whole range of primary school experiences.

The measures used by the project 'established that there were marked differences between the 50 schools in their effects upon pupils' progress and development' (ILEA, 1986). For example, the study showed that those schools deemed effective 'had pupils absent 7.5 days fewer per year than expected; the least effective school had an absence rate 7 days worse than predicted' (Reynolds, 1985b).

We now concentrate on identifying those aspects which may contribute to such school differences based on the ILEA Study's findings. Before considering the identified factors, it is worth noting that the project team are aware that some schools, by reason of their location, size, stability of staff and status, are more advantaged than others. However, though these aspects form a favourable framework, they are not in themselves a guarantee of school effectiveness. The team drew attention to those critical aspects of schooling which are in the control of the head and staff. These include:

1 Purposeful leadership of the staff by the headteacher.
2 The involvement of the deputy head in planning and decision-making.
3 The involvement of teachers in the running of the school.
4 Consistency among teachers about behaviour and their aims and objectives.
5 Structured sessions.
6 Intellectually challenging teaching.
7 A work-centred environment.
8 Limited focus within sessions.
9 Maximum communication between teachers and pupils.
10 Accurate and maintained record keeping.
11 Parental involvement.
12 A positive climate or school ethos. (ILEA, 1986).

We now propose to look at these factors in more detail and highlight some of the issues raised.

1 *Purposeful leadership of the staff by the headteacher*
Important aspects of headteacher's leadership were seen to centre around active involvement in the work of the school, in discussing curriculum policy and guidelines with teachers, and guiding staff on to suitable in-service courses. The head emphasised record keeping as part of a systematic monitoring policy.

2 *The involvement of the deputy head*
The deputy headteacher's role in the primary school may be somewhat problematic, sometimes leading to role-conflict. For example, is the role one of class teacher or administrator? The effec-

tive school headteachers delegated to deputies and involved them in 'a sharing of responsibilities'.

3 *The involvement of teachers in the running of the school*
In the effective school, teachers were involved in curriculum decision making. Consultation was important too, so that teachers felt they have a part in school policy.

4 *Consistency amongst teachers about behaviour and their aims and objectives*
Continuity of staff was found to have 'positive effects'. However, we would also wish to draw attention to the importance of continuity and consistency within teaching approaches, emphasising the need for clearly agreed school policies and guidelines.

5 *Structured sessions*
Pupils benefited from a positively structured and organised framework to their activities, where they 'were not given unlimited responsibility for planning their own programme of work'.

6 *Intellectually challenging teaching*
Children's progress appeared to be promoted when teachers were interesting and stimulating, asking 'open-ended' questions which encouraged a creative response from their pupils. Frequent direction of work had a negative impact. 'What was crucial was the level of the communication between teacher and pupils.' Progress was also linked to high teacher expectations of pupils. This led to teachers allowing pupils some measure of independence over their work.

7 *A work-centred environment*
Progress was assisted in schools where teachers spent a shorter time discussing routine matters with their pupils and 'more of their time discussing content'.

8 *Limited focus within sessions*
This is an important factor for new entrants to teaching. It is suggested by the

survey that learning activities centred in one curriculum area during a session promote better pupil progress. When attempts to organise sessions to include two or three distinct curriculum areas predominated, learning was not so successful. This is not to suggest that all children ought to be doing identical work at the same time. Indeed, appropriate 'match' of level of work to pupils is another important factor in promoting progress. Work may be undertaken in the one area in a variety of ways.

9 *Maximum communication between teachers and pupils*

Pupils benefited from a greater degree of teacher communication. Therefore, the teacher who attempted 'individual' contact clearly limited herself to a minimum time with each child. 'Whole class' contact increased the 'overall number of contacts with pupils'.

Therefore, a balance between individual and class contact is suggested. Referring to point 8 above the Report states:

> Furthermore, where children worked in a single curriculum area within sessions (even if they were engaged on individual or group tasks) it was easier for teachers to raise an intellectually challenging point with *all* pupils.

10 *Accurate and maintained record keeping*

Where teachers reported that they kept written records of pupils' work progress . . . the effect on the pupils was positive.

Though it is sometimes seemingly a laborious task, the benefit to the teacher of a record of children's work is highlighted here. In our experience it is easier to plan with purpose, to match work and to diagnose areas of difficulty if suitable records are kept. Like Clift *et al.* (1981), we are at pains to emphasise the professional nature of teaching and regard record keeping as a part of good professional practice.

11 *Parental involvement*

In keeping with much recent work, parental involvement was seen to aid pupil progress. This took many forms, such as helping in classrooms, meetings to discuss children's progress and assisting with reading at home. The presence of a formal PTA did not seem to be related to pupil progress. It could be that a formally constituted PTA which may see its brief in terms of fund raising or as a social focus for parents, is not necessarily linked to the specifically 'educational' work of the school; a province perhaps traditionally regarded as the exclusive domain of headteacher and staff. Many parents in primary schools may indeed have little to do with a formal PTA (see Chapter 12).

12 *Positive climate or school ethos*

Like most studies undertaken in the United States (Reid, Hopkins and Holly, 1987), the researchers found that an effective school has a positive school ethos or climate. This ethos was evidenced in the amount of emphasis on praise and reward rather than on punishment and on firm and fair discipline. Teacher's enthusiasm and interest communicated itself to pupils. There was also evidence of extra-curricula activities; trips and visits as well as 'the use of the local environment as a learning resource'.

When teachers had non-teaching time allocated, this helped progress. So the leadership of the head in creating a positive and helpful working atmosphere for teachers in turn communicated itself to pupils.

Another way of looking at primary schools is to use the HMI schedules reproduced in Figure 18.1. These provide a framework for making professional judgements. In particular, they examine children's learning experiences and organisation inside schools. Interestingly enough, HMI is concerned with matters of how children's learning is encouraged as well as matters of content. In Figure 18.2 we have included a framework which may help you to analyse these reports. You will see that the framework is divided into five main areas. Each of these is divided into positive and negative aspects sometimes called facilitators and constraints. This schedule may form a useful starting point in beginning to think about a school.

Figure 18.1 *Summary of HMI schedules*

Reproduced by permission of the Controller, HM Stationery Office, from Department of Education and Science, *Primary Education in England*, a Survey by HM Inspectors of Schools, HMSO, 1978, pp. 209–19.

AESTHETIC AND PHYSICAL EDUCATION

i. *Art and crafts*

(1) The extent to which children make use of the following starting points and resources in the development of aesthetic awareness: the immediate outdoor environment, arrangements and displays inside the school and the classroom, natural and man-made objects, a range of media for two- and three-dimensional work, visits to local art galleries, exhibitions or museums, visits by local craftsmen or artists.

(2) The quality of the following resources: the arrangements and displays within the classroom including man-made objects, a range of media for drawing and print-making, materials and textiles, three-dimensional constructional materials.

(3) The emphasis given to art and crafts within the whole curriculum.

(4) Evidence that children are learning to observe carefully in relation to form, texture, pattern and colour.

(5) Evidence that children may turn readily to paint, clay or other media when they have something to express which is personal to them.

(6) Evidence of the use of form, texture, pattern and colour in children's work.

(7) Evidence that children are learning to select materials with discrimination.

(8) Evidence that the children are learning to handle tools, apparatus and materials carefully and safely and with a sense of fitness for their purpose.

(9) The use made of drawing and modelling techniques and skills to record observations or information in other areas of the curriculum.

ii. *Music*

(10) The extent to which children make use of the following starting points and resources for musical experience: recorded music, television, radio, untuned and tuned percussion instruments, visits to concerts or to hear outside choirs, visits to the school by musicians.

(11) The emphasis given to music within the whole curriculum.

(12) The extent to which opportunities are taken to develop singing, listening, the learning of notation and creative music-making as aspects of musical experience.

(13) The quality of the songs chosen.

(14) The extent to which music is related to other areas of the curriculum.

(15) The provision for children in the class to play musical instruments.

iii. *Physical education*

(16) The extent to which children make use of the following starting points and resources for physical education: television, radio, gymnastic equipment of all kinds, games equipment and associated small apparatus.

(17) The emphasis given to the full range of movement activities within the whole curriculum.

(18) The extent to which opportunities are taken to develop gymnastics, dance,

games and swimming within the range of physical activities.

(19) Evidence that the children are developing skilful performance in gymnastics, skill in games or a games-like context, awareness and sensitivity in the use of expressive movement.

LANGUAGE AND LITERACY

(1) The extent to which children make use of the following starting points and resources to develop and extend their language, whether spoken, written or through reading:

- a experiences out of school which have not been planned by the school
- b experiences in school including the display of materials and objects, the keeping of animals and plants, imaginative play, constructional activities
- c book collections or libraries
- d television, radio, cine film, slides, pre-recorded material for listening, tape recordings by the children.
- e reading schemes and courses, assignment cards, language course kits, textbooks
- f stories and poems read or told by the teacher
- g visiting speakers
- h the immediate outdoor environment, visits and school journeys.

(2) The quality of the following: the arrangement of displays, book collections or libraries, pre-recorded material for listening, cine film and slides, assignment cards, stories and poems read by the teacher.

(3) The extent to which opportunities are taken to develop the language used in other areas of the curriculum.

(4) Evidence that children are being taught to do the following: follow instructions, follow the plot of a story, listen to poetry, comprehend the main ideas and the details in information they are given, follow a discussion or the line of an argument and contribute appropriately.

(5) The emphasis given to talking between the children and teachers, and the children and other adults.

(6) The emphasis given to informal discussion among children during the working day and the provision of more formal, structured arrangements for discussion and exchange between children.

(7) Evidence that children are encouraged to expand their spoken responses, that new vocabulary in introduced, that the use of more precise description is achieved, that children are helped to frame pertinent questions and that children are taught to use alternative and more appropriate structures in their talking.

i. Reading

(8) Evidence, where appropriate, that children's own speech is used to provide early reading material.

(9) Evidence that the children's own writing is used as part of their early reading material.

(10) The emphasis given to reading practice with main reading schemes and supplementary readers.

(11) The emphasis given to the reading of fiction and non-fiction related to curricular work and other reading not related to curricular work.

(12) The emphasis on the use of extended reading skills and children's comments on the material read.

(13) The emphasis on the selection of books by the children themselves.

(14) Evidence that children learn to turn readily and naturally to books for pleasure and that they use books with ease and confidence as a source of information.

(15) Evidence that the children read poetry and that some of the children

discuss books at more than a superficial level.

ii. *Writing*

(16) The emphasis given to self-chosen and prescribed topics for children's writing.

(17) The emphasis given to self-chosen and prescribed topics related to other curricular areas.

(18) The extent to which the following are used: copied writing, dictation and handwriting practice.

(19) The extent to which descriptive, expressive, narrative and expository styles or modes of prose writing are used by the children.

(20) The extent to which descriptive, expressive and narrative styles or modes of poetry writing are used by the children.

(21) Evidence that the children's writing is used for the following purposes: to share information or experience with other children, as samples of work used by the teacher to monitor progress, as a basis for learning language, spelling, syntax and style.

(22) Where French is taught, the number of sessions and total time per week which is spent on this subject.

MATHEMATICS

(1) The extent to which children make use of the following starting points and resources in the learning of mathematics:

    a television and radio
    b textbooks, commercial and school-made work-cards
    c investigations arising from questions asked by the children or initiated by the teachers
    d practice of skills directed from the blackboard.

(2) Evidence of sustained work on any mathematical topic.

(3) Evidence of profitable links with other areas of the curriculum.

(4) The emphasis given to the following aspects of mathematics during the current school year:

    a qualitative mathematical description; unambiguous description of the properties of number, size, shape and position
    b recognition of relationships and logical deduction applied to everyday things, geometrical shapes, number and ordering
    c appreciation of place value and recognition of simple number patterns (e.g. odds and evens, multiples, divisors, squares, etc.)
    d appreciation of some broader aspects of number (e.g. bases other than 10, number sequences, tests of divisibility)
    e use of various forms of visual presentation (e.g. three-dimensional and diagrammatic forms, statistical charts, tables of data, networks, etc.)
    f use of models, maps, scale drawings, etc.
    g use of algebraic symbols; notations such as 'box' and arrow diagrams
    h sensible estimation and use of measurements of length, weight, area, volume and time
    i understanding of money and sense of values regarding simple purchases
    j quantitative description; sensible use of number in counting, describing and estimating
    k practical activities involving the ideas of $+$, $-$, $\times$ and $\div$
    l suitable calculations involving $+$, $-$, $\times$ and $\div$ with whole numbers
    m examples involving four rules of number including two places of decimals (as in pounds and pence and measures)

n calculations involving the four rules applied to the decimal system
o use of fractions (including the idea of equivalence) in the discussion of everyday things
p competence in calculations involving the four rules applied to fractions

SCIENCE
(1) The extent to which children make use of the following starting points and resources in learning science:

a children's experience out of school
b experience of materials, plants and animals in school
c television and radio
d reference books, textbooks, commercial and school-made assignment cards
e the immediate outdoor environment.

(2) Quality of the overall provision of resources for scientific investigation.
(3) The emphasis given to science within the whole curriculum.
(4) The quality of assignment cards, reference books and materials available for scientific investigation.
(5) Evidence of investigations arising from questions asked by the children.
(6) Evidence that the children are using description arising from direct observation.
(7) Evidence that the children are learning about the following:

a notions of stability and change in relation to living things and materials
b knowledge of some of the characteristics of living things including differences and similarities
c reproduction, growth and developing in succeeding generations
d forms of energy sources and storage

e factors which influence personal and community health, including safety
f respect and care for living things.

(8) The extent to which children are encouraged to identify significant patterns (e.g. the way plants react to light, the way materials react to heat, bird migration, the position of leaves on a plant stem, etc.).

SOCIAL ABILITIES

i. *Social, moral and religious education*
(1) The extent to which situations are planned to encourage the development of moral and ethical values in the following aspects:

a the use of initiative and making informed choices
b the exercise of responsibility and self-assessment in behaviour and work
c emotional development and sympathetic identification with others
d respect for other people
e respect for plants and animals
f respect for things
g contribution and participation as a member of a group
h the exercise of qualities of leadership.

(2) The extent to which most children appear to be involved in the development of religious ideas and moral or ethical rules and values during the school assembly.
(3) The extent to which children learn about man's attempt to frame religious and moral or ethical rules and values in the following aspects of their work:

a history and geography
b the Old and New Testaments
c writings of other religions
d myths and legends
e other literature and drama.

ii. *Geography and history*

(4) The extent to which children make use of the following starting points and resources to develop historical and geographical awareness:

a the memories of people known to the children

b artefacts, historical documents and the use of historical aspects of the local area

c historical programmes on television and radio

d history textbooks, work-cards or assignment cards

e stories with an historical setting

f history reference books

g weather study

h use of geographical features of the local area

i geographical programmes on television and radio

j geography textbooks, work-cards or assignment cards

k stories with an interesting geographical setting

l geography reference books.

(5) The quality of the content of school-made assignment cards for history and geography.

(6) The quality of history and geography reference books.

(7) The emphasis given to developing children's awareness and appreciation of the past.

(8) The extent to which children are becoming aware of historical change and the causal factors in relation to people's material circumstances, the way people behaved and the things people believed in the past.

(9) The degree to which children are engaged in the following activities:

a understanding the nature of historical statements

b developing sympathy with the predicament of other people

c developing an awareness of the need for evidence.

(10) The emphasis given to geographical aspects of children's learning within the whole curriculum.

(11) The degree to which the following geographical aspects were included in children's work during the current academic year both within and outside the locality:

a population and settlements

b agriculture and industry

c transport

d geographical land features

e natural resources.

(12) The extent to which the children's work reveals an appreciation of man's dependence on natural phenomena and resources.

(13) Evidence that children are becoming familiar with maps of the locality, atlases and globes.

ORGANISATION AND METHODS OF WORKING

(1) The emphasis given to cognitive, social, emotional and physical development as judged by the quality of the children's work.

(2) The degree to which posts carrying particular organisational or curricular responsibilities influence the work of the school as a whole.

(3) The extent to which didactic and exploratory approaches to teaching were observed in the survey classes.

(4) Evidence of effective interaction between the basic skills of numeracy and literacy and the more imaginative aspects of the children's work.

(5) Evidence that children are encouraged to follow a sustained interest in the course of their work.

(6) The extent to which a quiet working atmosphere is established when this is appropriate.

(7) The degree of control over the children's use of resources in the classroom.

(8) The degree to which the content of

the children's work is prescribed by the teacher.

(9) Evidence that satisfactory educational use is made of spontaneous incidents which may arise.

(10) The attention given to creating an intellectually stimulating environment inside and outside the school.

(11) Evidence that vandalism outside school hours limits the creation of an aesthetically pleasing environment.

(12) The extent to which the accommodation facilitates or inhibits the children's work.

(13) The extent to which the adequacy of resources facilitates or inhibits the children's work.

(14) Type of catchment area and whether there is evidence of marked social difficulties.

Good practice: an HMI view

In *Primary Schools: some aspects of good practice* (HMI, 1987), the most significant characteristics of good practice in primary education are outlined. These are drawn from the observations of HMI in the course of their visits to a wide range of primary schools in England. The main features identified in the publication are considered below, first from

Figure 18.2

HMI Report on .... School. Date of Report ....

	Positive (Facilitators)	*Negative* (Constraints)
Headteacher Management 'Policy', 'guidelines', 'consultation'.		
Staff Postholder's role, Deputy's role, pedagogy. Correction of work 'process'.		
Curriculum Breadth, balance, 'match' consistency. Record keeping.		
Organisation Class groupings, use of resources. Classroom environment		
Social World Relation with/in community. Parents.		

the perspective of the school and then from that of the classroom.

Good practice: the whole school

Good practice flourished where the head and staff shared a sense of purpose. Curriculum guidelines had been 'carefully thought out' and drawn up after consultation. They were the subject of regular review.

Good management and organisation over the years had contributed to 'an adequate and suitable variety of resources'. Internal arrangements allowed members of staff to share expertise with colleagues, sometimes working alongside each other in classrooms.

Good practice: the classroom

Good practice within classrooms was typified by the nurturing of 'a sense of self-discipline'. Pupil movement around the classroom, therefore, showed consideration for other children. Pupils were 'keenly interested in their work', a result of high-quality teaching. Such successful teachers knew their pupils well and were deeply concerned that they made progress. They consistently asked themselves the question: 'Is that a sufficiently high standard for that particular child?'

A clear view of the objectives of the school formed the sound basis from which good school and classroom practice sprang. HMI concluded, 'the overriding characteristic is that of agreed, clear aims and purposeful teaching'.

Implications

This discussion provides a framework in which all participants in primary school life (teachers, parents, governors, pupils) can make a positive contribution. By contrast, it does not provide a blueprint around which a school can be evaluated. There is a very real danger that findings from such research can be misused by unqualified or unscrupulous third parties for their own purposes. Although

the ILEA Study has uncovered much valuable data, it is worth remembering that most studies of 'effectiveness' have been located in English and American secondary schools and that our knowledge of the effective primary school remains very slight (Reynolds, 1985a; Reid, Hopkins and Holly, 1987). Although we can identify factors such as the 12 in the ILEA Study, 'we do not know what actually generates the factors within a school' (Reynolds, 1985a). Nor do we know for sure which factors are causal and which are simply associated with effectiveness. In other words although we might begin to identify those factors in a primary school which contribute to its effectiveness we do not know how these factors operate. We do not know how to make a school a good one.

Reynolds (1985b) suggests that the key may lie in the headteacher. Sadly, this statement has massive implications. If change in a school is linked to a change of headteacher, then ultimately improvement will only take place after the eventual appointment of a new headteacher. Clearly, this is only one aspect of a very important problem as effecting change is never easy especially in an era when headteachers, and teachers for that matter, are remaining in post longer. Significantly, the ILEA Study (1986) pointed to the lessened effectiveness of schools where the head had remained in post for a long period. Therefore to wait for a change in personnel to induce change in schools is not practical. 'How one reaches the poor school without any personnel change is clearly the vital issue of the 1980s' (Reynolds, 1985b).

If it is hard to define a truly effective school, it is sometimes less difficult to agree on an ineffective one. The problem was highlighted in the William Tyndale School Enquiry of 1976.

This North London Primary School was managed by a head who had been in post a short time, and who adopted so-called 'progressive' methods which led to internal and external conflict. Matters culminated in an Official Enquiry conducted by Robin Auld, QC, in 1976. The difficulty for Mr Auld was that although conflict was apparent and parents were voicing open dissatisfaction with the school, there existed no criteria on which he could base his judgement as to what actually constitutes a good primary school.

Gretton and Jackson (1976) quote Mr Auld:

> Thus, if a headteacher is convinced that a particular educational policy or method is right for his school, and the district inspector is equally convinced that he is wrong, by what yardstick does the inspector judge and seek to advise the Head that he is wrong?

They go on to comment:

> Mr Auld had been gaily talking about efficiency and 'suitability' but was forced to recognise that, in practice – and London was no different in this respect from most other authorities – 'the authority has no policy:
>
> (1) as to the standards of attainment at which its primary school should aim;
> (2) as to the aims and objectives of the primary education being provided in its schools . . .;
> (3) as to the methods of teaching to be adopted in its schools.'

In the absence of such a yardstick 'Mr Auld was forced on what he called "the formidable weight of the evidence"' (Gretton and Jackson, 1976) and the head was removed from office.

Few other clues in British research exist on effective primary education. The study by Heal (1978) found that primary schools differed significantly in the levels of misbehaviour reported. Misbehaviour was higher in those schools which had more formal systems of punishment and in schools in which a large increase in pupil numbers had been met by the provision of temporary accommodation. Reid, Hopkins and Holly (1987) summarise findings from studies into school differences and effectiveness undertaken in elementary schools in the United States. Given the enormous situational and cultural differences which exist between these countries, considerable caution should be used when applying any of these findings to the British context, more especially to primary schools. Nevertheless, these findings do provide a kind of general overview which might be helpful to school managers when assessing the performance of their own schools.

Bibliography

ADVISORY COMMITTEE ON THE SUPPLY AND TRAINING OF TEACHERS (ACSTT) (1974) *In-Service Education and Training: Some Considerations*. London: HMSO.

ADVISORY COMMITTEE ON THE SUPPLY AND TRAINING OF TEACHERS (ACSTT) (1978) *Making INSET Work*. London: HMSO/WO.

ALEXANDER, R. J. (1984) *Primary Teaching*. London: Holt, Rinehart and Winston.

ARGYRIS, C. (1973) 'The Individual and Organization: Some Problems of Mutual Adjustment' in HOUGHTON, V. *et al*. (eds) *Management in Education*. London: Ward Lock Educational/Open University Press.

ARKWRIGHT, D., HEWITT, M. C., THORNE, K. and WEBB, W. (1975) 'Survey of Open Plan Primary Schools in Derbyshire' in BENNETT, N. *et al*. *Open Plan Primary Schools*. Slough: NFER.

ASHTON, P. (1978) 'What are primary teachers' aims?' in RICHARDS, C. (ed.) *Education 3–13 1973–1977*. London: Nafferton Books.

ASHTON, P. *et al*. (1981) *Teacher Education in the Classroom: Initial and In-Service*. London: Croom Helm.

ASTON UNIVERSITY (1981) *The Social Effects of Rural Primary School Organisation in England*. Birmingham: University of Aston.

AULD, M. (1976) *Report of the Committee of Inquiry into William Tyndale School*. London: ILEA.

BAILEY, C. and BRIDGES, D. (1983) *Mixed Ability Grouping*. London: George Allen and Unwin.

BAILEY, P. (1982) 'Falling rolls in the maintained secondary school: Towards a model for management', *Educational Management and Administration*, 10, 23–30.

BAKER, K. (1976) 'A review of current induction programmes for new teachers', *British Journal of In-Service Ed*. 2, 179–86.

BAKER, K. (1977) 'Helping probationers as staff development', *Journal of Applied Educational Studies*, 6, 2, 63–75.

BAKER, K. (1978) 'Survey findings from LEA induction programmes', *British Journal of In-Service Education*, 4, 3, 151–60.

BAKER, K. *et al*. (1982) *The Schools and In-Service Teacher Education Evaluation Project: Final Report*. University of Bristol.

BARKER-LUNN, J. (1970) *Streaming in the Primary School*. Slough: NFER.

BARKER-LUNN, J. (1982) 'Junior schools and their organizational policies', *Educational Research*, 24, 4, 259–60.

BARKER-LUNN, J. (1984) 'Junior school teachers: their methods and practices', *Educational Research*, 26, 3, 178–88.

BARNARD, C. I. (1938) *The Functions of the Executive*. Cambridge, Mass.: Harvard University Press.

BARRELL, G. R. (1978) *Teachers and the Law* (5th edition). London: Methuen.

BARRELL, G. R. (1983) 'Knowing the Law', in PAISEY, A. (ed.) *The Effective Teacher*. London: Ward Lock Educational.

BASTIANI, J. (ed.) (1978) *Written Communication between Home and School*. Report of the Community Education Working Party. University of Nottingham, School of Education.

BEALING, D. (1972) 'The Organisation of Junior School Classes', *Educational Research*, 14, 231–5.

BECHER, T., ERAUT, M., KNIGHT, J. (1981) *Policies for Educational Accountability*. London: Heinemann.

BENNETT, B. and MARTIN, K. (1980) *The Practice of Teaching – a positive start*. London: Harper and Row.

BENNETT, N. (1976) *Teaching Styles and Pupil Progress*. London: Open Books.

BENNETT, N., ANDREAE, J., HEGARTY, P. and WADE, B. (1975) 'An enquiry into Cumbria's open plan schools', in BENNETT, N. *et al. Open Plan Primary Schools*. Slough: NFER.

BENNETT, N. and HYLAND, T. (1979) 'Open plan – open education?', *British Education Research Journal*, 5, 2, 159–66.

BENNETT, N., ANDREAE, J., HEGARTY, P. *et al.* (1980) *Open Plan Schools: Teaching, Curriculum, Design*. Slough: NFER.

BENNETT, N., O'HARE, E. and LEE, J. (1983) 'Mixed Aged Classes in Primary Schools: a survey of practice', *British Educational Research Journal*, 9, 1, 41–56.

BERNBAUM, G., PATRICK, H. and REID, K. (1982) *The Structure and Process of Initial Teacher Education within Universities in England and Wales* (SPITE). Report of a sponsored DES Project. Leicester: University of Leicester, School of Education.

BERNBAUM, G., PATRICK, H. and REID, K. (1983) *The Probationary Year*. Report of a sponsored DES Project. Leicester: University of Leicester, School of Education.

BERNBAUM, G., PATRICK, H. and REID, K. (1985a) 'Postgraduate initial teacher in England and Wales: Perspective from the SPITE Project', in HOPKINS, D. and REID, K. (eds) *Rethinking Teacher Education*. London: Croom Helm.

BERNBAUM, G., PATRICK, H., JACKSON, S. and REID, K. (1985b) 'A history of postgraduate initial teacher education in England and Wales, 1880–1980', in HOPKINS, D. and REID, K. (eds) *Rethinking Teacher Education*. London: Croom Helm.

BIDWELL, C. E. (1965) 'The school as a formal organisation', in MARCH, J. G. (ed.) *Handbook of Organisations*. Chicago: Rand-McNally.

BLENKIN, G. M. and KELLY, A. V. (eds) (1983) *The Primary School Curriculum in Action*. London: Harper and Row.

BLENKIN, G. M. and KELLY, A. V. (1987) *The Primary School Curriculum* (2nd ed.). London: Harper and Row.

BLYTH, E. and MILNER, J. (1987) 'Non-attendance and the law: the confused role of the Social Services and Education Departments' in REID, K. (ed.) *Combating School Absenteeism*. London: Hodder and Stoughton.

BOLAM, R. (1981) 'Evaluative research. A case study of the teacher induction pilot schemes project', *Journal of Education for Teaching*, 8, 1, 70–83.

BOLAM, R. (1982a) *In-Service Education and Training of Teachers*. Paris: OECD/CERI.

BOLAM, R. (ed.) (1982b) *School-Focussed In-Service Training*. London: Heinemann.

BOLAM, R., BAKER, K. and MCMAHON, A. (1979) *The Teacher Induction Pilot Schemes Project National Evaluation Report*. University of Bristol, School of Education (mimeo).

BOLAM, R. *et al.* (1979) *LEA Advisers and the Mechanisms of Innovation*. Slough: NFER.

BOYDELL, D. (1979) *The Primary Teacher in Action*. London: Open Books.

BOYDELL, D. (1980) 'The organisation of junior school classrooms: a follow-up survey', *Educational Research*, 23, 14–19.

BRADLEY, H. (1974) *In-Service Education after the White Paper: A Survey of the Opinion of Teachers*. University of Nottingham, School of Education.

BRADLEY, H. (1981) 'Introduction to Part II' of DONOUGHUE *et al. In-Service, the Teacher and the School*. London: Kogan Page.

BRADLEY, H. W. and EGGLESTON, J. F. (1978) 'An induction year experiment', *Educational Research*, 20, 2, 89–98.

BRANSTON, P. and PROVIS, M. (1986) *Children and Parents Enjoying Reading*. London: Hodder and Stoughton.

BREARLEY, M. (1983) 'The making of teachers', *NAPE Journal*, 8, 4.

BRIGHOUSE, T. (1981) 'The Oxfordshire Secondment Scheme: A New Diploma for Serving Teachers', in DONOUGHUE, C. *et al. In-Service: The Teacher and the School*. London: Kogan Page.

BRINTON, E. and WATSON, L.E. (1975) 'The probationary year: An annotated bibliography', *British Journal of In-Service Ed*, 1, 3, 60–7.

BRODIE, M. (1983) 'Understanding organization and management', in PAISEY, A. (ed.) *The Effective Teacher*. London: Ward Lock Educational.

BROGDEN, M. (1983) 'Open plan primary schools: rhetoric and reality', *School Organization*, 3, 1, 27–41.

BROWN, D. (1987) 'The attitudes of parents to education and the school attendance of their children', chapter in REID, K. (ed.) (1987) *Combating School Absenteeism*. London: Hodder and Stoughton.

BROWNE, S. (1979) 'The Accountability of HM Inspectorate (England)', in LELLO, J. (ed.) *Accountability in Education*. London: Ward Lock Educational.

BRUNEL INSTITUTE OF ORGANISATION AND SOCIAL SERVICES (1977). *The Family and Child Guidance Clinic*. Educational Studies Unit, Brunel University, Institute of Organisation and Social Studies.

BURGESS, T. (ed.) (1985). *Education for Capability*. Windsor: NFER-Nelson.

BUSH, T. (1981) 'Key Roles in School Management' Block 4, Part 3, *Open University E323 Management and the School*. Milton Keynes: Open University Press.

BUSH, T. (1986) *Theories of Educational Management*. London: Harper and Row.

BUTCHER, H. J. (1965) 'The attitude of student teachers to education', *British Journal of Social and Clinical Psychology*, IV, 48, III.

CALDERHEAD, J. (1979) 'Teachers' classroom decision-making: its relationship to teachers' perceptions of pupils and to classroom interaction'. Unpublished PhD thesis, University of Stirling.

CALDERHEAD, J. (1984) *Teachers' Classroom Decision-making*. London: Holt, Rinehart and Winston.

CAMPBELL, R. J. (1984) 'In-school development: The role

of the curriculum postholder, *School Organisation*, 4, 4, 345–57.

CAMPBELL, R. J. (1985) *Developing the Primary School Curriculum*. London: Holt, Rinehart and Winston.

CANE, B. (1969) *In-Service Training: A Study of Teachers' Views and Preferences*. Slough: NFER.

CANE, B. (1973) 'Meeting teachers' needs', in WATKINS, R. (ed.) *In-Service Training: Structure and Content*. London: Ward Lock.

CAVE, J. and CAVE, R. (1982) 'Strategies for supporting small schools', *Education 3–13*, 10, 1, 40–3.

CENTRE FOR APPLIED RESEARCH IN EDUCATION (CARE) (1975) *The Ford Teaching Project*. Norwich: Centre for Applied Research in Education, University of East Anglia.

CHILD, J. (1984) *Organization: A Guide to Problems and Practice*. London: Harper and Row.

CLARE, J. (1986) 'Baker tells Brent to drop hearing', *The Times*, 17.12.86.

CLARE, J. (1987a) 'The Schools that must try harder', *The Times*, 16.1.87.

CLARE, J. (1987b) 'School computers fail to make grade', *The Times*, 22.1.87.

CLARK, J. and REID, K. (1986). *The In-Service Training Needs of Primary Teachers in West Glamorgan*. Report of a sponsored Welsh Office Project. Swansea: West Glamorgan Institute of Higher Education.

CLARK, J. and REID, K. (1987) 'Recent developments in INSET: a review', *CORE Journal on Microfiche*.

CLARK, R. P. and NISBET, J. (1963) *The First Two Years of Teaching*. Aberdeen, Department of Education.

CLEAVE, S., JOWETT, S. and BATE, M. (1982) *And so to school*. Windsor: NFER Nelson.

CLIFT, P. (1981) 'Parental involvement in primary schools', *Primary Education Review*, 10, 2–4.

CLIFT, P. S., WEINER, G. G. and WILSON, E. L. (1981) *Record Keeping in Primary Schools*. London: Macmillan.

CLWYD LEA (1980) *In-Service Education for Teachers: An INSET Model for the 1980s*. Clwyd: Clwyd LEA.

COHEN, L. (1969) 'Functional dependence, exchange and power of influence', *International Journal of Educational Science*, 3, 48.

COHEN, L. (1976) *Educational Research in Classrooms and Schools*. London: Harper and Row.

COHEN, L. and MANION, L. (1981) *Perspectives on Classrooms and Schools*. London: Holt, Rinehart and Winston.

COLES, M. (1984) 'Leave the Baby in the Bath', *NAPE Journal*, 12, 6, 4.

COOPER, D. and EBBUTT, D. (1974) 'Participation in action research as an in-service experience', *Cambridge Journal of Education*, 4, 2, 65–71.

COOPER, I. (1982) 'The maintenance of order and use of space in primary school buildings', *British Journal of Sociology of Education*, 3, 3, 267–79.

COOPER, R. (1986) Papers presented at the *TRIST School and College Focussed INSET Conference*, Llandrindod Wells: 17–19 September.

COPE, E. (1971) *School Experience in Teacher Education*. Bristol, School of Education.

CORNWELL, J., *et al.* (1965) *The Probationary Year*. Birmingham: University Institute of Education.

CORTIS, G. A. and DEAN, A. J. (1970) 'Teaching skills of probationary primary teachers', *Educational Research*, 12, 230–4.

COULSON, A. (1974) 'The role of the deputy head in the primary school: Role conceptions of heads and deputy heads.' Unpublished MEd dissertation. Hull: University of Hull.

COULSON, A. (1976) 'The Role of the Primary Head', in PETERS, R. S. (ed.) *The Role of the Head*. London: Routledge and Kegan Paul.

COULSON, A. (1978) 'Power and decision-making in the primary school', in RICHARDS, C. (ed.) *Power and the Curriculum*. London: Nafferton Books.

COWAN, G. (1984) 'What makes a good primary school teacher?', *Journal of Education for Teaching*, 10, 3, 256–8.

CRAFT, M., RAYNOR, J. and COHEN, L. (eds) *Linking Home and School* (3rd Edition). London: Harper and Row.

CRC (1980) *Child Guidance Service: Report 1977–1979*. Scotland: Central Regional Council, Education Department.

CYSTER, R., CLIFT, P. S. and BATTLE, S. (1979) *Parental Involvement in Primary Schools*. Slough: NFER.

DADDS, M. (1986) 'Those being tortured . . .', *Cambridge Journal of Education*, 16, 2, 151–4.

DAVIE, R. (1973) 'Seven answers to Professor Wall and Professor Tizard', *London Educational Review*, 2, 2, 38–60.

DAVIE, R., BUTLER, N. and GOLDSTEIN, H. (1972) *From Birth to Seven*. London: Longman.

DAVIES, D. (1976) 'Schools as Organizations, Unit 3, E321', *Management in Education*. Milton Keynes: The Open University Press.

DAVIES, E. (1975) 'The small primary school: Problem or paradigm', *Forum*, Summer, 17, 76–8.

DAVIES, J. H. (1979) 'INSET in Clwyd', *Education*, 11, 544–5.

DAVIES, L. F. (1976) 'Education welfare: the patchwork service', *Community Care*, 98, 16–17.

DAVIES, W. B. (1973) 'On the contribution of organisation analysis to the study of educational institutions' in BROWN, R. (ed.) *Knowledge, Education and Cultural Change*. London: Tavistock.

DAVIS, O. J. (1979) *The Liverpool Induction Pilot Scheme: A Summative Report*. University of Liverpool, School of Education (mimeo).

DAWSON, A. J. (1979) 'Criteria for the creation of in-service education programmes', *Canadian Journal of Education*, 3, 1, 49–59.

DAY, C. (1981) 'Classroom Based In-Service Teacher Education; The Development and Evaluation of a Client-centred Model', *Occasional Paper 9*, University of Sussex Education Area, Brighton.

DAY, C., JOHNSTON, D. and WHITAKER, P. (1985) *Managing Primary Schools*. London: Harper and Row.

DEAN, J. (1983) *Organising Learning in the Primary School.* London: Croom Helm.

DEMAINE, J. (1980) 'Compensatory Education and Social Policy', chapter, in CRAFT *et al.* (eds) *Linking Home and School* (3rd Edition). London: Harper and Row.

DENHAM, C. and LIEBERMAN, A. (1980) 'Time to learn'. New York National Institute of Education, in DEAN, J. *Organising Learning in the Primary School.* London: Croom Helm.

DES CIRCULARS: 14/77, 3/83, 4/84, 6/86. London: HMSO.

DES (1967a) *Primary Education in Wales: A Report of the Central Advisory Council for Education (Wales)* (Gittins Report). London: HMSO.

DES (1967b) *Children and their Primary Schools* (Plowden Report). London: HMSO.

DES (1970) *Survey of In-Service Training for Teachers 1967.* (Townsend Survey) Statistics of Education Special Services No. 2. London: HMSO.

DES (1972a) *Teacher Education and Training* (James Report). London: HMSO.

DES (1972b) *Education: a Framework for Expansion.* London: HMSO.

DES (1973) *The Role and Training of Education Welfare Offices* (Ralphs Report). London: HMSO.

DES (1975) *A Language for Life* (Bullock Report). London: HMSO.

DES (1976a) Advisory Committee on the Supply and Training of Teachers (INIST) *'Towards a National Policy for the Induction and In-Service Training of Teachers in Schools'.* London: HMSO.

DES (1976b) *Helping New Teachers: the Induction Year.* Report No. 84. London: DES.

DES (1977a) *Teacher Induction: Pilot Schemes' Progress. Report on Education.* No. 89. London: DES.

DES (1977b) *A New Partnership for our Schools* (Taylor Report). London: HMSO.

DES (1978a) *Making INSET Work.* London: HMSO.

DES (1978b) *Primary Education in England. A Survey by HM Inspectors of Schools.* London: HMSO.

DES (1980) *Special Needs in Education.* White Paper, command 7996. London: HMSO.

DES (1981) *Statistics of Education – Schools.* Darlington: Department of Education and Science.

DES (1982a) *Education 5–9: an Illustrative Survey of 80 First Schools in England.* London: HMSO.

DES (1982b) *The New Teacher in School.* London: HMSO.

DES (1982c) *Mathematics Counts* (Cockcroft Report). London: HMSO.

DES (1983a) *9–13 Middle Schools: an Illustrative Survey.* London: HMSO.

DES (1983b) *HM Inspectors today: Standards in Education.* London: HMSO.

DES (1983c) *The work of HM Inspectorate in England and Wales.* A policy statement by the Secretary of State for Education and Science and the Secretary of State for Wales. London: HMSO.

DES (1983d) *Teaching Quality.* London: HMSO.

DES (1984a) *Advisory Committee on the Supply and Education of Teachers 'The In-Service Education, Training and Professional Development of Schoolteachers'.* London: HMSO.

DES (1984b) *Statistics of Education.* Darlington: Department of Education and Science.

DES (1985a) *Better Schools.* London: HMSO.

DES (1985b) *The Curriculum from 5–16 Curriculum Matters* 2. An HMI Series. London: HMSO.

DES (1985c) *Mathematics from 5–16 Curriculum Matters* 3. An HMI Series. London: HMSO.

DES (1985d) *Report by Her Majesty's Inspectors on the Effects of Local Authority Expenditure Policies on Education Provision in England – 1984.* London: HMSO.

DES (1986a) 'Techniques for Appraising Teacher Performance' in *Better Schools Evaluation and Appraisal Conference. Birmingham 14–15 November, 1985, Proceedings.* London: HMSO.

DES (1986b) 'Inspection' in *Better Schools Evaluation and Appraisal Conference. Birmingham 14–15 November, 1985, Proceedings.* London: HMSO.

DONOUGHUE, C. *et al.* (1981) *In-Service, Teacher and the School.* London: Kogan Page.

DOWD, M. (1986) 'Manifesto on small schools derided', *The Times,* 30.12. 86.

DURNER, V. (1979) 'The induction year – A confrontation with reality', *Cambridge Journal of Education,* 9, 2 and 3, 145–52.

EDGAR, D. and WARREN, R. (1969) 'Power and autonomy in teacher socialization', *Sociology of Education,* XLII, 47.

EDUCATION (1985) 'Editorial on Appraisal', *Education,* 166, 18, 381–2.

EISNER, E. (1972) *Educating Artistic Vision.* New York: Macmillan Publishing Co. Inc.

EISNER, E. (1974) 'English Primary Schools: Some Observations and Assessment', National Association for the Education of Young Children, in RICHARDS, C. *The Study of Primary Education: A Source Book Volume 2.* Lewes: Falmer Press.

ELLIOTT, J. (1978) *The Classroom Action Research Newsletter.* Cambridge: Cambridge Institute of Education.

ELLIOTT, J. (1981) *Action-Research: A Framework for Self Evaluation in Schools.* Schools Council Working Programme 2, Working Paper 1.

ELLIOTT-KEMP, J. and ROGERS, C. (1982) *The Effective Teacher.* Sheffield: Sheffield City Polytechnic.

EMANUEL, J. (1983) *A Pattern for Learning.* London: Christian Schiller Memorial Lecture.

ERAUT, M. (1972) *In-Service Education for Innovation,* Occasional Paper 4, National Council for Educational Technology.

ERAUT, M. (1978) 'Some perspective on consultancy in in-service education', *British Journal of In-Service Education,* 4, 1, 95–9.

ERAUT, M. (1982) 'What is learned in in-service education and how? A knowledge-use perspective',

British Journal of In-Science Education, 9, 3, 6–13.

EVANS, K. (1979) 'The physical form of the school – school design as rhetoric', *British Journal of Educational Studies*, 37, 1, 29–41.

EVANS, K. (1985) *The Development and Structure of the English School System*. London: Hodder and Stoughton.

EVERARD, K. B. and MORRIS, G. (1985) *Effective School Management*. London: Harper and Row.

FAWCETT, R. (1979) 'The educational psychologist and child guidance', *Journal of the Association of Educational Psychologists*, 5, 1, 8–11.

FITZHERBERT, K. (1977) *Child Care Services and the Teacher*. London: Temple Smith.

FLETCHER, T. J. (1983) *Microcomputers and Mathematics in Schools*. London: Department of Education and Science.

FORSYTHE, D. (1983) *The Rural Community and the Small School*. Aberdeen: Aberdeen University Press.

FOWLER, G. (1980) 'Falling School Rolls and Home–School Links', in CRAFT *et al.* (eds) *Linking Home and School* (3rd edition). London: Harper and Row.

FRENCH, N. and RAVEN, J. (1959) 'The Bases of Social Power' in CARTWRIGHT, D. (ed.) *Studies in Social Power*. Ann Arbor, Michigan: Institute of Social Research.

FRUDE, N. (1984) 'Framework for analysis' in FRUDE, N. and GAULT, H. (eds) *Disruptive behaviour in schools*. Chichester: John Wiley.

FULLAN, M. (1979). 'School-Focussed In-Service Education in Canada'. Paper for *CERI/OECD Project on In-Service Education for Teachers*, Ontario.

GAGE, N. (1978) *The Scientific Basis of the Art of Teaching*. New York: Teachers College Press.

GALTON, M. and SIMON, B. (eds) (1980) *Progress and Performance in the Primary School*. London: Routledge and Kegan Paul.

GALTON, M., SIMON, B., CROLL, P. (1980) *Inside the Primary Classroom*. London: Routledge and Kegan Paul.

GARLAND, R. (1983) 'The primary school and the microcomputer: Some policy issues', *Education 3–13*, 11, 1, 33–7.

GARNER, J. (1986) 'Parental preference – four years on', *Home and School, NCPTA Magazine*, No. 1, 17–19.

GARNHAM, A. (1981) 'Professional Partnership in Practice in the South West' in DONOUGHUE, C. *et al. In-Service, the Teacher and the School*. London: Kogan Page.

GENTLE, K. (1985) *Children and Art Teaching*. London: Croom Helm Teaching 5–13 Series.

GOLBY, M. (1981) 'The primary curriculum', *Aspects of Education*, 26, 44–7.

GORDON, C. (1986) *Resource organisation in Primary Schools* (2nd Edition). London: Council for Educational Technology.

GOULD, C. (1985) 'The dilemmas of the student-teacher: a study of the patterns of influence and allegiance in science teacher training in one university department of education'. Unpublished PhD thesis. Sheffield: University of Sheffield.

GRACE, G. (1978) *Teachers, Ideology and Control*. London: Routledge and Kegan Paul.

GRAHAM, D. (1986) 'Teacher Appraisal; in DES (1986) *Better Schools Evaluation and Appraisal Conference. Birmingham 14–15 November, 1985, Proceedings*. London: HMSO.

GRAY, H. L. (1975) 'Exchange and Conflict in the School', in HOUGHTON, V. *et al.* (eds) *Management in Education*. London: Ward Lock Educational/Open University Press.

GRAY, H. L. (1985) *The School as an Organisation* (2nd Edition). Stoke-on-Trent: Deanhouse Ltd.

GRETTON, J. and JACKSON, M. (1976) *William Tyndale – Collapse of a School or a system?* London: George Allen and Unwin.

GULBENKIAN REPORT (1982) *The Arts in Schools*. Calouste Gulbenkian Foundation.

HAGEDORN, J. (1986) 'The Select Committee', *Times Educational Supplement*, 26 September 1986.

HALPIN, A. W. (1966) 'The organisational climate of schools', in HALPIN, A. W. (ed.) *Theory and Research in Administration*. New York: Macmillan.

HAMILTON, D. (1977) *In Search of Structure*. Edinburgh: Scottish Council for Research in Education.

HANNAM, C. *et al.* (1976) *The First Year of Teaching*. Harmondsworth: Penguin Books.

HARGREAVES, A. (1982) 'The Rhetoric of School-centred Innovation', *Journal of Curriculum Studies*, 14, 3, 251–66.

HARRISON, G. and BLOY, D. (1980) *Essential Law for Teachers*. London: Oyez Publishing Ltd.

HEAL, K. H. (1978) 'Misbehaviourism among schoolchildren: the role of the school in strategies for prevention', *Policy and Politics*, 6, 321–32.

HENDERSON, E. S. (1978) *The Evaluation of In-Service Training*. Beckenham: Croom Helm.

HENDERSON, E. S. (1979) 'The concept of school-focussed in-service education and training', *British Journal of Teacher Education*, 5, 1, 17–25.

HENDERSON, E. S. and PERRY, G. W. (1981) *Change and Development in Schools*. Maidenhead: McGraw-Hill.

HICKS, H. G. (1972) *The Management of Organizations*. New York: McGraw-Hill Book Co.

HILL, D. (1975) 'Experiments in Induction: New Approaches to the Probationary Year', *British Journal of Teacher Ed*, 1, 29–40.

HILLGATE GROUP (1987) 'Whose Schools? A Radical Manifesto', in MEIKLE, J. (1987) 'Privatization of State Schools Urged', *The Times Educational Supplement*, 2.1.87.

HILSUM, S. and START, K. B. (1974) *Promotion and Careers in Teaching*. Slough: NFER.

HIRST, P. H. (1965) 'Liberal Education and the Nature of Knowledge', in ARCHAMBAULT, R. D. (ed.) *Philosophical Analysis and Education*. London: Routledge and Kegan Paul.

HIRST, P. H. and PETERS, T. S. (1970) *The Logic of Education*. London: Routledge and Kegan Paul.

HMI (1987) *Primary Schools: Some aspects of good practice*. London: HMSO.

HOPKINS, Delyth, (1985) *Leadership in the Small Primary School. Dilemmas and Decisions related to Mixed Age Classes*. Swansea: West Glamorgan Institute of Higher Education.

HOPKINS, D. (1982) 'Doing research in your own classroom', *Phi Delta Kappan*, 64, 4, 274–5.

HOPKINS, D. (1985) *A Teacher's Guide to Classroom Research*. Milton Keynes: OUP.

HOPKINS, D. (ed.) (1987) *Improving the Quality of Schooling*. Lewes: Falmer Press.

HOPKINS, D. and REID, K. (1985) *Rethinking Teacher Education*. London: Croom Helm.

HOPKINS, D. and WIDEEN, M. (1984) *Alternative Perspectives on School Improvement*. Lewes: Falmer Press.

HORNSTEIN, D. *et al.* (1968) 'Influence and satisfaction in organizations: a replication', *Sociology of Education*, 412, 380–9.

HOWELL, A., WALKER, R. and FLETCHER, H. (1982) *Mathematics for Schools Series* (2nd Edition). London: Addison-Wesley.

HOWELLS, R. A. (1982) 'Problems of Curriculum Provision in the Small School and Possible Solutions', Cambridge Occasional Paper, Cambridge Institute of Education.

HOWEY, K., and JOYCE, B. (1979) 'A Data Base for Future Directions in In-Service Education', *Theory into Practice*, XVII, 3, 206–11.

HOYLE, E. (1970) 'Organizational change', *Research in Education*, May 3, 1–22.

HOYLE, E. (1973) 'The study of schools as organisations', in BUTCHER, H. J. and POUT, H. (eds) *Educational Research in Britain*, III. London: University of London Press.

HOYLE, E. (1974) 'Professionality, Professionalism and Control in teaching', in HOUGHTON, V. *et al. Management in Education*. London: Ward Lock Educational/Open University Press.

HOYLE, E. (1976) Reading 5, Innovation, the School and the Teacher Unit 30, 57–61 in Course E203 *Curriculum Design and Development*. Milton Keynes: Open University Press.

HOYLE, E. (1981) 'The Process of Management', *Block 3, Part 1, E323, Management and the School*. Milton Keynes: Open University Press.

HUGGETT, F. E. (1986) *Teachers*. London: Weidenfeld and Nicolson Ltd.

HUGHES, M. G. (1978) 'Reconciling Professional and Administrative Concerns', in BUSH, T. *et al. Approaches to School Management*. London: Harper and Row.

HUGILL, B. (1986a) '"Racism" label hinders discipline of Brent pupils says NUT chief', *Times Educational Supplement*, 29.8.86.

HUGILL, B. (1986b) 'Rotten borough or champion of racial equality', *Times Educational Supplement*, 21.11.86.

HUGILL, B. and MIEKLE, J. (1986) 'Heads set to quit over race discipline row', *Times Educational Supplement*, 3.10.86.

HUNTER, C. and HEIGHWAY, P. (1980) 'Morale, motivation and management in middle schools', in BUSH, T. *et al.* (eds) *Approaches to School Management'*. London: Harper and Row.

HURLIN, A. (1975) 'Open plan schools and inquiry/discovery learning', *Cambridge Journal of Education*, 5, 2, 98–103.

ILEA (1981) *Perspectives on attendance*. Research and Statistics Branch, Document RS 749–80. London: ILEA.

ILEA (1985) *Improving Primary Schools*. Report of the Committee on Primary Education, The Thomas Report. London: Inner London Education Authority.

ILEA (1986) *The Junior School Project*. London: ILEA, Research and Statistics Branch.

JONES, R. (1980) *Primary School Management*. Newton Abbot: David and Charles.

JOYCE, B. and SHOWERS, B. (1984) 'Transfer of Training: the Contribution of Coaching', in HOPKINS, D. and WIDEEN, M. *Alternative Perspectives on School Improvement*. Lewes: Falmer Press.

JUNIOR EDUCATION (1985) 'Appraisal can work – LEA Report', *Junior Education*, October, 7.

KEEBLE, D. (1967) 'Models of Economic Development', in CHORLEY, R. and HAGGETT, P. (eds) *Models in Geography*. London: Methuen.

KELLY, A. V. (1986) *Knowledge and Curriculum Planning*. London: Harper and Row.

KING, C. (1986) 'The burden of appraisal', *Times Educational Supplement*, 8.8.86.

KIRKHAM, S. (1986) 'Tracing roots of truancy beyond the school wall', *Times Educational Supplement*, 28.3.86.

KLEINBERG, S. M. and CROZIER, S. (1979) 'Art education: Some issues', *Education in the North*, 16, 22–31.

LACEY, C. (1977) *The Socialization of Teachers*. London: Methuen.

LANCASTER, J. (ed.) (1986) *Art, Craft and Design in the Primary School*. Leicester: NSEAD.

LAWTON, D. (1973) *Social Change, Educational Theory and Curriculum Planning*. London: University of London Press.

LAWTON, D. (1975) *Class, Culture and the Curriculum*. London: Routledge and Kegan Paul.

LAWTON, D. (1977) *Education and Social Justice*. London: Sage Publications.

LAWTON, D. (1981a) 'The Politics of the Curriculum, in GORDON, P. (ed.) *The Study of the Curriculum*. London: Batsford.

LAWTON, D. (1981b) 'Organization of Knowledge', in GORDON, P. (ed.) *The Study of the Curriculum*. London: Batsford.

LAWTON, D. (1981c) 'Models of Planning', in GORDON, P. (ed.) *The Study of the Curriculum*. London: Batsford.

LEWIS, I. (1976) 'In-service development: Institutional or radical', *British Journal of In-Service Education*, 2, 3, 50–9.

LEWIS, I. (1984) 'Towards a new map of in-service education', *British Journal of In-Service Education*, 10, 2, 6–13.

LIGHT, A. (1980) 'The conduct of in-service education in schools', in BRAND, J. and HUGHES, J. (eds) *Evaluation, INSET and the Teachers' Centre*. Sheffield University: Papers in Educational Management.

LIKERT, R. (1967) *Human Organization: Its management and value*. New York: McGraw-Hill.

LOMAX, P., MCDONALD, B. and MURPHY, P. (1980) 'Kinpol Inset Project: Richmond Teachers' Perspectives on INSET', *Working paper 2/81*, Division of Educational Studies, Kingston Polytechnic.

LORTIE, D. C. (1969) The balance of control and autonomy in elementary school teaching', in ETZIONI, A. (ed.) *The Semi-Professions and their Organization*. New York: Free Press.

LORTIE, D. C. (1975) *The Schoolmaster*. Chicago: University of Chicago Press.

LOWENFELD, V. and LAMBERT-BRITTAIN, W. (1982) *Creative and Mental Growth* (7th Edition). London: Collier Macmillan.

LYNCH, J. and BURNS, B. (1984) 'Non-attenders at INSET functions: some comparisons with attenders', *Journal of Education for Teaching*, 10, 2, 164–77.

MACMILLAN, H. (1957) 'Speech on the financial situation, 20th July, 1957', in COHEN, J. M. and M. J. *Dictionary of Modern Quotations*. Harmondsworth: Penguin Books.

MACMILLAN, K. (1977) *Education Welfare: Strategy and Structure*. London: Longman.

MARSH, L. (1970) *Alongside the Child in the Primary School*. London: A. & C. Black Ltd.

MARSHALL, S. (1963) *An Experiment In Education*. Cambridge: Cambridge University Press.

MAY, J. and GREER, A. (1970) *A Student's Guide to the Development of Education in England and Wales*. Middlesex: St Mary's College of Education.

MCCABE, C. (1978) 'A new look at problems of the probationary year', *British Journal of In-Service Education*, 4, 3, 144–50.

MCCABE, C. (1979) 'Some implications of induction for initial teacher training', *British Journal Teacher Education*, 5, 2, 157–64.

MCCABE, J. J. C. (1978) 'Attitudes, personality and induction – A research note', *British Journal of Teacher Education*, 4, 2, 143–5.

MCGEENEY, P. (1980) 'The Involvement of Parents', in CRAFT *et al.* (eds) *Linking Home and School* (3rd Edition). London: Harper and Row.

MCGREGOR, D. (1960) *The Human Side of Enterprise*. New York: McGraw-Hill.

MCLAUGHLIN, M. and MARSH, D. (1978) 'Staff development and school change', *Teachers' College Record*, 80, 1, 69–94.

MCLEISH, J. (1970) *Students' Attitudes and College Environments*. Cambridge: Cambridge Institute of Education.

MCMAHON, A., BOLAM, R., ABBOTT, R. and HOLLY, P. (1984) *Guidelines for Review and Internal Development in Schools*. Primary and Secondary School Handbooks. York: Longman/Schools Council.

MEAD, S. and MEAD, D. (1975) 'Treatment opportunities in child guidance clinics', *Social Work Today*, 5, 24, 734–40.

MEIKLE, J. (1986a) 'Governors support head in race row', *Times Educational Supplement*, 29.8.86.

MEIKLE, J. (1986b) 'Headhunting headaches for small primaries', *Times Educational Supplement*, 11.7.86.

MEIKLE, J. (1987) 'Privatization of state schools urged', *Times Educational Supplement*, 2.1.87.

MORGAN, C. and TURNER, C. (1976) 'Role, the Education Manager and the Individual in the Organisation' Unit 14, E321, *Management in Education*. Milton Keynes: Open University Press.

MORGAN, R. and LYON, E. (1979) 'Paired reading: a preliminary report on a technique for parental tuition of reading retarded children', *Journal of Child Psychology and Psychiatry*, 20, 151–60.

MORRIS, R. (1985) 'Quality leadership in the primary school', chapter in *West Glamorgan Institute of Higher Education (1986) Teacher Fellowship Report*. Swansea: West Glamorgan.

MORRISON, A. and MCINTYRE, D. (1967) 'Changes in opinions about education during the first year of training', *British Journal of Social and Clinical Psychology*, 6.

MORTIMORE, P. and TEAM (1985) 'The ILEA Junior School Study: An Introduction', in REYNOLDS, D. (ed.) *Studying School Effectiveness*. Lewes: The Falmer Press.

MOUNTFORD, B. (1984) 'The Management of Change in Small Schools', *Educational Management and Administration*, 12, 63–6.

MOYLE, D. (1981) *Language Patterns, Readiness to Stage 3*, Teachers' Resource Book. London: Holt, Rinehart and Winston.

MOYLE, D. (1982) *Language Patterns, Stages 3–6*, Teachers' Resource Book. London: Holt, Rinehart and Winston.

MUSGRAVE, P. W. (1976) *The School as an Organisation*. London: Macmillan.

NAHT (1975) 'The Teaching Head', in SCOTT, C. 'The small rural primary school: an appraisal', *Education 3–13*, 10, 1, 43–8.

NAHT (1985) *Mathematics in the Primary School* National Association of Headteachers. Haywards Heath: NAHT.

NASH, I. (1986) 'Appraisal pilots ready for take-off', *Times Educational Supplement*, 5.12.86.

NATIONAL ASSOCIATION OF SCHOOLMASTER/UNION OF WOMEN TEACHERS (1987) *The New Contract: Working Hours*. London: NAS/UWT.

NATIONAL CONFEDERATION OF PARENT TEACHER

ASSOCIATIONS (1985) *The State of Schools in England and Wales: A Report.* NCPTA, 43 Stonebridge Road, Northfleet, Gravesend, Kent.

NEWSOM, J. and NEWSOM, E. (1983) 'Child and parent, school and culture: issues in identification', BRAHAM, M. (ed.) *Aspects of Education.* Chichester: Wiley.

NEWSOM, J. and NEWSOM, E. (1984) 'Parents' Perspectives on Children's Behaviour at School', in FRUDE, N. and GAULT, H. (eds) *Disruptive Behaviour in Schools.* Chichester: John Wiley and Sons.

NFER (1985) 'LEA Advisers: New research at NFER', *Educational Research News,* No. 43, Autumn.

NIAS, J. (1980) 'Leadership Styles and Job Satisfaction in Primary Schools', in BUSH *et al.* (eds) *Approaches to School Management.* London: Harper and Row.

NISBET, J. (1986) 'Appraising Appraisal' in GREIG, D. 'Time for Appraisal'. *Education,* 168, 8, 166.

NUT (1981) *A Guide to First Appointment and Probationary Year Procedures.* London: NUS/NUT.

NUTTALL, D. (1986) 'Appraising Appraisal', in GREIG, D. 'Time for Appraisal', *Education,* 168, 8, 166.

OLIVER, R. A. C. and BUTCHER, H. J. (1965) 'Teachers' Attitudes to Education – the Structure of Educational Attitudes', *British Journal of Social and Clinical Psychology,* 1, 48–59.

OLIVER, R. A. C. and BUTCHER, H. J. (1968) 'Teachers' Attitudes to Education', *British Journal of Ed Psych,* 38, 48–59.

OTTY, N. (1972) *Learner Teacher.* Harmondsworth: Penguin Books.

OWENS, R. G. (1970) *Organizational Behaviour in Schools.* Englewood Cliffs, N.J.: Prentice-Hall Inc.

PACKWOOD, T. (1977) 'The School as Hierarchy' in BUSH, T. *et al.* (eds) *Approaches to School Management.* London: Harper and Row.

PAISEY, A. (1981a) *The Management of Primary and Middle Schools.* Windsor: NFER/Nelson.

PAISEY, A. (1981b) *Organisation and Management in Schools.* Harlow: Longman.

PARTINGTON, J. (1985) *Law and the New Teacher.* London: Holt, Rinehart and Winston.

PATON, R., BONN, S., SPEAR, R., CHAPMAN, J., FLOYD, M. and HAMWEE, J. (eds) (1984) *Organizations: Cases, Issues, Concepts.* London: Harper and Row in association with The Open University.

PATRICK, H. (1985) *Small Schools: a report.* Bristol, National Development Centre for School Management Training Newsletter.

PATRICK, H., BERNBAUM, G. and REID, K. (1982) *The Structure and Process of Initial Teacher Education within Universities in England and Wales.* Report to the DES, Leicester, University of Leicester School of Education.

PATRICK, H., BERNBAUM, G. and REID, K. (1983a) *The Probationary Year: An Interim Report* presented at the DES/University of Leicester Conference on Teacher Education, Oxford, September 1983.

PATRICK, H., BERNBAUM, G. and REID, K. (1983b) 'The PGCE and the probationary year', *British Journal of In-Service Teacher Education,* 10, 3, 47–53.

PEARCE, J. (1979) 'Advisers and Inspectors', in LELLO, J. (ed.) *Accountability in Education.* London: Ward Lock Educational.

PEDLEY, F. (1975) 'Beyond the truant', *New Society,* 31, 650, 723–4.

PICKARD, J. (1985) 'Teacher Appraisal', *Junior Education,* October, 8.

PLOWDEN, B. (1983) 'Primary education. Looking back and glancing forward – A personal view', *NAPE Journal,* 11, 8.

POLLARD, A. (1985) *The Social World of the Primary School.* London: Holt, Rinehart and Winston.

PRICE, M. (1985) 'Perspectives of headteachers and teachers on teacher participation in decision-making in primary schools'. Unpublished MPhil thesis. Swansea: West Glamorgan Institute of Higher Education.

PRICE, M. and REID, K. (1987a) 'Differences between headteachers' and teachers' views on aspects of decision-making in primary schools', *Research in Education,* in press.

PRICE, M. and REID, K. (1987b) 'School size related to differences between headteachers' and teachers' views on teacher participation in primary schools', *School Organisation,* in press.

PRICE, M. and REID, K. (1987c) 'Personal variables in decision-making in primary schools', *School Organisation,* in press.

PRICE, M. and REID, K. (1987d) 'Sex differences between headteachers' and teachers' views on teacher participation in decision-making in primary schools', Unpublished paper. Swansea: West Glamorgan Institute of Higher Education.

PRING, R. (1978) 'Teacher as researcher', in LAWTON, D., GORDON, P., ING, M., GIBBY, B., PRING, R. and MOORE, T. (eds) *Theory and Practice of Curriculum Studies.* London: RKP.

RAVENETTE, A. T. (1972) 'Psychologists, teachers and children: how many ways to understand?', *Journal of the Association of Educational Psychologists,* 3, 2, 41–7.

RAWLINSON, J. (1982) 'The Changing Role of Postholders': text of talk given to primary school teachers. Beaumanor Hall, Leicestershire, October.

REDFORD, R. (1986) *Hear to Read.* London: National Book League.

REID, K. (1983) 'The management of decline: a discussion paper', *School Organization,* 3, 4, 361–70.

REID, K. (1984a) 'Teaching Practice Report: Results of a Survey on Teaching Practice 1983/1984', Unpublished paper. Swansea: West Glamorgan Institute of Higher Education.

REID, K. (1984b) 'The Probationary Year: Facts, Fallacies, Research and the Practical implications', *CORE Journal on Microfiche.*

REID, K. (1985a) *Truancy and School Absenteeism.* London: Hodder and Stoughton.

REID, K. (1985b) 'Recent research and developments in teacher education in England and Wales; in HOPKINS, D. and REID, K. *Rethinking Teacher Education*, London: Croom Helm.

REID, K. (1985c) 'The postgraduate certificate of education, teaching practice, and the probationary year', in HOPKINS, D. and REID, K. *Rethinking Teacher Education*. London: Croom Helm.

REID, K. (1986) *Disaffection From School*. London: Methuen.

REID, K. (ed.) (1987a) *Combating School Absenteeism*. London: Hodder and Stoughton.

REID, K. (1987b) 'The Education Welfare Service – some issues and suggestions', in REID, K. (ed.) *Combating School Absenteeism*. London: Hodder and Stoughton.

REID, K., BERNBAUM, G. and PATRICK, H. (1981) 'On Course: Students and the PGCE', Unpublished paper given at the UCET Conference, Oxford, October.

REID, K., BERNBAUM, G. and PATRICK, H. (1982) 'Future Research Issues in Teacher Education', *Educational Review*, 33, 2, 143–50.

REID, K., HOPKINS, D. and HOLLY, P. (1987) *Towards the Effective school*. Oxford: Blackwell.

REID, K., JONES, K. and O'SULLIVAN, F. (1987) 'Implementing changing in-service'. *Educational Review*, in press.

REID, K. and PATRICK, H. (1980) 'The Structure and Process of Initial Teacher Education within Universities in England and Wales', in ALEXANDER, R. and WHITTAKER, J. (eds) *Recent Developments in PGCE Courses*. Teacher Education Study Group. SRHE.

REID, K., PATRICK, H. and BERNBAUM, G. (1981) 'Future research issues in teacher education', *Educational Review*, 32, 2, 143–50.

REYNOLDS, D. (1976) 'The deliquent school', in HAMMERSLEY, M. and WOODS, P. (eds) *The Process of Schooling: a Sociological Reader*. London: RKP.

REYNOLDS, D. (1982) 'School effectiveness research – a review of the literature', *School Organisation and Management Abstracts*, 1, 1, 5–14.

REYNOLDS, D. (ed.) (1985a) *Studying School Effectiveness*. Lewes: The Falmer Press.

REYNOLDS, D. (1985b) 'The Effective School', *Times Educational Supplement*, 20.9.85.

REYNOLDS, D., JONES, D. and ST LEGER, S. (1976) *Schools do make a difference*. ('Education' 3rd Edition, 1981) A New Society Social Studies Reader. London: New Society.

REYNOLDS, D. and MURGATROYD, S. (1984) 'The Creative Consultant: The Potential Use of Consultancy as a Method of Teacher Education', *School Organisation*, 4, 4, 321–35.

REYNOLDS, D. and REID, K. (1985) 'The second stage: towards a reconceptualization of theory and methodology in school effectiveness research', chapter in REYNOLDS, D. (ed.) *Studying School Effectiveness*. Lewes: Falmer.

RICHARDS, C. (1982a) 'Primary Education 1974–80; in RICHARDS, C. (ed.) *New Directions in Primary Education*. Lewes: Falmer Press.

RICHARDS, C. (1982b) 'Curriculum Consistency', in RICHARDS, C. (ed.) *New Directions in Primary Education*. Lewes: Falmer Press.

RICHARDS, C. (1986) 'The Curriculum from 5–16', *Education 3–13*, 14, 1, Spring, 3–8.

RICHARDS, R., COLLIS, M. and KINCAID, D. (1980) *Learning Through Science: Formulating a School Policy*, London: Macdonald Educational for the Schools Council.

RICHARDSON, G. A. (1981a) 'Student-Teacher attitudes towards decision-making in schools before and after taking up their first appointments', *Educational Studies*, 7, 1, 7–15.

RICHARDSON, G. A. (1981b) 'Personal variables in student-teacher attitudes towards teacher participation in school decision-making.' *Durham and Newcastle Research Review*, 9, 47, 285–92.

RIDLEY, K. and TREMBATH, D. (1983) 'Primary school organization: some rhetoric and some reason', *School Organization*, 3, 1, 43–50.

ROBERTS, J. (1988) 'Small schools: A clustering experiment'. Unpublished MEd Dissertation. Swansea: West Glamorgan Institute of Higher Education.

ROBERTS, K. (1980) 'Schools, Parents and Social Class', in CRAFT *et al.* (eds) *Linking Home and School* (3rd Edition). London: Harper and Row.

ROY, W. (1983) *Teaching Under Attack*. London: Croom Helm.

RUBINSTEIN, D. (1969) *School Attendance in London, 1870–1904*. Hull: Hull University Press.

RUDD, W. E. A. and WISEMAN, S. (1962) 'Sources of Dissatisfaction Among a Group of Teachers', *British Journal of Educational Psychology*, 32, 45ff.

RUDDUCK, J. (1981) *Making the Most of the Short In-Service Course*, Schools Council Working Paper 71. London: Methuen.

RUDDUCK, J. (1984) 'Introducing innovation to pupils', in HOPKINS, D. and WIDEEN, M. (eds) *Alternative Perspectives on School Improvement*. Lewes: Falmer.

RUTTER, M., MAUGHAN, B., MORTIMORE, P., OUSTON, J. with SMITH, A. (1979) *Fifteen Thousand Hours*. London: Open Books.

SALLIS, J. (1985) *The School in its setting* (4th Revised Edition). London: Advisory Centre for Education.

SALLIS, J. (1987) 'Good news, bad news', *Times Educational Supplement*, 9.1.87.

SALTER, B. and TAPPER, T. (1981) *Education, Politics and the State*. London: Grant McIntyre.

SAYER, J. (1979) 'INSET strategy of a large comprehensive school', *Cambridge Journal of Education*, 9. 2, 95.

SCHMUCK, R. A. (1974) 'Interventions for Strengthening the School's Creativity', in NISBET, J. (ed.) *Creativity of the School*. Paris: OECD.

SCHOOLS COUNCIL (1975) 'Small Schools Study'. Unpublished Paper.

SCHOOLS COUNCIL (1978) *Art 7–11*. Occasional Bulletin from the Subjects Committee.

SCHOOLS COUNCIL (1981) *Resources for Visual Education 7–13*. Occasional Bulletin from the Subjects Committee.

SCHOOLS COUNCIL (1982) *Small Schools in Concert: Report of the Llanwrtyd Wells Conference*. London: Schools Council.

SCHOOLS COUNCIL (1983) *Primary Practice: Working Paper 75*. London: Methuen Educational for the Schools Council.

SCRUTON, R. (1986) 'Exam figures and facts', *The Times* 30.12.86.

SEFTON-DAVIES, R. W. (1982) 'Providing INSET Consultancies for Schools' in BOLAM, R. (ed.) *School-focused In-Service Training*. London: Heinemann.

SHARROCK, A. (1980) 'Research on Home–School Relations', in CRAFT *et al.* (eds) *Linking Home and School* (3rd Edition). London: Harper and Row.

SIMMONS, L. M. (1980) 'Staff development in schools', *Curriculum*, 1, 1.

SIMON, B. and WILLCOCKS, J. (eds) (1980) *Research and Practice in the Primary Classroom*. London: Routledge and Kegan Paul.

SKILLING, D. (1984) 'Mathematics Co-ordinators: Co-ordinating Mathematics', *British Journal of In-Service Education*, 11, 1, 26–31.

SKINNER, J. (1981) 'Regional Collaborative Schemes and National INSET Provision', in DONOUGHUE, C. *et al.* (eds) *In-Service the Teacher and the School*. London: Kogan Page.

SPENCER, D. (1986) 'Judge backs McGoldrick', *Times Educational Supplement*, 24.10.86.

SPOONER, R. (1984) 'In praise of doing good by stealth', *Education*, 163, 16, 325.

STENHOUSE, L. (1975) *An Introduction to Curriculum Research and Development*. London: Heinemann.

STENHOUSE, L. (1980) 'Curriculum Research and the Art of the Teacher', *Curriculum*, 1, 1, 40–4.

STILLMAN, A. and GRANT, M. (1986) 'The challenge of change: structures, policies and working practices in LEA advisory services'. Unpublished paper given at the NFER Annual Conference, Slough, 1986.

SUFFOLK (1985) *Those having torches: Teacher Appraisal: a study*. Ipswich: Suffolk Education Department.

TANN, S. (1981) 'Grouping and group work', in SIMON and WILLCOCKS (eds) *Research and Practice in the Primary Classroom*. London: Routledge and Kegan Paul.

TAYLOR F. (1980) *A School Prospectus Planning Kit*, ACE, 18 Victoria Park Square, London E2.

TAYLOR, F. (1981) *Choosing a School* (2nd Edition). ACE, 18 Victoria Park Square, London E2.

TAYLOR, J. K. and DALE, I. R. (1971) *A Survey of Teachers in Their First Year of Service*. School of Education, University of Bristol.

TAYLOR, W. (1985) 'The future for teacher education', in

HOPKINS, D. and REID, K. (eds) *Rethinking Teacher Education*. London: Croom Helm.

TES (1986) 'McGoldrick returns but could still be ousted', *Times Educational Supplement*, 7 November 1986.

TES (1986) 'Brent assurance', *Times Educational Supplement*, 14 November 1986.

TES (1986) 'Following the Suffolk Signposts', *Times Educational Supplement*, 5 December 1986.

TES (1987) 'New threat from the new Right', *Times Educational Supplement*, 2 January 1987.

THOMPSON, D. (1971) 'Season of birth and academic success', *Educational Research*, Vol. 14.

TIZARD, J. (1973) 'Maladjusted children and the child guidance service', *London Educational Review*, 2, 2, 29–39.

TOPPING, K. (1978) 'Consumer confusion and professional conflict in educational psychology', *Bulletin British Psychological Society*, 31, 265–7.

UPTON, G. and GOBELL, A. (eds) (1980) *Behaviour problems in the comprehensive school*. University College, Cardiff, Faculty of Education.

WALKER, D. (1986) 'So who really governs Britain's schools?', *Daily Telegraph*, 17.11.86.

WALSH, K., DUNNE, R., STOTEN, B. and STEWART, J. D. (1984) *Falling School Rolls and the Management of the Teaching Profession*. Windsor: NFER/Nelson.

WARWICK, D. (1974) *Team Teaching*. London: University of London Press.

WATERS, D. (1979) *Management and Headship in the Primary School*. London: Ward Lock Educational.

WATKINS, R. (ed.) (1973) *In-Service Training: Structure and Content*. London: Ward Lock Educational.

WEBB, S. (1980) 'Teething trouble: questions about the early days of units for disruptive pupils'. Unpublished paper. London: Education Welfare Service, ILEA.

WEDELL, K. and LAMBOURNE, R. (1980) *Psychological services for children in England and Wales*. Occasional Paper 4, 1 and 2. Leicester: British Psychological Society.

WEEKES, D. R. (1973) 'Organisation theory – some themes and distinctions', in SALAMAN, G. and THOMPSON, K. (eds) *People and Organisations*. London: Longman/Open University.

WEICK, K. (1976) 'Educational organizations as loosely coupled systems', *Administrative Science Quarterly*, 21, 1–19.

WELSH OFFICE (1984) *Curriculum and Organisation of Primary Schools in Wales*. London: HMSO.

WELSH OFFICE (1985) *Leadership in Primary Schools*. Primary Education in Wales. HMI (Wales) Occasional Paper, June 1985. Cardiff: Welsh Office.

WELSH OFFICE (1986) *Taking Stock: Primary Schools*. A commentary on HMI reports published during 1983, 1984 and 1985. Cardiff: HMSO.

WEST GLAMORGAN COUNTY COUNCIL (1985) *Resourcing the Small School*. A Report by the Primary Curriculum Working Group: Sub-Group 5. Swansea: West Glamorgan County Council.

WEST GLAMORGAN COUNTY COUNCIL (1987) *Primary Curriculum Working Party Sub-Group 2: Language, Reading and English Guidelines*. In preparation.

WEST GLAMORGAN INSTITUTE OF HIGHER EDUCATION (1986) *Parental Involvement in Primary Schools*, Teacher Fellowship Report, Swansea, WGIHE.

WHITAKER, P. (1980) *The Primary Head*. London: Heinemann.

WHITE, J. (1975) 'The End of the Compulsory Curriculum', Studies in Education 2. *The Doris Lee Lectures 1975*. London: University of London Institute of Education.

WHITE, J. (1979) 'Aims and Curricula: Do heads and teachers have the right to decide?', *Primary Education Review*, 7, 6–8.

WILCOX, B. (1985a) 'Clarifying the role of the adviser', *Education*, 165, 15, 331.

WILCOX, B. (1985b) 'Revolution and rose-water', *Times Educational Supplement*, 20.9.85.

WILCOX, B. (1986) 'Appraising Appraisal' in GREIG, D. 'Time for Appraisal', *Education*, 168, 8, 166.

WINKLEY, D. (1985) *Diplomats and detectives: LEA advisers at work*. London: Robert Royce.

WISEMAN, S. and START, K. (1965) 'A Follow-up of Teachers Five Years After Completing Their Training', *British Journal of Ed Psych*, XXXV, 45ff.

WOLFENDALE, S. (1983) *Parental Participation in Children's Development and Education*. London: Gordon and Breach.

WOOD, J. (1981) 'The behavioural approach to non-attendance cases' in DUNN, J. (ed.) *Partnership in Education and Social Sciences: some school problems*. Joint Occasional Publication No. 2, University of Lancaster.

WRAGG, E. (1984) 'Brave New World', *NAPE Journal*, 11, 3.

WRAGG, E. and PARTINGTON, J. A. (1985) *Handbook for School Governors*. London: Methuen.

WRIGHT, H. J. and PAYNE, T. A. N. (1979) *An evaluation of a school psychological services; the Portsmouth pattern*. Hampshire: Hampshire Education Authority.

YEOMANS, A. (1983) 'Collaborative group work in primary and secondary schools: Britain and the USA', *The Durham and Newcastle Research Review*, X, 51, 99–105.

YOUNG, M. F. D. (ed.) (1971) *Knowledge and Control*. London: Collier Macmillan.

Acknowledgments

We wish to thank and acknowledge the contributions and help of the following teachers, headteachers and lecturers during the data gathering and proof-reading stages of this book – Janet Clark, Gill Figg, Hilary Hipkin, Delyth Hopkins, Rosalind Morris, Diane O'Sullivan, Glyn Ellis, Basil Morgan, Robert Platt, Fergus O'Sullivan and John Roberts. We should also like to thank those teachers and headteachers who consented to our visiting their schools and taking part in fact-finding tours as well as in structured and semi-structured interviews. We are grateful to you all.

The HMI schedules from the 1978 Primary Survey are reproduced with the permission of the Controller of Her Majesty's Stationery Office.

We should like to thank the Council for Educational Technology for permission to reproduce Celia Gordon's table from *Resource Organisation in Primary Schools* on the link between colour coding and the Dewey classification.

The table reproduced from Cyster *et al.* (1979), *Parental Involvement in Primary Schools*, is included by permission of NFER Nelson, Windsor.

Last, but certainly not least, we should like to thank Judith Hyde for her good humour and indefatigable patience in typing and retyping the manuscript and making sense of some fairly indecipherable handwriting.

The authors and publishers would also like to thank the following for permission to reproduce photographs: Sally and Richard Greenhill (pp. 2, 3, 19, 94 (top), 105, 109, 125 and 176 and cover); Janine Wiedel (pp. 62 and 79); Nance Fyson (pp. 94 (bottom) and 175).

Index

a pattern of observation 97–8
abbreviations ix
accidents 136–8
action research 64
advertising 40–5
advisers 111–17
advisory teachers 117–18
analysis of needs 152–60
anthologies 129
anti-racism 12
attendance registers 135
autonomy 9–10
   of the headteacher 10–11

Baker Pay Deal vii, 7
benefits of parental involvement 127–8
better schools 7
bibliography 196–206
Board of Education 10
book resources 104–6
box systems 73–4
Bullock Report 7
Burnham Regulations 32, 33

calculators 108
capitation 107
case data 165–6
case studies vii, 1, 2, 3, 6, 24–6, 86–90, 96–101,
   174–81
child guidance service 122–3
children in classroom organisation 109–10
children's work 98–9
choice of schools 126–7
classroom observation 14, 16, 57
clustering 83, 86, 88

Cockcroft Report 7, 47
collection after school 138–9
collegial ideas 11
colour coding 104–5
committees 54–5
communication 61–3
community 87
confidentiality 16
consultants 157–9
contract (1987) 8, 18
control and discipline 140
Council for the Accreditation of Teacher Education
   54
curriculum (also referred to at appropriate points
   throughout book in most chapters) 91–101
  leaders 49–50
  skills 49

decision-making 57–61
decision-making and authority 59–61
defining probation 162–3
definition of an organisation 4
delegation 56
deputy head 81–2
Dewey system 105–6
difficult pupils 119–20
directed time 8

education 16, 17
Education Acts, 1976, 1980 and 1981 7
Education Act, 1986 7, 8, 9, 12, 32
Education Welfare Officers 63, 120–2
Education Welfare Service 120–2

effective
  primary schools   184–95
  teachers   174–83
  teaching in primary schools   172–83
effectiveness   172–95
electronic resources   108–9
evaluation   15, 113–14
external agencies   111–23

finance   9
financial resources   106–7

good practice   93–101, 193–4
Great Debate   6
GRIST   7, 142–60

Her Majesty's Inspectorate   118–19
HMI schedules   188–94
Homeland Junior   24–6
human resources   103–4

ILEA Junior School Project   18, 91, 184–8
individual work   75
induction   165
industry   15
INSET   63, 142–60
  and the school   150–1
  in school time   156–7
  analysis of needs   152–60
  developments   143–4
  effective courses   145–6, 148–50
  implementation   159–60
  levels of co-ordination   145
  policy and planning   144–5
  stages   147–8
  teachers' surveys   146–7
institutional influences   65
interpersonal skills   49
interviews   14, 50

job descriptions   40–9
job details   40–6
junior education   16

language patterns   77
large groups   76–7
law   134–41
LEA reorganisation   7
Learning Through Science   77
leaving the school premises   139
listening centres   109
literacy and numeracy   99–100
Local Government Act, 1966   27

materials   104
Mathematics For Schools   77
McGoldrick case   11–13
microcomputers   108
mixed-age classes   83–90
moderation   15
monitoring   15
MSC   7
multiple responsibilities   36–7

needy pupils   119–20
new INSET   7, 11, 142–60
New Teacher in School, The   55, 161–71
new teachers   161–71
Newcastle Report   13
newsletters   129
non-teaching staff   37–9
noticeboard   129
notion of quality   96–7
number of schools   18–30
NUT   12

open-plan classrooms   73–4
open-plan schools   6, 65–9, 74
ORACLE   74–5, 76, 77, 185
organisation of classes   69–77, 100–101, 109–10
organisation within classes   72, 100–101
organisational policies of junior schools   6
Organisations   3, 4
organising for learning   74–5
organising the curriculum   91–101

paired working   75–6
parent governors   126
parental involvement   100, 124–33
parents and children learning together   131–2
parents' rights   126
personal and social interaction   100
physical education   139–40
physical provision   98
plan of schools   65–9
'points' scores   32
preparation   14
primary survey   6, 7, 10, 35
probationary teachers   55–6, 161–71
probationary year myths   163–4
pupil–teacher ratios   27–30

research on parental involvement   132–3
resource management   102–3
resources   10–11, 16, 80–1, 102–10
rural schools   72, 78–90

scale posts   2, 18–30, 31–39, 40–51
school-based parental involvement   129–31
school
    brochures   129
    buildings   65–9
    effectiveness   172–95
    hierarchy   21–6
    psychological service   122
    reports   129
schools and industry   123
schools as organisations   3–6
secondary school liaison   48
single-age classes   70–1
single classrooms   73–4
sizes of schools   18–30
small groups   76
small schools   78–90
staff
    deployment   34–9
    in the small primary school   82–3
    management   52–64
    meetings   52–5
    organisation   21–30, 31–9, 40–51
    selection   40–51
staffing primary schools   26–30
streaming   71
student teachers   140–1
Suffolk   14, 16

supervision   135–6
supervision before school   138

Tameside   12
Taylor Report   7
teacher appraisal   13–17
teacher-as-researcher concept   63–4
teacher autonomy   11
teachers' surveys   146–7
teaching heads   79–90
theft prevention   108
time is money   107
Times Educational Supplement   12, 13, 17
TRIST   7
TVEI   7
types of parental involvement   128–9
types of schools   19–21, 26

vertical grouped classes   72

Welsh Office INSET Project   154–7
West Glamorgan Institute of Higher Education   54
William Tyndale School   7
working in threes   76
working parties   54–5
written communication   129

YTS   7